Principles
in Practic

MW01098137

The Principles in Practice imprint offers teachers concrete illustrations of effective classroom practices based in NCTE research briefs and policy statements. Each book discusses the research on a specific topic, links the research to an NCTE brief or policy statement, and then demonstrates how those principles come alive in practice: by showcasing actual classroom practices that demonstrate the policies in action; by talking about research in practical, teacher-friendly language; and by offering teachers possibilities for rethinking their own practices in light of the ideas presented in the books. Books within the imprint are grouped in strands, each strand focused on a significant topic of interest.

Adolescent Literacy Strand

Adolescent Literacy at Risk? The Impact of Standards (2009) Rebecca Bowers Sipe

Adolescents and Digital Literacies: Learning Alongside Our Students (2010) Sara Kajder

Adolescent Literacy and the Teaching of Reading: Lessons for Teachers of Literature (2010) Deborah Appleman

Rethinking the "Adolescent" in Adolescent Literacy (2017) Sophia Tatiana Sarigianides, Robert Petrone, and Mark A. Lewis

Restorative Justice in the English Language Arts Classroom (2019) Maisha T. Winn, Hannah Graham, and Rita Renjitham Alfred

Writing in Today's Classrooms Strand

Writing in the Dialogical Classroom: Students and Teachers Responding to the Texts of Their Lives (2011) Bob Fecho

Becoming Writers in the Elementary Classroom: Visions and Decisions (2011) Katie Van Sluys

Writing Instruction in the Culturally Relevant Classroom (2011) Maisha T. Winn and Latrise P. Johnson

Writing Can Change Everything: Middle Level Kids Writing Themselves into the World (2020) Shelbie Witte, editor

Growing Writers: Principles for High School Writers and Their Teachers (2021) Anne Elrod Whitney

Literacy Assessment Strand

Our Better Judgment: Teacher Leadership for Writing Assessment (2012) Chris W. Gallagher and Eric D. Turley

Beyond Standardized Truth: Improving Teaching and Learning through Inquiry-Based Reading Assessment (2012) Scott Filkins

Reading Assessment: Artful Teachers, Successful Students (2013) Diane Stephens, editor

Going Public with Assessment: A Community Practice Approach (2018) Kathryn Mitchell Pierce and Rosario Ordoñez-Jasis

Literacies of the Disciplines Strand

Entering the Conversations: Practicing Literacy in the Disciplines (2014) Patricia Lambert Stock, Trace Schillinger, and Andrew Stock

Real-World Literacies: Disciplinary Teaching in the High School Classroom (2014) Heather Lattimer

Doing and Making Authentic Literacies (2014) Linda Denstaedt, Laura Jane Roop, and Stephen Best

Reading in Today's Classrooms Strand

Connected Reading: Teaching Adolescent Readers in a Digital World (2015) Kristen Hawley
Turner and Troy Hicks
Digital Reading: What's Essential in Grades 3–8 (2015) William L. Bass II and Franki Sibberson
Teaching Reading with YA Literature: Complex Texts, Complex Lives (2016) Jennifer Buehler

Teaching English Language Learners Strand

*Beyond "Teaching to the Test": Rethinking Accountability and Assessment for English Language
Learners* (2017) Betsy Gilliland and Shannon Pella
Community Literacies en Confianza: Learning from Bilingual After-School Programs (2017)
Steven Alvarez
Understanding Language: Supporting ELL Students in Responsive ELA Classrooms (2017)
Melinda J. McBee Orzulak
*Writing across Culture and Language: Inclusive Strategies for Working with ELL Writers in the
ELA Classroom* (2017) Christina Ortmeier-Hooper

Students' Rights to Read and Write Strand

Adventurous Thinking: Fostering Students' Rights to Read and Write in Secondary ELA Classrooms
(2019) Mollie V. Blackburn, editor
In the Pursuit of Justice: Students' Rights to Read and Write in Elementary School (2020) Mariana
Souto-Manning, editor
*Already Readers and Writers: Honoring Students' Rights to Read and Write in the Middle Grade
Classroom* (2020) Jennifer Ochoa, editor

Children's and YA Literature Strand

*Challenging Traditional Classroom Spaces with YA Literature: Students in Community as Course
Co-Designers* (2022) Ricki Ginsberg

Technology in the Classroom Strand

Reimiagining Literacies in the Digital Age: Multimodal Strategies to Teach with Technology (2022)
Pauline S. Schmidt and Matthew J. Kruger-Ross

Reimagining Literacies in the Digital Age

Multimodal Strategies to Teach with Technology

Pauline S. Schmidt
West Chester University of Pennsylvania

Matthew J. Kruger-Ross
West Chester University of Pennsylvania

National Council of Teachers of English
340 N. Neil St., Suite #104, Champaign, Illinois 61820
www.ncte.org

Staff Editor: Cynthia Gomez
Imprint Editor: Cathy Fleischer
Interior Design: Victoria Pohlmann
Interior Photos: Kyle Tucker
Cover Design: Pat Mayer
Cover Image: iStock.com/Halfpoint

ISBN 978-0-8141-3201-2; eISBN 978-0-8141-3203-6

Library of Congress Control Number: 2022946264

This book is dedicated to the teachers, preservice teachers, and students who persevered through the pandemic. We see you and hope this book helps us rebuild education together.

Dear Reader,

As a former high school teacher, I remember the frustration I felt when the gap between Research (and that is how I always thought of it: Research with a capital R) and my own practice seemed too wide to ever cross. So many research studies were easy to ignore, in part because they were so distant from my practice and in part because I had no one to help me see how that research would make sense in my everyday practice.

That gap informs the thinking behind this book imprint. Designed for busy teachers, Principles in Practice publishes books that look carefully at NCTE's research reports and policy statements and put those policies to the test in actual classrooms. The goal: to familiarize teachers with important teaching issues, the research behind those issues, and potential resources, and—most of all—make the research and policies come alive for teacher-readers.

This book is part of a new strand, one that focuses on Technology in Today's Classrooms. Each book in the strand highlights a different aspect of this important topic and is organized in a similar way: immersing you first in the research principles surrounding technology use (as laid out in NCTE's *Beliefs for Integrating Technology into the English Language Arts Classroom)* and then taking you into actual classrooms, teacher discussions, and student work to see how the principles play out. Each book closes with a teacher-friendly annotated bibliography to offer you even more resources.

Good teaching is connected to strong research. We hope these books help you continue the good teaching that you're doing, think hard about ways to adapt and adjust your practice, and grow even stronger and more confident in the vital work you do with kids every day.

Best of luck,

Cathy Fleischer
Imprint Editor

Contents

Preface

Who We Are

We want to begin our journey together by introducing ourselves and our relationship to literacy and technology. As former teachers of grades 5–12 and current teacher educators, we have thought a lot about the connections among literacy, technology, and pedagogy, and so we begin by sharing some of our thinking and clarifying our beliefs and stances so that you will understand what led us to write this book and share our ideas with you.

As authors, you will see we generally write with one voice, but you will occasionally notice that our examples focus on one of us in particular because of our backgrounds. Thus, Pauline's voice primarily shares examples that focus on ELA content, and Matthew will chime in on content more related to educational technologies. The book is truly cowritten, but we rely on our own strengths and expertise in these areas.

We start by recalling some of our own memories of teaching with technology to illustrate why we are such passionate advocates of embedding technologies into authentic literacy experiences. Our stories may seem laughable to some of our younger colleagues, while others will find a confirmation of their own experiences. You may also notice that we have tried to specifically highlight and include examples of relevance given the importance of antiracist and social justice pedagogies. We hope that these can continue to help our ELA and teacher education colleagues to situate justice meaningfully in our classrooms.

As readers, we think of you as colleagues. We ask that you be open to our ideas and consider the possibilities of adapting them to your own specific culture and contexts. Since March 2020, educators and students all over the country—and even some of you—may have implemented technologies without really understanding how or why you were doing it. This book should help reframe those experiences. In this book, we share our vision of technology in the literacy classroom, highly influenced by what we experienced during the pandemic as the technology we used grew and changed in ways we could not have imagined. We start by explaining the core structure of the book.

Before we jump into the intersection of technological tools and literacies of the present, let's take a short trip to the past and explore just how quickly technology has emerged and evolved in classrooms.

Listen to us introduce ourselves!

Visit the *Notorious Pedagogues*, "Going Virtual" series on Anchor.fm

Pauline: When I was teaching ninth-grade English in Western New York, my rural school district had just made a huge financial investment in technology. It was the early 2000s, and I remember one summer we had to pack everything and protect our personal belongings from the dust, as every classroom was going to be wired. We didn't know what that meant, but we found that when we returned to school in August, we had new docking stations for teacher laptops at our desks, and I had five student computers at the back of my classroom. I wasn't entirely sure what I'd do or how (or if) I'd make good use out of this new equipment, but I was curious and tried a few things out over the course of the year.

While I was preparing to be observed for my tenure review, the pressure was on to impress the superintendent with something based on technology. I planned what I thought was an engaging, technology-based lesson only to discover that the network was down that day. My beloved department chair, John, walked past my classroom and rolled a piece of chalk across the floor. At the time, I'd thought he was trying to make me smile and relax about the tenure observation, but I wonder now what he'd really meant. Was he trying to send a message about technology itself? About the importance of placing pedagogy first? That experience led me to further reflect on the tension that exists between integrating technologies. I realize that in that particular time frame, technology was new and exciting, and maybe some experienced teachers thought it was a trend that would soon fade away. Further, some probably believed that simply placing technological devices into the classroom would, by the power of osmosis, sponsor educational innovation. Without explicit pedagogical training, some teachers reacted with fear and resistance. Now, two decades into the twenty-first century, I think we can all agree that technology isn't going anywhere any time soon, so buckle up!

Matthew: In the mid-2000s, when I began teaching middle school, my colleagues and I were beginning to feel the pressure to evaluate and integrate emerging Web 2.0 technologies into our classrooms. I was one of fifteen teachers in the middle school, and we shared one projector that was located on a rolling cart and locked in a closet when not in use. In this era of educational technology, each teacher had a desktop computer and two classrooms had three desktop computers for student use. My classroom was one of the rooms that housed the computers for student use, and having students from another class gently knock on the door during my own class time to ask for permission to use the computers was the norm. The integration of technology was based on the day-to-day availability of the projector and whether or not the website or web-based tool being used was allowed past the school's sensitive firewalls.

I remember the time I had planned an elaborate and interactive lesson. I had booked the projector, brought my own personal laptop, and made sure I had the right adapter. I got the students settled and explained the activity, and then I turned to load the website. The page turned red, and I was informed that this type of website had been deemed inappropriate or too risky by the school's internet filters. As a teacher, I had to reconsider and reevaluate my planned lesson activity at warp speed—a phenomenon that will be familiar to many other teachers. The ability to adapt and select technologies to truly benefit learning and teaching has become a staple in my own teaching and in my preparation of future teachers.

BOTH: Picture how you were feeling in January 2020. Perhaps you were, like us, feeling awesome! We had just been to Walt Disney World with our families, we had signed this book contract, our research ethics proposal had been approved, and we knew we were looking forward to our co-taught class Technology in the Secondary English Classroom (more on that class in a moment). It was our fourth time teaching this class, so we had made improvements and tweaks to the assignments and pacing. We were on the top of the world and had entered the spring 2020 semester with a plan. The plan was working . . . until spring break. Then COVID-19 hit. Our spring break was extended to give faculty an opportunity to reconfigure face-to-face classes to a remote format. To be honest, even for two people completely comfortable with technology, we faltered. Big time. But then we stepped back and learned from the experience as we crafted this book.

Acknowledgments

Since most of this manuscript was written while we were working from home, we start by acknowledging our families: Frederik, Brian, Robert, and Emma. Thank you for tolerating our Zoom sessions, overcoming pandemic-related challenges, and helping us keep things in perspective.

We are profoundly grateful to our professional families as well. Our colleagues at West Chester University, West Chester Writing Project, PCTELA, and NCTE have provided sound advice and encouragement throughout this process.

To all the participants who gave up their time to be interviewed, we appreciate your contributions and reflections and were continually moved by your inventiveness, creativity, and commitment to your students.

To our graduate assistants, Bobby and Jen, thank you for your support with the minutiae of book publishing, from spelling errors to QR codes. We specifically thank you for the annotated bibliography at the end of this book.

To Kyle Tucker and Maria Mejia, thank you for helping us secure amazing photographs for the book.

To the creators, writers, leaders, and artists we have cited and mentioned here, we hope that we have honored your work, elevated your voice, and expanded the reach of your influence.

To our editor, Cathy Fleischer, we cannot thank you enough for shepherding us through this process. We used to look upon editorial acknowledgments and find them rather over the top, but on the other side of this book-writing journey, we struggle to express the fullness of our gratitude.

To the editorial team at NCTE, thank you for trusting our unique approach to creating a multimodal text.

To the WRH 325 class itself. This book would not exist without us having had the opportunity to co-teach this unique and rewarding course.

Finally, to our students taking WRH 325 in spring 2022. You enthusiastically read through our chapter drafts and asked questions that helped us with the final revisions. Your energy, curiosity, and confidence make us optimistic about the future of our profession.

Beliefs for Integrating Technology into the English Language Arts Classroom

This statement, formerly known as Beliefs about Technology and the Preparation of English Teachers, was updated in October 2018 with the new title, Beliefs for Integrating Technology into the English Language Arts Classroom.

Originally developed in July 2005, revised by the ELATE Commission on Digital Literacy in Teacher Education (D-LITE), October 2018

Preamble

What it means to communicate, create, and participate in society seems to change constantly as we increasingly rely on computers, smartphones, and the Web to do so. Despite this change, the challenge that renews itself — for teachers, teacher educators, and researchers — is to be responsive to such changes in meaningful ways without abandoning the kinds of practices and principles that we as English educators have come to value and know to work.

That's why we created this document — a complete update and overhaul of a 2005 document published on behalf of the Conference on English Education, "Beliefs about Technology and the Preparation of English Teachers: Beginning the Conversation," published in *Contemporary Issues in Technology and Teacher Education*. With some members of that original working group, as well as with many colleagues who have emerged in our field since that time, we offer a layered framework to support colleagues in their efforts to confidently and creatively explore networked, ubiquitous technologies in a way that deepens and expands the core principles of practice that have emerged over the last century in English and literacy education.

We begin by articulating four belief statements, crafted by this working group, composed of teachers as well as teacher educators and researchers. Then, we unpack each of the four belief statements in the form of an accessible summary paragraph followed by specific suggestions for K–12 teachers, teacher educators, and researchers. We conclude each section with a sampling of related scholarship. As you read, you will notice that the beliefs are interwoven and echo each other necessarily; they are recursive but not redundant. We anticipate that as you read, you will see ways that they complement (or even conflict with) each other in theory or practice. Our field is complex, as is human experience. Our goal is to offer the field something well researched, usable, and empowering. If any of those words occur to you while reading, we will have considered our task complete, for now.

All contributors have offered their time, talent, and energy. Without the people noted at this document's conclusion, this simply would not have happened. Moreover, we thank our four external reviewers whose feedback was thorough and thoughtful, and contributed with expertise, collegiality, and aplomb.

Tom Liam Lynch, Pace University   Troy Hicks, Central Michigan University

Beliefs for Integrating Technology into the English Language Arts Classroom

1. **Literacy means *literacies*.** Literacy is more than reading, writing, speaking, listening, and viewing as traditionally defined. It is more useful to think of literacies, which are social practices that transcend individual modes of communication.

2. **Consider literacies before technologies.** New technologies should be considered only when it is clear how they can enhance, expand, and/or deepen engaging and sound practices related to literacies instruction.

3. **Technologies provide new ways to consume and produce texts.** What it means to consume and produce texts is changing as digital technologies offer new opportunities to read, write, listen, view, record, compose, and interact with both the texts themselves and with other people.

4. **Technologies and their associated literacies are not neutral.** While access to technology and the internet has the potential to lessen issues of inequity, they can also perpetuate and even accelerate discrimination based on gender, race, socioeconomic status, and other factors.

The Beliefs Expanded

Belief 1: Literacy means *literacies*.

Literacy is more than reading, writing, speaking, listening, and viewing as traditionally defined. It is more useful to think of literacies, *which are social practices that transcend individual modes of communication.* In today's world, it is insufficient to define literacy as only skills-based reading, writing, speaking, listening, and viewing. Even though common standards documents, textbook series, and views on instruction may maintain the traditional definition of literacy as print-based, researchers are clear that it is more accurate to approach literacy as *literacies* or *literacy practices*. (We'll use the former here.)

There are multiple ways people communicate in a variety of social contexts. What's more, the way people communicate increasingly necessitates networked, technological mediation. To that end, relying exclusively on traditional definitions of literacy unnecessarily limits the ways students can communicate and the ways educators can imagine curriculum and pedagogy.

Understanding the complexities of literacies, we believe:

1. K–12 English teachers, with their students, should
   - engage literacies as social practices by sponsoring students in digital writing and connected reading to collaboratively construct knowledge, participate in immersive learning experiences, and reach out to their own community and a global audience.
   - encourage multimodal digital communication while modeling how to effectively compose images, presentations, graphics, or other media productions by combining video clips, images, sound, music, voice-overs, and other media.
   - promote digital citizenship by modeling and mentoring students' use of devices, tools, social media, and apps to create media and interact with others.
   - develop information literacies to determine the validity and relevance of media for academic argument including varied sources (e.g., blogs, Wikipedia, online databases, YouTube, mainstream news sites, niche news sites).

- foster critical media literacies by engaging students in analysis of both commercial media corporations and social media by examining information-reporting strategies, advertising of products or experiences, and portrayals of individuals in terms of gender, race, socioeconomic status, physical and cognitive ability, and other factors.

2. English teacher educators, with preservice and inservice teachers, should
   - critically evaluate a variety of texts (across genres and media) using a variety of theoretical perspectives (e.g., social semiotics, connectivism, constructivism, post-humanism).
   - consider the influence of digital technologies/networks in English language arts (ELA) methods courses to help preservice and inservice teachers foster use of digital/multimodal/critical literacies to support their students' learning.
   - model classroom use of literacy practices for creating and critiquing texts as well as for engaging with digital and networked technologies.
   - design assignments, activities, and assessments that encourage interdisciplinary thinking, community and civic engagement, and technological integration informed by theories relevant to ELA.

3. English and literacy researchers should
   - study *literacies* as more than general reading and writing abilities and move toward an understanding of teaching and learning within expanded frames of literacies and literacy practices (e.g., new literacies, multiliteracies, and socially situated literacies).
   - question how technologies shape and mediate literacy practices in different scenes and spaces for activating user agency and making change.
   - examine to what degree access to and support of digital tools/technologies and instruction in schools reflects and/or perpetuates inequality.
   - explore how students and/or teachers negotiate the use of various literacies for various purposes.
   - make explicit the ways technologies and literacies intersect with various user identities and understandings about and across different disciplines.
   - articulate how policies and financial support at various levels (local, state, and national) inform both the infrastructure and the capacities for intellectual freedom to engage with literacies in personally and socially transformative ways.

Some Related Scholarship

Bartels, J. (2017). Snapchat and the sophistication of multimodal composition. *English Journal, 106*(5), 90–92.

Beach, R., Campano, G., Edmiston, B., & Borgmann, M. (2010). *Literacy tools in the classroom: Teaching through critical inquiry, grades 5–12.* New York, NY: Teachers College Press.

Coiro, J., Knobel, M., Lankshear, C., & Leu, D. J. (Eds.). (2014). *Handbook of research on new literacies.* New York, NY: Routledge.

Gee, J. P. (2015). Social linguistics and literacies: *Ideology in discourses* (5th ed.). New York, NY: Routledge.

Hicks, T., Young, C. A., Kajder, S. B., & Hunt, B. (2012). Same as it ever was: Enacting the promise of teaching, writing, and new media. *English Journal, 101*(3), 68–74.

Kist, W. (2000). Beginning to create the new literacy classroom: What does the new literacy look like? *Journal of Adolescent & Adult Literacy, 43*(8), 710–718.

Kucer, S. B. (2014). *Dimensions of literacy: A conceptual base for teaching reading and writing in school settings* (4th ed.). New York, NY: Routledge.

Leander, K. (2009). Composing with old and new media: Toward a parallel pedagogy. In V. Carrington & M. Robinson (Eds.), *Digital literacies: Social learning and classroom practices* (pp. 147–163). London, England: SAGE.

Lynch, T. L. (2015). *The hidden role of software in educational research: Policy to practice.* New York: Routledge.

Piotrowski, A., & Witte. S. (2016). Flipped learning and TPACK construction in English education. *International Journal of Technology in Teaching and Learning, 12*(1), 33–46.

Rheingold, H. (2012). *Net smart: How to thrive online.* Cambridge, MA: The MIT Press.

Rish, R. M., & Pytash, K. E. (2015). Kindling the pedagogic imagination: Preservice teachers writing with social media. *Voices from the Middle, 23*(2), 37–42.

Rodesiler, L., & Pace, B. (2015). English teachers' online participation as professional development: A narrative study. *English Education, 47*(4), 347–378.

Turner, K. H., & Hicks, T. (2015). *Connected reading: Teaching adolescent readers in a digital world.* National Council of Teachers of English.

Belief 2: Consider literacies before technologies.

New technologies should be considered only when it is clear how they can enhance, expand, and/or deepen engaging and sound practices related to literacies instruction.

In news releases and on school websites, it is not uncommon for educators to promote new technologies that appear to be more engaging for students or efficient for teachers. Engagement and efficiency are worthwhile pursuits, but it is also necessary to ensure that any use of a new technology serves intentional and sound instructional practices. Further, educators must be mindful to experiment with new technologies before using them with students, and at scale, in order to avoid overshadowing sound instruction with technical troubleshooting.

Finally, many new technologies can be used both inside and outside school, so educators should gain a good understanding of both the instructional potential (e.g., accessing class materials from home) and problems (e.g., issues of data privacy or cyber-bullying) of any potential technology use. Technological decisions must be guided by our theoretical and practical understanding of literacies as social practices.

Understanding this need to focus on instructional strategies that promote mindful literacy practices when using technologies, we believe:

1. K–12 English teachers, with their students, should
   - identify the unique purposes, audiences, and contexts related to online/e-book reading as well as digital writing, moving beyond historical conceptions of literature and composition in more narrowly defined, text-centric ways.
   - explore an expanded definition of "text" in a digital world which includes alphabetic text as well as multimodal texts such as images, charts, videos, maps, and hypertexts.
   - discuss issues of intellectual property and licensing in the context of multimodal reading and writing, including concepts related to copyright, fair use, Creative Commons, and the public domain.

2. English teacher educators, with preservice and inservice teachers, should

- recognize the role of out-of-school literacies and consider the place of students' own language uses in mediated spaces, including the use of abbreviations, acronyms, emojis, and other forms of "digitalk."
- model instructional practices and engage in new literacies that teachers themselves will employ with their own K–12 students such as composing, publishing, and reflecting on a video documentary or digital story.
- focus on affordances and constraints of technologies that can be used for varied purposes (e.g., the use of a collaborative word processor for individual writing with peer feedback, for group brainstorming, or for whole-class content curation) over fixed uses of limited tools such as online quiz systems, basic reading comprehension tests, or grammar games.

3. English and literacy researchers should
- consider how existing paradigms such as New Literacy Studies, New Literacies, and the Pedagogy of Multiliteracies can help to understand how students themselves experience technology, as well as how to use technology to enhance student learning.
- develop research agendas that examine best practices in K–12 classrooms where teachers leverage the power of literacies and technologies to help foster student voice and activism.
- build on a rich ethnographic tradition in our field to discover how literacy practices—for teachers and for students—change across time, space, and location.
- focus on inquiry that balances the novelty of digital tools with the overarching importance of teaching and learning for deep meaning-making, substantive conversation, and critical thinking.

Some Related Scholarship

Garcia, A., Seglem, R., & Share, J. (2013). Transforming teaching and learning through critical media literacy pedagogy. *Learning Landscapes, 6*(2),109–124.

Hammer, R., & Kellner, D. (Eds.). (2009). *Media/cultural studies: Critical approaches.* New York, NY: Peter Lang.

Hicks, T. (2009). *The digital writing workshop.* Portsmouth, NH: Heinemann.

Jones, R. H., & Hafner, C. A. (2012). *Understanding digital literacies: A practical introduction.* Milton Park, Abingdon, Oxon; New York: Routledge.

Kolb, L. (2017). *Learning first, technology second: The educator's guide to designing authentic lessons.* Portland, OR: International Society for Technology in Education.

Kress, G. (2010). *Multimodality: A social semiotic approach to contemporary communication.* London, England: Routledge.

Lankshear, C., & Knobel, M. (2011). *New literacies: Everyday practices and social learning* (3rd Ed.). Berkshire, England ; New York, NY: Open University Press.

Merkley, D. J., Schmidt, D. A., & Allen, G. (2001). Addressing the English language arts technology standard in a secondary reading methodology course. *Journal of Adolescent & Adult Literacy, 45*(3), 220–231.

Mills, K. A. (2010). A review of the "digital turn" in the new literacy studies. *Review of Educational Research, 80*(2), 246–271.

Belief 3: Technologies provide new ways to consume and produce texts.

What it means to consume and produce texts is changing as digital technologies offer new opportunities to read, write, listen, view, record, compose, and interact with both the texts themselves and with other people.

As digital technologies have become more ubiquitous, so too has the ability to consume and produce texts in exciting new ways. To be clear, some academic tasks do not change. Whether a text is a paper-based book or a film clip, what it means to create a strong thesis statement or to ask a critical question about the text remains consistent. Further, some principles of consumption and production transfer across different types of texts, like the idea that an author (or a filmmaker, or a website designer) intentionally composed their text using specific techniques.

However, some things do change. For example, students can collaborate virtually on their reading (e.g., annotating a shared text even when not in the same physical space) and their writing (e.g., using collaborative document applications to work remotely on a text at the same time). Educators should be always aware of the above dynamics and plan instruction accordingly.

Understanding that there are dynamic literacy practices at work in the consumption and production of texts, we believe:

1. K–12 English teachers, with their students, should
   - teach students the principles of design and composition, as well as theories connected to issues of power and representation in visual imagery, music, and sound.
   - introduce students to the idea of audience through authentic assignments that have shared purpose and reach beyond the classroom to other youth as well as across generations.
   - ask students to repurpose a variety of digital media (e.g., images, video, music, text) to create a multimodal mashup or explore other emerging media genres (e.g., digital storytelling, infographics, annotated visuals, screencasts) that reflect concepts in literature such as theme, character, and setting.
   - direct students to use a note-taking tool to post text and images connected to a piece of literature they are reading in the form of a character's diary or a reader response journal.
   - immerse students in the world of transmedia storytelling by having them trace the origin and evolution of a character, storyline, issue, or event across multiple online platforms including a photo essay, a timeline, and an interactive game.
   - invite students to investigate their stance on social issues through the multimodal inquiry methods involved in digital storytelling, documentary video, or podcasting.

2. English teacher educators, with preservice and inservice teachers, should
   - harness online platforms for collaborative writing to invite teacher candidates to examine the composing practices of students and create peer feedback partnerships.
   - read, annotate, and discuss both alphabetic and visual texts, leading to substantive discussion about issues of plot, theme, and character development.
   - explore how practicing teachers are facilitating multimodal composition and sharing student writing with audiences beyond the classroom.
   - encourage teacher candidates to design instruction that integrates digital composing and multimodalities with canonical literature.

3. English and literacy researchers should
    - examine the affordances and constraints of multimodal composition, points of tension with traditional academic literacies, and the role that teachers of writing play in assessment and evaluation of multimodal compositions.
    - describe and articulate ideas related to authentic writing experiences beyond the classroom, including a better account of audiences for whom students are writing and purposes other than academic argument.
    - explore what constitutes critical literacy—paying attention to the construction of individual and cultural identities—when composing multimodally with visuals, music, and sound.

Some Related Scholarship

Alpers, M., & Herr-Stephenson, R. (2013). Transmedia play: Literacy across America. *Journal of Media Literacy Education, 5*(2), 366–369.

Bishop, P., Falk-Ross, F., Andrews, G., Cronenberg, S., Moran, C. M., & Weiler, C. (2017). Digital technologies in the middle grades. In S. B. Mertens, & M. M. Caskey (Eds.), *Handbook of resources in middle level education*. Charlotte, NC: Information Age Publishing.

Brandt, D. (2015). *The rise of writing: Redefining mass literacy*. Cambridge, England: Cambridge University Press.

Brownell, C., & Wargo, J. (2017). (Re)educating the senses to multicultural communities: Prospective teachers using digital media and sonic cartography to listen for culture. *Multicultural Education Review, 9*(3), 201–214.

Connors, S. P. (2016). Designing meaning: A multimodal perspective on comics reading. In C. Hill (Ed.), *Teaching comics through multiple lenses: Critical perspectives* (pp. 13–29). London, England: Routledge.

Doerr-Stevens, C. (2017). Embracing the messiness of research: Documentary video composition as embodied, critical media literacy. *English Journal, 106*(3), 56–62.

Garcia, A. (Ed.). (2014). *Teaching in the connected learning classroom*. Irvine, CA: Digital Media and Learning Research Hub.

Hicks, T. (2013). *Crafting digital writing: Composing texts across media and genres*. Portsmouth, NH: Heinemann.

Hobbs, R. (2011). *Digital and media literacy: Connecting culture and classroom*. Thousand Oaks, CA: Corwin.

Ito, M., Gutiérrez, K., Livingstone, S., Penuel, B., Rhodes, J., Salen, K., Schor, J., Sefton-Green, J., & Watkins, S. (2013). *Connected learning: An agenda for research and design*. Digital Media and Learning Research Hub.

Kajder, S. (2010). *Adolescents and digital literacies: Learning alongside our students*. Urbana, IL: NCTE.

Krutka, D. G., & Damico, N. (2017). Tweeting with intention: Developing a social media pedagogy for teacher education. In *Society for Information Technology & Teacher Education International Conference* (pp. 1674–1678). Association for the Advancement of Computing in Education (AACE).

Moran, C. M. (2016). Telling our story: Using digital scrapbooks to celebrate cultural capital. *International Journal of Designs for Learning, 7*(3), 88–94.

Rodesiler, L., & Kelley, B. (2017). Toward a readership of "real" people: A case for authentic writing opportunities. *English Journal, 106*(6), 22–28.

Rybakova, K. (2016, March). Using Screencasting as a Feedback Tool in Teacher Education. In *Society for Information Technology & Teacher Education International Conference* (pp. 1355–1358). Association for the Advancement of Computing in Education (AACE).

Smith, A., West-Puckett, S., Cantrill, C., & Zamora, M. (2016). Remix as professional learning: Educators' iterative literacy practice in CLMOOC. *Educational Sciences, 6*(12).

Sullivan, S. R., & Clarke, T. (2017). Teachers first: Hands-on PD with digital writing. *English Journal, 106*(3), 69–74.

Yancey, K. B. (2009). 2008 NCTE Presidential address: The impulse to compose and the age of composition. *Research in the Teaching of English, 43*(3), 316–338.

Young, C. A., & Moran, C. M. (2017). *Applying the flipped classroom model to English language arts education.* Hershey, PA: IGI Global.

Belief 4: Technologies and their associated literacies are not neutral.

While access to technology and the internet has the potential to lessen issues of inequity, they can also perpetuate and even accelerate discrimination based on gender, race, socioeconomic status, and other factors. It is common to hear digital technologies discussed in positive, progressive, and expansive terms; those who speak with enthusiasm may be doing so without an awareness that technology can also deepen societal inequities. Students who have access to technology at home, for example, might appear to understand a subject presented with a digital device faster than those who do not have access to similar devices outside of school.

As another example, some technologies that enable systems like "credit recovery courses" and remedial literacy software — which are frequently used more heavily in "struggling" schools that serve students who are poor and/or of color — can often reduce pedagogy to the mere coverage of shallow content and completion of basic assessments, rather than providing robust innovation for students to creatively represent their learning.

Understanding the complexity of learning how to use technology, and one's own social, political, and personal relationship to issues of gender, race, socioeconomic status, and other factors, we believe:

1. K–12 English teachers, with their students, should
   - promote and demonstrate critical thinking through discussion and identification of the rhetoric of written and digital materials (e.g., political propaganda and groupthink through social media posts and commentary).
   - introduce research skills that complicate and expand upon the trends of online authorship and identity (e.g., censorship, fair use, privacy, and legalities).
   - explore and measure the impact of a digital footprint on readers by analyzing different online identities (e.g., fanfiction, social media, professional websites).
   - choose technology products and services with an intentional awareness toward equity, including the affordances and constraints evident in free/open source, freemium, and subscription-based offerings.

2. English teacher educators, with preservice and inservice teachers, should
   - demonstrate how inequality affects access to technology throughout communities (e.g. policies, funding, stereotyping).
   - advocate for technology in marginalized communities through, for example, grant writing, community outreach programs, and family-oriented workshops.

- model research-driven practices and methods that integrate technology into the English language arts in ways that underscore the learning of conceptual, procedural, and attitudinal and/or value-based knowledge (e.g., lesson and curriculum planning).
- define and provide examples of technology use for educational equity that expand beyond gender, race, and socioeconomic status to include mental health, ableism, immigration status, exceptionality, and (dis)ability.

3. English and literacy researchers should
   - design research studies that problematize popular assumptions about the nature of societal inequity, as well as issues of power and authority in knowledge production.
   - introduce, examine, and question theoretical frameworks that provide principles and concepts which attempt to acknowledge and name inequality in society.
   - build methodological frameworks that account for hidden issues of power and stance in research questions, methods, the role of researcher(s), and identification of findings.
   - advocate for equitable solutions that employ technology in culturally responsive ways, drawing on students' and teachers' existing funds of knowledge related to literacy, learning, and using digital devices/networks.

Some Related Scholarship

Drucker, M. J. (2006). Commentary: Crossing the digital divide: How race, class, and culture matter. *Contemporary Issues in Technology and Teacher Education, 6*(1), 43–45.

Hicks, T. (2015). (Digital) literacy advocacy: A rationale for creating shifts in policy, infrastructure, and instruction. In E. Morrell & L. Scherff (Eds.), *New directions in teaching English: Reimagining teaching, teacher education, and research (pp. 143–156)*. Lanham, MD: Rowman & Littlefield.

Levitov, D. (2017). Using the Women's March to examine freedom of speech, social justice, and social action through information literacy. *Teacher Librarian, 44*(4), 12–15.

Lewis, C., & Causey, L. (2015). Critical engagement through digital media production: A nexus of practice. In E. Morrell & L. Scherff (Eds.), *New directions in teaching English: Reimagining teaching, teacher education, and research* (pp. 123–142). Lanham, MD: Rowman & Littlefield.

McGrail, E. (2006). "It's a double-edged sword, this technology business": Secondary English teachers' perspectives on a schoolwide laptop technology initiative. *Teachers College Record, 108(*6), 1055–1079.

Morrell, E. (2008). *Critical literacy and urban youth: Pedagogies of access, dissent, and liberation.* New York, NY: Routledge.

Norris, P. (2001). *Digital divide: Civic engagement, information poverty, and the Internet worldwide.* Cambridge, England: Cambridge University Press.

Pasternak, D. L., Hallman, H. L., Caughlan, S., Renzi, L., Rush, L. S., & Meineke, H. (2016). Learning and teaching technology in English teacher education: Findings from a national study. *Contemporary Issues in Technology & Teacher Education, 16*(4).

Price-Dennis, D. (2016). Developing curriculum to support black girls' literacies in digital spaces. *English Education, 48*(4), 337–361.

Rice, M., & Rice, B. (2015). Conceptualising teachers' advocacy as comedic trickster behaviour: Implications for teacher education. *The European Journal of Humour Research, 3*(4), 9–23.

Thompson, S. (2004). An imitation of life: Deconstructing racial stereotypes in popular culture. In K. D. McBride (Ed.), *Visual media and the humanities: A pedagogy of representation* (1st ed.). Knoxville, TN: University of Tennessee Press.

Wargo, J. M., & De Costa, P. (2017). Tracing academic literacies across contemporary literacy sponsorscapes: Mobilities, ideologies, identities, and technologies. *London Review of Education, 15*(1), 101–114.

Warschauer, M. (2004). *Technology and social inclusion: Rethinking the digital divide.* Cambridge, MA: MIT Press.

Summary

In offering these four belief statements and numerous examples, the scholars and educators involved in writing this document recognize that we, too, are both informed — and limited — by our own experiences, assumptions, and daily literacy practices. It is our sincere hope that this substantially revised document can be a tool for opening up new conversations, opportunities for instruction, and lines of inquiry within the field of English language arts.

Contributors

Working Group Members

Jonathan Bartels, University of Alaska Anchorage

Richard Beach, University of Minnesota (Emeritus)

Sean Connors, University of Arkansas

Nicole Damico, University of Central Florida

Candance Doerr-Stevens, University of Wisconsin-Milwaukee

Troy Hicks, Central Michigan University

Karen Labonte, independent educational consultant

Stephanie Loomis, Georgia State University

Tom Liam Lynch, Pace University

Ewa McGrail, Georgia State University

Clarice Moran, Kennesaw State University

Donna Pasternak, University of Wisconsin-Milwaukee

Amy Piotrowski, Utah State University

Mary Rice, University of Kansas

Ryan Rish, University of Buffalo

Luke Rodesiler, Purdue University Fort Wayne

Katie Rybakova, Thomas University

Sunshine Sullivan, Houghton College

Mark Sulzer, University of Cincinnati

Stephanie Thompson, Purdue University Global

Carl Young, North Carolina State University

Lauren Zucker, Northern Highlands Regional High School (Allendale, NJ)

External Reviewers

Nadia Behizadeh, Georgia State University

Nicole Mirra, Rutgers, The State University of New Jersey

Ian O'Byrne, College of Charleston

Dawn Reed, Okemos High School (MI)

Introduction: Premise of the Book

This book captures our understanding of literacies and technologies based on our decades of teaching and learning with our students. We invite you to join us as we share our co-teaching journey. In spring 2017, we became colleagues at West Chester University of Pennsylvania, working in teacher education. We were given the opportunity to co-teach a class called WRH 325: Technology in the Secondary English Classroom.

To this course, required for English education majors, Matthew brought his expertise in educational technology and Pauline brought her knowledge in secondary English. With a title like Technology in the Secondary English Classroom, you might think the course would be on the cutting edge of transforming teaching with technology—in some ways, it was and still is. The syllabus we inherited had several solid elements as it invited preservice teachers (PSTs) to create podcasts, lesson plans, digital video production, and online portfolios. But the original syllabus had problems as well: the pieces were loosely strung together by technology and were not really grounded in practical pedagogical applications in secondary English classrooms. We've now taught together for six years, and as reflective practitioners, we have yet to stop revising our assignments and our pedagogical approach to this specific content. In this book, we share some of the critical lessons and reflections about secondary teaching and technology that we've learned and experienced.

To learn more about us as co-teachers, listen to Season 1, Episode 3.

We would be remiss in failing to mention the 2020 and 2021 iterations of our own teaching, which included teaching our course remotely, and the new set of challenges that a fully remote teaching mode presents. In addition, that time period witnessed a shift in the national conversation around police violence and racism in the United States, which influenced our approaches to literacy and technology. Throughout the book, then, we highlight lessons and activities that speak to our developing understandings and indicate how these played out in face-to-face and remote settings. We include the voices of several inservice high school English teachers, many of whom are our former students, who have generously shared what they are doing in their classrooms. We have also chronicled our teaching and learning with technologies in a podcast that is publicly available entitled *Notorious Pedagogues*. Throughout this book, QR codes link to relevant episodes. Join us in rethinking the implementation and impact of technology on literacies in both the face-to-face and remote classroom.

NCTE Position Statement

We were so excited by the release of the 2018 NCTE Position Statement: *Beliefs for Integrating Technology into the English Language Arts Classroom*, upon which this book is based, because it more accurately reflects the reality of the classroom environment teachers find themselves in with regard to new literacies and technologies. We are aware that in a few years, even this updated statement may well be obsolete.

It is ironic that as an institution, education moves at a glacial pace, while new technologies hit like hurricanes, leaving a lot of teachers flying blind with digital tools. But the revised position statement has truly helped us reimagine our course over the last few years and, as a result, has affected how our PSTs envision their approaches to teaching. In particular, we have been guided by the following four beliefs that are at the center of the Position Statement:

1. **Literacy means** *literacies*.

   In this text, we begin with the presumption that literacy is inherently plural: literacies. As the statement suggests, "Literacy is more than reading, writing, speaking, listening, and viewing as traditionally defined. It is more useful to think of *literacies*, which are social practices that transcend individual modes of communication." We fully embrace and acknowledge the ways in which we are simultaneously exploring information on multiple levels. In this book, we specifically isolate visual and aural literacies (before considering multi-modality as a whole) as social practices and artifacts to consider them fully and address them in isolation. Thus, we highlight pedagogical strategies and activities, such as podcasting and augmented reality, that exemplify this component of the statement.

2. **Consider literacies before technologies.**

   One of the pitfalls we hope teachers avoid is merely thinking of technologies as add-ons or flashy tools. Again, according to the statement, "New technologies should be considered only when it is clear how they can enhance, expand, and/or deepen engaging and sound practices related to literacies instruction." By foregrounding literacies in our pedagogy, we demonstrate throughout the book the meaningful application of such tools in both face-to-face and remote classroom settings. For example, we describe in Chapter 11 how working with students as they create digital videos mirrors the writing process in a variety of ways. We aim to help teachers reflect on and consider the pedagogy behind selecting a particular tool, that is, to help them purposefully identify the right tool at the right time for optimum learning.

3. **Technologies provide new ways to consume and produce texts.**

    The Position Statement offers this advice: "What it means to consume and produce texts is changing as digital technologies offer new opportunities to read, write, listen, view, record, compose, and interact with both the texts themselves and with other people." Undoubtedly, the explosion of digital tools has pushed our imaginations beyond the pages of traditional texts. In this book, we share ways to help the next generation of students utilize technology to enhance their capacity for reading and responding to texts in multiple ways. We also explore the rights and responsibilities of producers in digital spaces to create accurate, fact-based artifacts. Specifically, in Chapters 4 and 5, we focus on how secondary students can engage with and write their own texts via digital art forms.

4. **Technologies and their associated literacies are not neutral.**

    Too often overlooked is the lack of access to digital tools and information. "While access to technology and the Internet has the potential to lessen issues of inequity," the statement reminds us, "they can also perpetuate and even accelerate discrimination based on gender, race, socioeconomic status, and other factors." In other words, we focus on how to integrate a multimodal approach to literacy beyond just the digital. We provide many examples in the text that follows for preservice and inservice teachers to identify and challenge inequities in their classrooms. Digital inequities remain a challenging and wicked problem of our current times, and this was sadly amplified at the start of the pandemic. If the pandemic taught us anything, it's that there remains a cavernous gap when it comes to access to quality/reliable technology across the country's school systems.

Road Map to the Book

The text as a whole embraces our developing understanding of different ways of using technology and how each impacts teachers in the classroom. To that end, we divide the book into three parts based on types of literacies (visual, aural, and multimodal) to illustrate how we isolate and blend literacies in the classroom. This parsing helps us approach, demonstrate, and critically assess the integration of technologies for PSTs. In each of the sections we will demonstrate what we mean by providing examples from our own teaching at the university level and the kinds of assignments our PSTs complete. We will also call upon the voices of classroom teachers committed to the work of integrating technology and literacy. These teachers generously share their stories about the lessons, activities, and reflections that they have implemented in their own classrooms. You will notice we use QR codes that will link you to additional examples and other resources.

Margin Memos

Be on the lookout for these text boxes that provide commentary on how various elements of each chapter or activity align with and are informed by the NCTE Position Statement.

Each of the three literacy sections begins with a focus chapter that is followed by two application chapters—one that highlights consuming texts and a second that showcases producing texts. For example, Part II, Visual Literacies, opens with a focus chapter (Chapter 3) that summarizes and presents the relevant scholarship and research in this area. This chapter is then followed by two application chapters—one that highlights activities and skills related to consuming visual texts (Chapter 4, on memes) and another that focuses on producing visual texts (Chapter 5, on infographics).

However, we embrace the philosophy of reading like a writer and encourage you to consume like a producer. Neither of these activities exists in isolation; we are always moving through consuming and producing. Within each application chapter, we have chosen to use a common layout. These chapters include the following elements.

Introduction

In the introduction to each chapter, we connect its topic to the theme of the section and contextualize the topic in a way that you will understand its connection to the overall purpose of the text.

Focus on Literacies

This part dives deeper into our thinking related to literacies and how the technological example best exemplifies that specific literacy. Relative to the Position Statement, this section ensures that we consider literacies before technologies.

Educating PSTs

Our collaboration draws primarily on our work together as teacher educators; thus, in this section, we draw on our own higher education teaching experience with PSTs. This section is particularly written to be accessible to preservice and early career teachers as we share insights about the focus of the chapter in such a way that is relevant to the novice teacher. Where possible, we include specific examples and samples of our conversations with our PSTs to highlight their experiences.

From the University to the Secondary Classroom

Building on our work with PSTs, we have continued to engage with secondary classroom teachers to explore how the activities and ideas presented in this book are transferable to the 8–12 classroom. This section is written with the experienced teacher in mind. Readers in this section can build on the recommendations for preservice and early career teachers as they often have greater confidence in trying new things, whether pedagogical strategies or new technological tools. Where possible, we include specific examples and samples of our conversations with secondary teachers to showcase their stories.

Concluding Thoughts

In the final section, we conclude and wrap up the chapter by briefly summarizing the key points offered throughout.

QR Codes

When possible, we link to audio, video, or other digital files that illustrate the content of that particular section; some will include *Notorious Pedagogues* podcast episodes. By sharing this work, we aim to embody the lessons and strategies presented within this text. For example, we argue that aurality is an important and often undervalued literacy. Instead of reading about an early career teacher using audiobooks in their classroom, the QR code will allow you to listen to that story instead. We hope that this feature of the book enhances its interactivity.

Reflection Box

We also use these boxes to record questions and thought experiments for you to think further about your practice.

How to Read This Book:
A Challenge to the Reader

We know there also exists a spectrum of interest when it comes to teachers integrating technology, from those who try to avoid using technology in their classrooms at all costs to those who are only interested in using technology for the sake of using the latest and greatest new tool. Neither extreme is productive or practical. Where do you fall on the spectrum? Maybe you went into survival mode and pushed fast-forward on the technology button during the 2020–2021 school year, without feeling confident in what you were doing. Maybe you have avoided technology or don't even know where to start. Or maybe you are already confidently using technology. No matter where you are on the spectrum, reading our book will help you assess yourself, consider how you and your students are using technology, and perhaps be inspired. We've embedded the existing research, our teaching, and the voices of countless preservice and inservice teachers to give you some new ideas.

We are teacher educators with forty years of combined experience, and our hearts are set on helping teachers integrate technology into their classrooms in meaningful and productive ways. In this text, we hope to appeal to the vast majority of teachers who fall in the middle of the spectrum; that is, educators who want to use technology in ways that are appropriately tied to pedagogy and will result in their students' peak engagement.

Annotated Bibliography

Moving beyond the three literacies, we consider how teachers and students engage with technologies inside and outside the classroom as digital citizens. The book concludes with an annotated bibliography of useful resources and references for teachers that collates those previously mentioned throughout the text and also includes others not already referenced.

We also acknowledge that teachers today are overwhelmed by their growing responsibilities, and we want to avoid you thinking of technology as one more thing you need to add to your daily tasks. We'd like to share our learning and successes as well as the failures and frustration we've experienced while teaching through a global pandemic. We want teachers to be able to read this book and think about how to embed technology in meaningful ways into what they are already doing in the classroom. We also hope to push the thinking of classroom teachers so that they are picking the right tool for the right moment. We, ourselves, are wary of simply using technology for technology's sake; we aim to share practical applications here that should help teachers consider the product and the process equally.

We know you are ready to get started, and we are excited to get started as well. We are committed to our work as teachers and teacher educators and hope that the

following text reflects our love of the profession and honors the important work
teachers contribute to the world.

Reflection Box

Take a moment to think about your own classroom and your use of technology. What do you feel
confident about? What questions do you have? Are you reluctant to try new technologies? Are
there specific things you are afraid of?

- How does a transformed understanding of literacies impact the integration of technologies
  into the classroom?
- How are you using technology in your teaching?
- How are your students using technology to support their learning?
- Are there pedagogical and practical applications for the integration of technology?

Part I
Foundations

On Literacies

(Re)Considering Literacy

Literacy, as it is traditionally understood, must be dramatically expanded to incorporate the ways that digital technologies have transformed the landscape of texts and reading. Drawing inspiration from the first two beliefs in the NCTE Position Statement, we take this opportunity to unpack some ideas. The first belief notes that "literacy means literacies," and the second argues to "consider literacies before technologies." This expanded understanding of literacy is described in the *Standards for the English Language Arts* (1996), which was published by NCTE and the International Reading Association over twenty-five years ago, and is reiterated in the NCTE *Belief Statement* revision (2018) that shapes the framework of this text. Rather than use *reading and writing* to describe this expanded understanding of literacy, we choose to use the terms *consuming* and *producing* because we want you to immediately grasp this broader conceptualization in order to reframe our understanding of texts and media. Thus, when we mention *consuming*, we are referring to reading, listening, and viewing. When we mention *producing*, we are referring to writing, speaking, and designing.

When we first started teaching Technology in the Secondary English Classroom and were handed a copy of the existing syllabus, we realized our co-taught version of the course needed more connections between ELA content and digital tools. We also needed to challenge our own assumptions, particularly those around our students' knowledge of and expertise in technologies. We started by going back to the basics and reflected on the traditional strands of the ELA standards—reading, writing, listening, speaking, and viewing—and wondered how we could see them as linked rather than as separate strands, especially in terms of their technological possibilities. We now see these five strands as three sets of consuming/producing pairs, especially when we added the strand *designing* to the mix. In what follows, we explore this seemingly simple, yet multilayered, idea: *developing teachers and students to read and write, listen and speak, and view and design multimodal texts* (see Figure 1.1).

FIGURE 1.1. Rethinking literacy as consuming and producing.

Consuming	Producing
Reading	Writing
Listening	Speaking
Viewing	Designing

Reading is no longer simply black text on a white page, read in isolation. Reading also includes digital video and infographics and other multimodal texts! Think about this: we are bombarded by images on websites with ads off to one side and print-based comments at the bottom of the page. There are images and videos embedded in social media streams that we need to learn how to read and understand. Take this example from news media. Even just watching the news, we now have the reporter on-screen but there is a line of print scrolling at the bottom of the screen and frequently numbers or graphs off to the side, updating the viewer on a relevant vote count or COVID-19 cases.

How is a person to understand all of this input at once? In education, we assume that our students will simply get it. We assume that because our students have been born into a digital and multimodal world, they are equipped to read and understand all of the media and information that swirls around them. But they are not. This is the myth of the digital native (Prensky, 2001). Students need to slow down, pause, and develop skills in visual literacies and aural literacies in isolation before piecing them back together. Once they are stronger in these areas, they are better equipped to handle our multimodal world. Thus, when students are bombarded by the multimodal world, they can truly grasp it with critical thinking and tact.

We argue (and explain why below) that defining literacy as understanding letters/ characters, words, and the reading practices of printed text (i.e., on paper and in books) must be shifted to include all of the ways that human beings are now engaging with, experiencing, creating, and experimenting with language. For our purposes here, texts include—but are not limited to—books, poems, podcasts, digital videos, songs, photographs, graphic novels, performances, and other works of art. In this book, when we refer to literacies, we are alerting the reader to this expanded and transformed understanding of literacy and text.

(Re)Considering Content

In addition to broadening the conventional definition of literacy, we also want to challenge the traditional notions of curriculum. By this, we mean not only disrupting the canon, but also shifting pedagogical approaches to include text sets, layered texts, and multimodal texts. For example, our PSTs already take a literature methods course, a writing methods course, several literature courses, and a young adult literature course (taught as a literature course, not as a methods course). We turned to *Workshopping the Canon* by Mary Styslinger (2017) to build upon their existing knowledge and create what we call book club to incorporate some of these strategies. Rather than reading a single classic text, as they've done in many of their previous classes, our PSTs read a pair of books: a canonical text alongside a contemporary book, such as *Lord of the Flies* and *Beauty Queens*. Throughout this book, we share the various assignments connected to this ongoing group project, including creating an infographic (Chapter 5), a podcast episode (Chapter 8), and lesson plans (appearing throughout the book). While this approach has assumed different iterations each time we have taught the course, most recently we have explored pairings with Shakespeare's *Hamlet*. Those interested in exploring this idea further should consult Styslinger's excellent book.

See *Workshopping the Canon* by Mary Styslinger.

See a snapshot of the book pairings we've used over the past few years.

Multimodality

By expanding our definition of literacy and challenging the curriculum, we open the door to rethinking multimodality. We know that we all experience the world multimodally, that is, we receive input and make meaning from all of our senses. But to be critical digital consumers of the world around us, we need to parse out and learn the skills and strategies that serve as the foundation of multimodality: aural and visual literacy. Thus, in this book we explicitly split multimodality into these two components to consider not only the characteristics of each but also their interconnections, particularly in approaching the high school English curriculum. While we think you will recognize many of our approaches, we hope you will consider multimodalities in a new light. By deconstructing the abstract notion of multimodality, we think your confidence in trying some of these strategies in your own classes will grow. We understand that teaching with multimodal texts can be tricky. We have seen some of our PSTs' visceral reactions to being asked to try some of these pedagogical shifts. Because pedagogy has not always transformed to meet this moment of multimodality, we all need to take some creative risks. By offering PSTs multiple exposures to multimodal approaches, we try to move teachers out of their classically trained comfort zone into a space that cultivates and encourages creativity and endless possibilities in terms of learning and assessment in classrooms. We ask:

- Could a student do a character analysis with a series of Instagram posts?
- Could a student analyze or problematize the plot of a canonical text by interviewing someone on a podcast?
- Could a student capture a poem's theme by creating a multimodal, digital video?

To achieve this, we build a scaffold so that PSTs can become accustomed to multimodal thinking by offering them supports. We model the experiences you will read about here and frequently remind students that they are both learners and PSTs.

A Multimodal Example

Take the example of teaching the poem "Still I Rise" by Maya Angelou (see Figure 1.2). Our students recognize it because they have read it in a class or read it independently as text.

FIGURE 1.2. Screenshot of Maya Angelou's ninetieth birthday Google Doodle.

Pauline: So, how would you teach this poem?
Moira (a PST in the class): I would photocopy the poem and hand it out to my students. And then we would read it out loud together.
Matthew: How would you do that? Would you have one student read or move through the room?
Moira: I think I would have one student volunteer to read it out loud.
Pauline: Would you give them any guided questions? Would you give them notes ahead of time? Would they need to know anything about Maya Angelou before reading it?

This dialogue represents a typical ELA poetry study. Consider how multimodality might add a new twist. Instead of using the printed text, students could also use the multimodal Google Doodle produced to commemorate Angelou's ninetieth birthday. They would see a variety of images float on a pop-out video while hearing a variety of contemporary voices (actors and singers whose names and voices they may recognize) and Maya Angelou herself recite this work of art. Further, there would be other narrative text below the video that includes biographical information for the reader. This example represents a complex multimodal text. We must ask how we can encourage our PSTs to embrace these texts and this way of teaching in their classrooms.

Watch the Google Doodle commemorating Dr. Maya Angelou's ninetieth birthday.

What we acknowledge is that a traditional focus on printed texts is only one approach. This book will help teachers layer digital elements on top of things they are likely already doing in their classrooms. Digital technologies greatly expand our ability to consume and produce texts but are an added option rather than a replacement. While these claims must remain tentative for now, we hope that you will give us the opportunity to provide additional background and supporting evidence for them throughout the book.

The Four I Multimodal Strategy (FIMS)

To provide the scaffolding for our PSTs to effectively teach multimodal texts, we developed the Four I Multimodal Strategy (FIMS). FIMS emerged from the study of our own teaching practice, our PSTs' learning, and our interviews with teachers (many of them our former students) in a variety of settings, all of whom were using technologies in their secondary classrooms. FIMS consists of four interrelated activities: identification, impact, influence, and imagination. We believe this strategy provides a much-needed language to help teachers and teacher educators as we explore digital literacies in our classrooms. FIMS connects to our emphasis on consuming and producing texts. As shown in the chart below (Figure 1.3), we see these steps developing in one direction when a student examines or experiences a text (consuming) and reversing direction when a student creates a text of their own (producing).

FIGURE 1.3. The FIMS for consuming and producing texts.

For CONSUMING texts, teachers lead students through the following steps:

- Identify →
- Impact →
- Influence →
- Imagine

These four steps can be broken down into the following prompts for further reflection and analysis:

Identify. What is this text? What do you literally experience as represented on the page/screen or in the sound? What genre is it? Whose voice is being highlighted? Can everyone access the text in its current form?

Impact. What stands out in this text? What do you first notice? What is striking about the image or sound? Are there any problems/stereotypes in the text? Would changing the mode/format change the text in any significant way?

Influence. What is the piece trying to communicate? Who is the intended audience? How do you know? Why this audience? How can you problematize the text? Why does this text enter classroom discussions?

Imagine. Can you imagine yourself within the text? Try to place yourself within the text: slow down, wonder, pause, and let your imagination engage. How can you push yourself to higher-order thinking? Are there other texts that speak to this theme or idea that come from a marginal perspective?

**Remember, imagination can seem abstract and broad in terms of application, so there are no right or wrong answers here.

For PRODUCING texts, we reverse the steps:

- Imagine →
- Influence →
- Impact →
- Identify

The reversed steps can then be broken down into the following prompts:

Imagine. How would you imagine what you are going to create? How would what you have imagined best be communicated?

Influence. What is the best format for communicating your meaning? Who are you trying to communicate with? What do you want to say? Can everyone access the text in its current form?

Impact. How can you engage the audience or impact the meaning? How can you best convey the intent of your text? How can you problematize the text?

Identify. Can you identify your successes? Can you reflect on what you did? What did you learn?

FIGURE 1.4. The FIMS image.

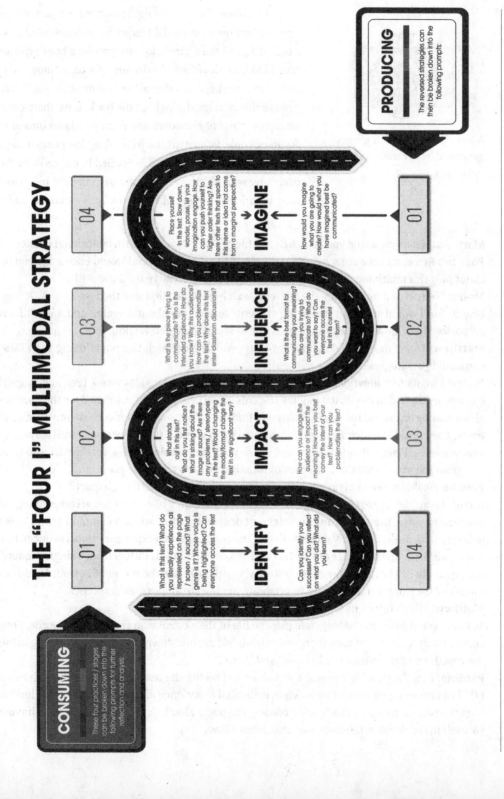

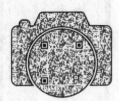

View alternative FIMS images generated by our students and colleagues.

Of course, this is not a rigid structure but part of a general strategy for how multimodal literacy instruction could proceed in a digital age. In the figure below, we present a brief explanation of how FIMS, a series of interpretive steps for consuming and producing texts, can take shape in a digital environment. As you'll see, we will use this strategy throughout the book as we share even more examples from our classroom and from the classrooms of others. As an example, let's revisit the Maya Angelou poem using the consuming practices of FIMS as applied in our class. In this first encounter with FIMS, we write the steps in bold italics to draw your attention to the use of the terms by our students and ourselves.

Matthew: Now, how would you approach teaching "Still I Rise" using this multimodal text?

Pauline: Remember, we are moving from a physical, printed text and would encourage you to think about how this multimodal representation can push your creative thinking skills.

Moira: Well, what about having the students watch the video first and then—

David: But I would still start by having students learn more about Angelou and, I don't know, preparing them for what they would be about to see in the video version.

Matthew: Okay, so Moira, do you want to try walking through the poem using the FIMS consuming strategies?

Moira: I would first *identify* that this is a Google Doodle that includes video, text, and sound; by consuming the text in this digital way, my students would hear different voices and see the words spoken aloud floating on and off the screen differently from how they would experience silently reading the poem. They would also *identify* that this is a poem written by a historical person named Maya Angelou, whose animated image they would see and whose voice they would hear—a female elder who is African American and whose mellifluous voice adds meaning to the words of the poem.

Pauline: Yeah, I agree. A great start. David, what about the second step, impact?

David: I consider *impact* by noting the power and resonance of each of the accompanying voices and how together they blend and complement one another to narrate a common poem. This text is different from a silent or individual reading of the poem, and this experience impacts understanding. This leads me to the *influence* of this text as a whole—and how it differs from a single reading of the poem—to celebrate her ninetieth birthday, to acknowledge the power of her words, to see the impact of the words on others, and to celebrate her life are all possible responses.

Matthew: Which brings us to imagine . . .

Moira: I could have my students *imagine* the life of the woman who crafted these words. They could also imagine when they themselves have felt pushed down by some force and be inspired by the repetition of the phrases "still I rise" and "I rise."

Pauline: Exactly. Hearing the multiple voices and seeing the text of the poem shows how using FIMS can provide you with a much richer, embodied experience of the poem. You could just read it on the page or hear Angelou's voice reading the poem aloud, but you would not have immersed yourself in the poem in the same way that FIMS allows.

This dialogue illustrates how FIMS provides both students and teachers with a group of strategies to help them deconstruct, interpret, and create their own multimodal texts. For producing multimodal texts, the FIMS strategies reverse to: imagine, influence, impact, and identify. Students would first *imagine* what their finished text would look and sound like, using the Angelou video as a mentor text. They wouldn't necessarily have to spend a lot of time considering the second part of *influence*, because we've assigned the digital video as the format, but they could get swept up in selecting images and background music to enhance their *impact* as they layer the reading of the poem over the visual elements. Finally, they could consider the success of the text by sharing with others and reflecting on the process of creation. Ultimately, they should be able to *identify* what they learned through this project.

As we were revising the manuscript, we shared sections with peers and our writing group for feedback. One of our colleagues, Kelly, created a list of student prompts that she thought would be a helpful addition to the FIMS strategy. You'll notice that each prompt begins with an "I" statement, such as "I see" or "I can create." This is in contrast to the questions we initially developed that teachers would ask themselves or use as verbal prompts for students in the classroom. With Kelly's "I" statements, she created a way for students to guide themselves through FIMS. Here is what she came up with:

> **Margin Memo**
>
> Throughout the remainder of the book, whenever we refer to the FIMS steps, we will italicize the terms to get your attention.

FIGURE 1.5. FIMS prompts for students.

CONSUMING	PRODUCING
Identify	Imagine
• I see . . .	• I can create . . .
• I hear . . .	• I imagine creating . . .
• I think . . .	Influence
Impact	• I want my audience to know/think/feel . . .
• I notice . . .	• I can do this by . . .
• This makes me think . . .	Impact
Influence	• I can communicate this by . . .
• I understand . . .	• I can impact my audience by . . .
• I realize . . .	Identify
• I notice . . .	• I feel proud of . . .
Imagine	• I learned . . .
• I see myself . . .	
• I imagine . . .	
• I wonder . . .	

Reflection Box

How has this chapter helped you so far to expand your definition of literacy? Make a chart with one column identifying what you are already actively doing in your classroom and one column naming what you'd like to try as you read this text.

Margin Memo

Belief #2: Consider literacies before technologies. *New technologies should be considered only when it is clear how they can enhance, expand, and/or deepen engaging and sound practices related to literacy instruction.* This Belief Statement pushes us to reframe the many kinds of literacies that constitute all students' learning and lives. This also stretches our definition of the purpose of our work in an English classroom beyond simply analyzing the words on a page. Using FIMS, we can effectively unpack literacies in new and exciting ways.

Conclusion

In this chapter, we shared our approach to literacy, multi-modality, and teaching using the FIMS strategy, focusing on the first two beliefs of the NCTE Position Statement: "literacy means literacies" and "consider literacies before technologies." As you read and consider your own practice, we hope you are already thinking of ways to expand and include a variety of modes and genres in your classroom.

We think that FIMS provides concrete practices that teachers can apply to more fully appreciate, analyze, and even create multimodal texts with their students. Of course, this strategy would amplify more traditional approaches to texts as well, but we want to suggest that focusing on them in a digital and multimodal world can enhance students' experiences with texts. In the next chapter, we turn to focusing on technology in the classroom.

On Technology

Chapter Two

Introduction

*I*n this chapter, we turn to the third and fourth beliefs in the NCTE Position
Statement and their focus on technologies. The third belief notes that "technologies
provide new ways to consume and produce texts," while the fourth argues that
"technologies and their associated literacies are not neutral." Building on these beliefs,
we begin by challenging the idea that today's students are all digital natives (Prensky,
2001). While that idea may seem commonsensical, it can easily be debunked. While
it's true that some of our PSTs might engage with social media and be glued to their
smartphones, we know that it is up to us to be the conduit to help them learn how to
harness technologies *for learning*, to help them understand the connections between
literacy, technology, and pedagogy so that once they become classroom teachers, they
can help their own students.

When we first teach our PSTs how to write lesson plans that effectively integrate
technology, it rarely goes as planned. Our students often think that using Flipgrid or
Google Slides without regard to the content or context "checks the box" for effective
technology use in the ELA classroom. While these may well be useful and productive

uses of technology in some contexts, we urge our PSTs to push beyond these initial ideas to evaluate critically how integrating technology into their future lessons can be informed by literacies, effective pedagogy, and best practices.

Models of Educational Technology That Inform Our Thinking

Two frameworks can help guide our path toward a thoughtful and intentional integration of technology and literacy teaching: TPACK and SAMR. TPACK is a theoretical model that describes teacher knowledge and stands for technological pedagogical content knowledge. SAMR is a framework for technology integration and is an acronym for substitution, augmentation, modification, and redefinition. We look at these models as two sides of the same coin, a two-pronged approach that ensures effective and meaningful teaching with technologies. The following sections are dense, but important, to help frame our work and your understanding of the book.

FIGURE 2.1. Acronyms for terms used in this chapter.

Acronym	Name	Description
TPACK	Technological pedagogical content knowledge	Framework for understanding teacher knowledge
PK	Pedagogical knowledge	
CK	Content knowledge	
TK	Technological knowledge	
PCK	Pedagogical content knowledge	
TCK	Technological content knowledge	
TPK	Technological pedagogical knowledge	
SAMR	Substitution, augmentation, modification, and redefinition	Model of technology integration

TPACK

TPACK (pronounced *tea-pack*) was originally developed as a model to describe teacher knowledge about teaching. If TPACK rings any bells in your mind, it might be because the model was inspired by Shulman's (1986) model of pedagogical content knowledge from the 1980s. Within a scholarly field that was at the time advocating for greater standardization and technical approaches to teaching, Schulman developed the idea of pedagogical content knowledge as a description of the robust body of thought and knowledge that teachers utilize in their daily work.

As technologies became increasingly accessible to teachers and students, Mishra and Khoeler (2006) updated Schulman's theoretical model to include technology, and they referred to this kind of understanding as technological knowledge. The addition of this new type of knowledge acknowledged the impact of new and emerging technologies but also grounded them in the ongoing recognition of the importance of pedagogy and content knowledge. TPACK is represented by the image in Figure 2.2.

FIGURE 2.2. Technological Pedagogical Content Knowledge (TPACK) diagram.

Again, building on pedagogical content knowledge, the introduction of technological knowledge adds complexity to the concept. For example, not only do we have the three different kinds of knowledge (technological knowledge, pedagogical knowledge, and content knowledge), but the different variations also overlap. Thus, there is *pedagogical content knowledge* (PCK), *technological pedagogical knowledge* (TPK) and *technological content knowledge* (TCK). These all overlap or culminate in what we call the sweet spot, where all three types of knowledge intersect: technological pedagogical content knowledge, or TPACK. In the sweet spot, a lesson or activity is planned that accounts for and synergizes content knowledge, pedagogical strategies, and the necessary technological tool.

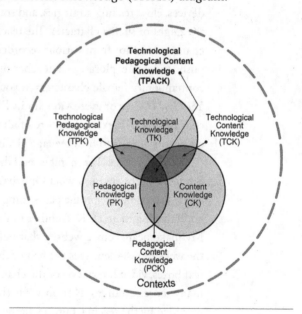

A few examples will help unpack this model further. Pedagogical knowledge means the *how* of teaching, while content knowledge denotes the *what* that we teach. Therefore, PCK encompasses teachers' understandings of specific and appropriate ways to teach certain content. For example, the experienced English teacher knows multiple ways of teaching the writing process. In this instance, the skills and practices around writing would be the *content knowledge*, and the method, Writer's Workshop, would exemplify an expression of *pedagogical knowledge*.

Things become more complicated when technological knowledge is integrated into the model, which results in TCK and TPK. In short, certain technologies and applications are more effective for certain content areas (TCK), and certain methods of teaching (i.e., pedagogies) are more aligned with a number of technologies (TPK).

The examples that we share to make this understanding clear for our PSTs draw on other subject areas: a teacher would not use a timeline app to teach multiplication (as a skill), nor would they use a tool like Google Slides to teach creative writing. Again, it isn't that a teacher could never use these technologies; rather, it is simply that they are neither the best nor the most effective choices for teaching those particular skills or disciplines.

The ultimate goal is to hit the TPACK sweet spot by creating a lesson or implementation that takes account of, and can argue for, all three types of knowledge simultaneously. For example, to teach the direct/indirect characterization of Ophelia in *Hamlet*, a teacher would have the content knowledge of the play to guide students to examine what Ophelia says, does, and thinks and how she interacts with the main character, Hamlet. A teacher would also have the pedagogical knowledge to scaffold that analysis with the students by using character webs, body biographies, mnemonic devices, close reading strategies, and so on to help them fully understand and appreciate the plight of such a character. The teacher might also share visual renditions of the character or clips from various recorded performances of the play or film. To further push students' exploration, a teacher might ask students to compare Ophelia to more contemporary female characters in young adult literature, like Starr in Angie Thomas's *The Hate U Give* or even Xiomara in Elizabeth Acevedo's *The Poet X*. Students could consider the context and culture of all three of these characters and critically reflect on what it means to be a teenage girl in society.

That same teacher might extend the students' collective thinking using technology. Students might envision what Ophelia's Instagram page would look like; they may create Facebook-like profile pages using evidence from the text itself. Thus, the teachers are activating their TCK. Another tool that could be utilized in this lesson would be MyShakespeare.com, a website that pulls all of these areas together. For example, on the website, a student sees the text of the original play along with pop-out vocabulary text boxes, video interviews of the characters, video performances of the characters, and many more resources. Not only has the content and pedagogical knowledge been provided by the teacher, but the digital literacies open the technological knowledge up for the students. In both activities, the social media profiles and MyShakespeare.com, the TPACK sweet spot can be met by the skillful teacher and engaged students. We think of TPACK as a heuristic for framing, planning, and executing meaningful lessons with technology. We will return to discuss this idea after presenting the second model that is the key to effective technology use in the classroom: SAMR.

SAMR

SAMR refers to differing levels of technological integration and is considered more of a model for implementing technologies in the classroom than a heuristic for teacher knowledge like TPACK (see Figure 2.3).

At the simplest level, the integration of technologies could be interpreted as substituting for other ways or modes of conducting activities. For example, the introduction of an overhead projector would, depending on its use, be understood as a *substitution* for the blackboard or chalkboard in a classroom. There is little to no transformation of the activity in question—only a switch in modality. One level up from substitution is *augmentation*, where the use of technology expands instruction and contributes something to the classroom and learning experience beyond mere substitution. The use of a projector and a laptop computer to project onto a whiteboard might best represent an augmentation.

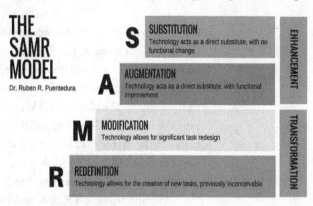

FIGURE 2.3. Substitution, augmentation, modification, and redefinition (SAMR) technology integration image.

A threshold is crossed when moving from augmentation to *modification*. A considerable modification must occur for there to be a shift from augmenting something to modifying it. Something must happen to shift into this mode—something new and different. For example, a typical or traditionally common task, such as presenting information on the board for students to see and consume, would have to be shifted. Consider the basic use of an interactive whiteboard or similar technology, like document cameras. Depending on the use, of course, this would be a modification since it goes above and beyond the traditional board or overhead projector.

To reach *redefinition*, a teacher must use a tool or technology that transforms the task in question, such as the use of not only an interactive whiteboard (and utilizing the full capabilities of the technology) but also tools like wireless display apps that allow you to broadcast and interact with the screen with little latency and low thresholds for students and teachers. The example we typically share with students to help them understand the redefinition stage is to try and imagine what it was like to teach in the 1990s or early 2000s, with limited internet and maybe one computer per classroom. If you would struggle to describe and explain your use of technology to a teacher from the 1990s—for example, explaining touchscreens, using your fingers to manipulate objects on the screen, and students being able to broadcast from tablets in their hands from across the room—you are probably in the redefinition zone!

Reflection Box

Consider how you have used technologies in your teaching in the past. Try to categorize them using the lenses of TPACK and SAMR.

Putting It All Together:
Using the Frameworks as Lenses

Given these frameworks, we work to establish with our students a common vocabulary situated in our work in the digital and multimodal world. We believe that this heuristic process—when implemented in the planning process, and even in the praxis of teaching—can dramatically shift conversations around the effectiveness of using technologies in the classroom. When we argue that technologies should be integrated into the classroom in meaningful and compelling ways, ways that connect and enhance the literacy skills that are at the heart of our practice, what we really mean is that both SAMR and TPACK have been considered and we can justify the decisions we have made pedagogically and technologically.

We find that the TPACK and SAMR models are the missing link in approaching the challenging task of effectively integrating technologies into the classroom. Here are the questions we ask our students (and ourselves!) in practice:

- In what way is this technology/tool/app substituting for something else?
- Augmenting? Modifying? Redefining?
- How do you know?
- Can you argue for and make your case?

At the same time, we ask students (and ourselves) to account for their integration of technology into their lessons according to TPACK. Thus, we ask:

- How does this chosen technology/app/tool best align with your understanding or knowledge of content and pedagogy?
- Does its use make sense?
- In what ways does the use of that technology hit the TPACK sweet spot (or not)?
- If it doesn't adhere to or exemplify one area of knowledge, how so and why?
- How are you accommodating for this in the results of your planned lesson?

TPACK and SAMR help make this distinction clearer. Return to the trusty overhead projector. Technologically, all you need to use this device is electricity, a working light bulb, transparencies, and markers. Pedagogically, and using the language of the SAMR model, most often the overhead projector is used simply as a substitution for either the chalkboard/whiteboard or poster paper hung on the walls. The overhead projector is used as a substitution within classroom instruction, replacing the blackboard or printed pieces of paper.

Turning to TPACK, to evaluate the use and effectiveness of the overhead projector, we would want to consider how the content and pedagogical knowledge are enhanced and addressed by the use of the technology. Once we consider this, we realize that the overhead projector was never there to spur on the learning or make it more interactive. It was a tool to directly share information that essentially all teachers had at one time. Even though it might seem like a technology, no technological knowledge was truly needed to operate it.

But there are new and emerging technologies that do require specific additional technological knowledge and facilitate our transition from simply substituting to modifying or redefining teaching and learning. An application such as *Kahoot!* that can be accessed via the internet or via a standalone application on a phone or tablet is an example of one such technology. *Kahoot!* is a game-based website and application that can be used for review that often inspires competition. The affordances and capabilities made available by *Kahoot!* are clearly different, and of a different magnitude, than an overhead projector. *Kahoot!* can be used as an example of technology that augments or modifies teaching and learning. For example, *Kahoot!* draws on existing content knowledge to structure the pedagogical strategy of addressing formative feedback in real time. *Kahoot!* also requires additional technological knowledge to know how to set up the application and understand the types of questions and activities that can be created. *Kahoot!* at least augments the learning activity and at best modifies it (in SAMR terms) by providing a teacher with immediate formative assessment data in real time. This type of learning activity would be almost unthinkable using a different technology, such as an overhead projector. Kahoot! also provides instant feedback for the students and teacher.

To apply this to a full-length work in the ELA classroom, let's turn to Shakespeare, whose works can be found in most secondary classrooms. Typically, these plays exist in a grade-level anthology or a class set purchased by the school, and students are able to read from their own copy. Sometimes they are able to take the book home; other times, they are only allowed to access the book during class time or while at school. When students read Shakespeare's plays in this manner, they are operating within a traditional literacy perspective (see Chapter 1). Even if students are performing the play in class and engaging in other multimodal or arts-based pedagogy, this is still an activity that does not utilize the power of technologies.

Imagine an alternative example that integrates technology into the lesson. A teacher selects one of Shakespeare's plays that exists on the MyShakespeare.com website. The play is available in digital format and can be accessed either online or on a smartphone/tablet. The entire text is present but also integrates images that can be opened and explored in detail. There are links to embedded videos, and the site itself offers the ability to highlight and leave notes in the digital margins that can be read aloud to students at the touch of a button. Some might argue, given the SAMR model, that we have substituted a paper copy for a digital one; however, we think using this platform not only effectively integrates technology into the lesson but also *modifies* and in some ways *redefines* the pedagogy. Students in this scenario are reading but they are also engaging multiple, multimodal literacies—from their ears and eyes to multimodal experiences with video. As mentioned, the affordances and capabilities made available by the digital text are clearly different, and of a different magnitude, than a physical book.

To be clear, we are not advocating for the overthrow of books en masse! Both of us have shared experiences with the felt sense of books, the feeling in our hands, the smell, and the feeling of a pencil or the perfect pen pressing against the paper. But we do think that there are affordances and capacities provided by technologies that allow us to engage with multimodal texts, and as ELA teachers, we should be embracing these new tools while simultaneously evaluating them in terms of technology frameworks such as TPACK and SAMR.

A Note on Technology Access, Multimodality, and FIMS

When we add FIMS to TPACK and SAMR, significant possibilities open up for teaching and learning literacies with technologies. As we crafted FIMS, we recalled our own meaningful experiences with texts, teaching, and learning; some of those experiences included technology, and others did not. In other words, FIMS exists with and without technology. We must be aware that there are districts, classrooms, and other contexts outside the school where access to technologies is severely limited or not available at all. This lack of access to high-speed internet and laptops/computers became especially evident during the COVID-19 pandemic. An image of elementary and middle school-aged children gathered outside a fast-food restaurant simply to access its free Wi-Fi in order to complete their remote schooling remains in our minds. Even as we are advocating for greater and more thoughtful integration of technologies into the secondary ELA classroom, we must also account for and speak to the challenges related to access and technologies.

Belief #4 points out that "technologies and their associated literacies are not neutral" and is of a different kind than the first three belief statements. Beliefs #1–3 direct our attention to the possibilities within literacies and technologies, whereas Belief #4 is a warning of sorts. Recall the Google Doodle example from Chapter 1, On Literacies, highlighting Maya Angelou's birthday. We shared this as an exemplary multimodal text and to show how FIMS can be used to interpret digital texts. Given the call to action provided by the fourth belief, we would still advocate for providing students access to the multimodal text, but rather than assuming they have access to strong and reliable Wi-Fi or one-to-one devices in a classroom setting, we would encourage our secondary ELA colleagues to rely on their pedagogical expertise to find ways to share and create multimodal texts with their students. In this way, we reinterpret Belief #2 ("consider literacies before technologies") as "consider pedagogies before technologies." If teachers maintain a strong footing within their planning and pedagogy, we still think multimodal texts can be consumed and produced even in contexts where access is lacking.

For example, teachers could share the Google Doodle using a projector and single device (such as a laptop). If a projector is unavailable, the multimodal text could be shared on a computer screen, and students could take turns in small groups to view/read the Doodle. Or, if the lesson or activity calls for it, the well-planned teacher could book access to the school's computer lab or laptop cart so that each student or pairs of students could view the text. We would even argue that we must not forget the power of arts-based pedagogies that can help support multimodal texts that do not need digital technologies. There are a number of examples in the upcoming focus chapters that highlight embodied and other forms of multimodality that could create the space for creative thinking about multimodality in the ELA classroom.

Conclusion

We will use SAMR and TPACK throughout this text to help situate the use of technology in the classroom. For example, in the focus chapters, we describe lessons and activities that would be appropriate in terms of their content and pedagogy. We think that many teachers will connect with these examples as they recognize them from their own classrooms. When considering speaking and listening, we describe common class discussion strategies. However, we want to help teachers understand that when technology is integrated in a lesson, it must strive to hit the TPACK sweet spot, where the technology is integrated in a way that supports the content and pedagogy. There are times when a lesson has, based on a study of the content and pedagogy, no need for the use of technology. We recommend that teachers use the TPACK Venn diagram as an ongoing lens to reflect on how they are (or are not) using technology in the classroom. We also want teachers to push beyond the substitution and augmentation of SAMR to explore ways that technology can *modify* and *redefine* teaching and learning. Ultimately, we want to encourage teachers to consider the sheer power of integrating technology into their lessons when it makes sense to consider both content and pedagogy.

By focusing on the last two beliefs of the NCTE Position Statement in this chapter, namely "technologies provide new ways to consume and produce texts" and "technologies and their associated literacies are not neutral," we have aimed to situate our approach and thinking related to teaching with technologies in ways that honor new and emerging multimodal texts but are also integrated effectively and meaningfully into ELA classrooms. In the next chapter, we jump into our first focus: visual literacies. We begin with the visual because it is likely the most familiar to most teachers and students. As we transition to the next section, we will apply the foundations from our opening chapters on literacies and technologies within a visual context.

Part II
Visual Literacies

Chapter Three

Focusing on Visual Literacies

Introduction

Two decades into the twenty-first century, we find ourselves inundated with images as we go about our daily lives. Visual literacy, or learning to read and create visual texts, is important in our visually saturated world. Traditional literacy often privileges text over images for a number of reasons. For example, some administrators, teachers, and community members may feel that printed texts are the backbone of study in an English class, or that reading a book or short story is the essence of an ELA experience. Other teachers may feel that visual texts are important, but they are unsure of how to include them in their curriculum and pedagogy. Still others may worry about how to defend their choice to use visual texts in an English class. Consider, for example, how often secondary ELA teachers have to defend the legitimacy of graphic novels. In this focus chapter, we want to help teachers and students shift their understanding of visual texts by thinking about how we perceive the world through different visual modes.

To contextualize and provide a foundation for our work with visual literacies, we begin by explaining what we mean by visual text and reading a visual text. A visual text is any combination of words and images that might come in a variety of formats. Key to a visual text, for us, is that images dominate the representation. Building from this, we define reading a visual text as the practice of synthesizing the meaning of the images within the text and determining how they contribute to an overall sense of the text. Understanding what a visual text is, learning how to read a visual text, and producing a visual text are the basic components of visual literacy.

Visual literacies build on the foundational work of Elliot Eisner (1989), who argues that the image is just as important as text in meaning making. Visual literacies pertain to our capacities to engage visually with the world, such as interpreting a wordless picture book or decoding the meaning of an image. Further, Eisner details the importance of visual literacy as arts-based pedagogy, saying:

> reading images as texts in order to reveal their political and often covert purposes is one form of reading. Another is developing the student's ability to use the arts to understand the values and life conditions of those living in a multicultural society. (2002, p. 29)

In this chapter, we introduce how to read or consume visual texts by starting with familiar in-class examples. In the following chapters, we consider ways to engage with visual literacies and texts, focusing on newer types of media like interpreting memes (Chapter 4) and designing infographics (Chapter 5).

Margin Memo

Belief #2: Consider literacies before technologies. *New technologies should be considered only when it is clear how they can enhance, expand, and/or deepen engaging and sound practices related to literacy instruction.* Our work in visual literacy draws heavily from the Belief Statement. Students need to apply traditional analytic skills to visual texts whether they are using technology or not. In this way, we keep our focus on literacies before technologies, while simultaneously embracing the shift from literacy to literacies.

Distinguishing Visual Literacies in the Classroom

Before considering how digital technologies have modified and redefined visual texts, we first explore the very concrete ways that secondary ELA teachers already draw on literacy skills to analyze visual texts. Remembering the interplay between consuming and producing texts, we offer examples of both in the chapters to come. Here, though, we focus first on the everyday practices we and other teachers utilize to stretch and expand our students' visual literacies through artwork, photography, and graphic novels.

Artwork

Trevor Bryan (2019) argues that even with "the rise of visual literacy, very little literature exists regarding how to explicitly teach students to engage meaningfully with and make meaning of visual texts" (p. 4). One way to begin to teach students explicit approaches is by paying attention to more traditional art. As Marshall and Donahue (2014) explain, we know that "art raises fundamental questions about meaning, students can engage with others in construction of understanding that would be harder to accomplish with familiar artwork that only requires what Dewey called 'recognition' rather than 'perception'" (p. 4). Our work builds on Dail et al. (2018), who asked: "Are we positioning students as consumers of the media they study, or are we inviting them to enter and contribute to the conversation through the production of their own texts?" (p. 3). Once students have examined artwork, they might be better able to respond to literature or to use artwork to illustrate their learning. Student-created visual texts must be recognized as valid assessments.

Check out some other student work from this visual literacy activity.

Let's start with an example of students producing art to illustrate their learning. To do this, we use a strategy with our PSTs for reading particularly dense, theoretical articles based on White's "sketch-to-stretch," where students move from text to sketch to understand what they are reading (Macro & Zoss, 2019, pp. 102–103). We have them first read these challenging articles for homework and then when we are together, the PSTs group up and "illustrate" what they have read. The visual artifact they create helps PSTs grasp some really complex concepts. During our remote teaching, this activity shifted to Jamboard, with our students working in breakout rooms. Figure 3.1 is a representation one of the PST groups created after reading Takayoshi and Selfe's (2007) article "Thinking about Multimodality."

FIGURE 3.1. Jamboard sketch from PSTs processing an article.

In an increasingly technological world, students need to be experienced and skilled not only in reading (consuming) texts employing multiple modalities, but also composing in multiple modalities, if they hope to communicate successfully within the digital communication networks that characterize workplaces, schools, and civic life, and span traditional and geographical borders.

This activity disarms the expectation that students will simply "get it" after reading a traditional text once; this also models an approach to differentiation and assessment for our PSTs. Based on their reading of the article and using FIMS, we can see from their Jamboard collage that they have identified three modes to highlight: audio, visual, and oral. They discerned from their reading that part of the impact of multimodality occurs across content areas. Their influence gets expressed in two key components we would highlight: (a) the redefinition of the book as oral, visual, and audio; and (b) the identification of a significant quote in the text and its inclusion in the lower left-hand corner. They have also chosen to include a mixture of images to represent their understanding.

While we could just quiz them on the articles, we prioritize visual literacy by having them collaborate to illustrate their learning. As we move through the room, we can offer assistance if there are questions or confusion. This activity pushes our PSTs even further by asking them to use their imaginations as they then jigsaw each groups'

FIGURE 3.2. Cover of *O*, the *Oprah Magazine* featuring Breonna Taylor, September 2020, as tweeted by the artist Alexis Franklin on December 30, 2020."

drawings to confirm their understanding of the article. The PSTs are seen as the experts, and it empowers them when they break down a challenging text, represent the meaning visually, and then have the opportunity to teach it to their peers. What is more, through the highlighting of FIMS, we can see the interplay between consuming and producing strategies, demonstrating the structure and rigor of this work.

As we drafted this chapter in the summer of 2020, we learned that for the first time in twenty years, Oprah would not appear on the cover of *O Magazine*. Breonna Taylor, the young woman who was murdered in Kentucky by police officers, was featured as the first person to appear on the cover besides Oprah herself (see Figure 3.2). This occurred even as calls to arrest Taylor's murderers still rang out in the streets months after her death. To honor Taylor and this historic moment, the magazine devoted an entire webpage to the development and design of the cover that is worth exploring.

When sharing this magazine cover with students, we might ask them to reflect on the *impact* of Oprah Winfrey selecting this image and then apply their *imagination* to engage in a critical and meaningful dialogue around #BlackLivesMatter and police brutality in the United States. In our visually dominated culture and society, visual texts matter—often-

Read more about the artist and her process of creating the image of Breonna Taylor.

times more than the mastheads and titles of articles. From advertisers to politicians, people in power know the impact that visual texts can have on the national conversation and tone/tenor of tense debates on key issues.

Visual texts humanize and ground abstract ideas, making viewers care and engaging them emotionally in an issue—representing the cultural zeitgeist like few other things can. These touchstone visual texts show up on the front pages of our news-papers, magazines, and flash on news screens and social media over and over again because of the ease of sharing them.

FIGURE 3.3. *Ophelia* by John Waterhouse, 1910.

Pauline: When I taught high school English, I would frequently bring in artwork as writing prompts or visual texts for students to examine as we read a particular text. When I left the classroom, I knew that I wanted to learn more about arts-based pedagogy. So, when I was collecting my dissertation data, I focused on identifying arts-based practices in the ELA classroom.

I observed one very poignant lesson where a high school classroom full of young women examined the painting Ophelia before they read Hamlet and made all sorts of observations, inferences, and assumptions about the woman depicted in John Waterhouse's gorgeous work of art (see Figure 3.3). For example, the students looked at her eyes and asked, "What is she looking at in the distance?" They examined her stance—her hand on a tree—and assumed she was running away. They wondered, "Who is she running to? Or, is she running from someone?"

In that moment, or maybe later when I was transcribing, writing my reflective memos, and drafting my dissertation, I realized I was never specifically taught to incorporate the arts into my classroom, but it always seemed a natural fit for me as a visual thinker and learner.

Another way of turning to arts-based pedagogy to further examine literature is to incorporate traditional art, such as paintings. Doing this kind of visual work requires attention and intention by the teacher whether we use traditional art, photographs, or even pop culture. We suggest that how we teach visual literacy matters more than *what* kind of art we use, and we should keep our options open. In that spirit, let's look next at another example that really centers the teaching of visual literacy: photographs.

Photographs

Right now, our smartphones have thousands of photographs stored on them. Our social media accounts probably feature hundreds of pictures that we have posted over the years. Our students' phones are no different; humans know that pictures tell a story, and so they share them as a form of visual literacy. Think of the work of photojournalists; they work tirelessly to capture a moment, a person, a story. Their work enhances newspaper headlines and graces the covers of magazines. Images are powerful, but do we have the tools to identify why certain images resonate with us? Do we have the vocabulary to unpack an image and identify the meaning behind it? Do we have the stamina to examine it beyond a quick glance? Do we have the tools to compose our own powerful images, too?

In *Focus Lessons*, Ralph Fletcher (2020) walks the reader through his process of engaging visual literacy—both personally and professionally—by connecting photography to writing and to the teaching of writing. In composing a photographic image, the photographer must first *imagine* how best to frame and shoot the image. Their *influence* reveals what they want to communicate and why the photograph is the modality of choice. The *impact* brings considerations of audience, purpose, and tone, mirroring the writing process. Finally, the photographer *identifies* their successes and reflects on their process. We've also observed teachers using photographs for students to analyze by zooming in and zooming out. Take, for example, a zoom in of this iconic photograph (Figure 3.4):

To begin the activity, using a FIMS approach, teachers could ask students the following questions:

- Can you *identify* what you see in this image?
- What is the *impact* of seeing the number two in the lower right-hand corner?
- How does the photographer *influence* the intended audience?
- What do you *imagine* about this person?

FIGURE 3.4. Zoomed in and cropped photo for FIMS visual literacy activity (CNN.com).

Pauline: As a writer and teacher of writers, I have kept a writer's notebook for years. As Fletcher points out, writers react to outside forces by recording them in their notebooks, just like we record moments, places, things, and people by taking photographs and storing them on our phones or on our computers (or both). I've used photographs as writing prompts in a variety of ways; years ago, I would have a stack of printed pictures and have students randomly select one and write about it as we started class.

I've recently transitioned to having students look at their phone and select a picture to write about. Sometimes I give them guidelines, like "pick the fifth picture from the bottom of your collection" so they don't spend writing time just scrolling through and then not having enough time for writing. I've also left it open to their selection by giving them a theme or general prompt to consider, like "find a photo that shows contentment or happiness and write about it." I've recently taken my writer's notebook up a notch, thanks to a suggestion that came from several teachers at the West Chester Writing Project. I now have a small photo printer, called a Sprocket, that is synced with my phone, and I can print 2 x 3 inch photo stickers to place next to my writing. This device has definitely added an extra element to my writing; sometimes I see something that captures my imagination and take the photo as a visual reminder to go back and write about it. At other times, I am writing about something and then go looking for the photograph that complements the writing I've already done.

FIGURE 3.5. Full photo for FIMS visual literacy activity.

Students may say the young man in the photo looks upset that he won second place in whatever event he just completed, they may debate what type of event it was, and they may wonder what year it was because the image is in black and white. These are all valid responses, but then we push students' thinking further by zooming out, looking at the whole photograph (Figure 3.5) as a visual text, and then repeating those questions/prompts.

All of a sudden, the white gentleman who earned second place, Australian athlete Peter Norman, is no longer the focus; our eyes are drawn to Tommie Smith (first place) and John Carlos (third place), the African American athletes on the podium. So, with the whole photograph in view, the *impact* has shifted.

Now, students may ask questions about the fists raised, students may or may not know the context of the photograph, and students may take an educated guess about the timing of this photograph—all things to consider. As Fletcher (2019) warns, "you cannot take any photo at face value. Photographs can be misleading" (p. 78).

Many have criticized Norman (the second-place athlete) for not joining in unity, with his own fist raised, yet if students zoom in closely enough, they may notice he is wearing an Olympic Project for Human Rights Badge on his uniform. Even though this photograph was taken at the 1968 Olympics in Mexico City, there are still unanswered questions about what transpired that day on the Olympic podium. This, we would highlight, is a question of *influence*. Was Norman an ally at that moment or was he a passive observer? The debate continues about the details in the photograph, and we would encourage students to research this moment and these men.

Consider, for example, the iconic nature of *Time Magazine* when it not only features a photograph to highlight a relevant person in the news but also frames the image in such a way that previews the story to follow. Take this cover from December 2017, honoring *Time*'s Person of the Year: "The Silence Breakers." At that time, the #MeToo movement had gained enough traction that several women had come forward to share their stories of sexual assault and harassment. Students may immediately *identify* Taylor Swift, since she is the youngest person pictured; they may consider the impact of all the women wearing black and who aren't really smiling for this particular photo shoot. They may notice the

FIGURE 3.6. *Time Magazine* cover, Person of the Year, 2017.

different skin tones represented, and if they look closely, they may also notice these women seem to all be different ages, too. Students might wonder what silence they have broken—who is this image trying to *influence*? The teacher may encourage discussion by sharing data illustrating how many times the magazine has chosen a woman as the person of the year compared to a man; they might also want to open up a conversation about the man/woman/person distinction. Such questions can activate students' *imaginations* as they examine the magazine cover (see Figure 3.6).

After this initial visual analysis, teachers could zoom in on the lower right corner of the image (see Figure 3.7). This would call on us to repeat, in part, FIMS and ask:

- Why is there only an elbow pictured (*identify/ impact*)?
- Who do you think the photographer is trying to *influence* with this artistic choice?
  - What do you *imagine* about this elbow

FIGURE 3.7. Zoom and crop of *Time Magazine* cover, Person of the Year, 2017.

and the person attached to it (who is technically outside of the frame)?

- Why would they not want to be photographed?
- What's at stake for people when they break the silence surrounding sexual assault, unwanted advances, and even harassment at work or in their lives?

These suggested questions are only the beginning of a courageous conversation that teachers could support. If teachers are looking for other photos to use in their classroom, they could consider exploring the series "What's Going On in This Picture?" that runs every Monday in *The New York Times* (Fletcher, 2019). Subtle details embedded in photographs will help students when they start analyzing and creating memes. The final phase of photography as a visual literacy would actually be composing the photographs, much like composing writing in our classrooms. Students would use the language and the mentor texts you've shared to create their own perfect shot.

This can take several forms and could be in response to literature or embedded in a creative writing prompt—the possibilities are endless. There's even a blank template for the cover of *Time Magazine* online, so students could play around with composing a cover photo and supplementary text.

Check out "What's Going On in This Picture?" in *The New York Times*.

View the blank *Time Magazine* cover template.

Graphic Novels

Graphic novels can be a gateway to encourage people to become lifelong readers. People often underestimate graphic novels and don't give them the credit they deserve, but John Lewis, Andrew Aydin, and Nate Powell's *March: Book Three* won the National Book Award in 2016, and in 2020, the Newbery Medal was awarded to Jerry Craft's graphic novel *New Kid*. For folks looking to bolster an argument in favor of using graphic novels in the classroom, they can look to these awards as validation. These awards demonstrate to skeptics that these visual texts are "real reading" and we need to help students have rich reading experiences with them. Here, we outline some strategies for you to apply to the reading of visual texts like graphic novels.

Reflection Box

Think about your current curriculum and identify three possible lessons where you could incorporate painting or photographs. How might this enhance your overall approach to visual literacy?

Gareth Hinds is an author and illustrator who graphically represents classics like *Romeo and Juliet* (2013) and *The Odyssey* (2010). We have found these editions not only visually stunning but also an effective way to differentiate learning within a classroom setting if your school/district is still including these canonical texts. These visual texts are an ideal supplement to the curriculum for students who need a little extra help to comprehend a complicated text. For many of us, trained in a mostly text-based world, reading graphic novels requires us to slow down our reading, pausing to look at the images and connecting those images to the words.

Laurie Halse Anderson reimagined her 1999 book, *Speak*, as a graphic novel in 2018. Page 341 captures so much of Melinda's pain and progress as embedded in the simple imagery of a tree (see QR code). By applying FIMS to reading this graphic novel, students would *identify* that the entire text is in black and white but the cover and end papers have green accents, perhaps leading them to consider the *impact* of that choice by the author, illustrator, and publisher. Students may also wonder about the *influence* of this format. And finally, they can *imagine* themselves in the world of Merryweather High School with Melinda and the Beast. This version of the book is just as powerful as the original but may engage readers in slightly different ways, thus adding a layer of differentiation in the reading classroom.

Former National Ambassador for Young People's Literature, Gene Luen Yang, writes graphic novels, and he revealed in a TED Talk that he used comics as a substitute teacher, noting:

See the images referenced in this part of the text here.

> In a comic, past, present and future all sit side by side on the same page. This means that the rate of information flow is firmly in the hands of the reader . . . So for certain students and certain kinds of information, these two aspects of the comics medium, its visual nature and its permanence, make it an incredibly powerful educational tool. (2016)

His latest work, *Dragon Hoops* (2020) is a Printz Award-winning book (along with other accolades) and would appeal to many sports-loving teenagers. Yang inserts himself into this story as a teacher who wanted to know more about the basketball culture—and sports culture in general—at his school. What starts out as curiosity on his behalf ends up as a fantastic story told through a graphic format.

See the images referenced in this part of the text here.

Another way to differentiate using classroom texts is to include more nonfiction. Do not let the description graphic "novel" lead you to believe that these visual texts are genre bound. In a wonderful nonfiction graphic novel titled *Becoming RBG: Ruth Bader Ginsburg's Journey to Justice* (2019), Debbie Levy reimagined the biography of late Supreme Court Justice Ruth Bader Ginsburg (affectionately known as "the Notorious RBG"). The text and images are almost all blue and white, with splashes of red. Students could examine that color palette and what impact it has on the reader. This book covers Ginsburg's early years, from birth to her appointment to the Supreme Court in 1993. The epilogue describes some of the high points of her tenure on the court.

Consider a spread that illustrates her first time presenting oral arguments to the Supreme Court (see QR code on this page). Readers might *identify* that the rectangles are the narrative, the ovals are what Ginsburg actually said that day, and the speech bubbles represent her *imagined* inner monologue that reveals how nervous she was. Students will likely be aware of RBG's presence in recent news media but may be unaware of her background and her journey. The novel describes the foundations of one of the most inimitable voices on the Supreme Court in modern history while incorporating a personal narrative. Her passing in 2020 revealed the extent of her influence on both of us; in fact, the name of our podcast, *Notorious Pedagogues*, is a nod to her nom du guerre.

Another phenomenal nonfiction text is the *MARCH* trilogy that documents the experience of the Civil Rights Movement through the eyes of the late Representative John Lewis. Most of the trilogy takes place in the 1960s during the movement, but the entire story is framed around John Lewis attending President Barack Obama's inauguration. The graphics are all done in black, white, and shades of gray, and the overall impact of this choice is not lost on the reader because we know that race relations in the United States have been simply black and white (see QR code). Consider the juxtaposition of two panels and the use of color.

Students might *identify* that the image on the left is dated January 20, 2009, the date of President Obama's inauguration; the page is almost all white, with song lyrics floating above the heads of the military choir. Compare that to the image on the right—what stands out? What is the *impact* of these pages, side by side? The entire page is almost all black, and the text shifts from black to white, with a diminutive illustration of the Edmund Pettus Bridge at the bottom. The largest word on the page is simply, "Selma," followed by a description of what was happening

See the images referenced in this part of the text here.

at that moment in history. How is the artist trying to *influence* us here? *Imagine* you are a part of either historical moment.

Similar to Ruth Bader Ginsburg, John Lewis is a historic figure whose sacrifices played an important role in ensuring every American has the right to vote. Further, by framing the book in Barack Obama's inauguration, the creators illustrate the importance of both men to one another, both historically and personally. Once again, graphic novels are a vital tool to help students hone their visual literacy skills: "Supporting students in responding to literature is one means of empowering them with interpretive authority as readers and creating a classroom culture where student contributions matter" (Dail et al., 2018, p. 4). Using sketching and blank panels can support student learning as they take inspiration from graphic novels as visual texts. For example, using FIMS for producing, teachers could consider having students create initial story panels to experiment with these visual literacy skills.

Students could then take an existing piece of literature, such as a scene from *The Joy Luck Club*, and then in groups summarize the scene in three panels. They would have to *imagine* how to represent the scenes graphically and in sections, asking themselves how to *influence* the viewer/reader and considering the *impact* of their interpretation. Through a reflection, they would *identify* the choices they made and their successes/challenges. This activity could also help students begin to transition into thinking about creating another kind of visual text, like infographics.

Conclusion— Now, Let's Shift to Application: Memes and Infographics

We know that incorporating visual texts and art in general supports the Common Core learning standards, but that shouldn't be our focus. If we are aiming for innovation in teaching and learning, we know that "what the arts have to offer is the capacity to truly engage all students in learning, and as such are effective strategies for changing school cultures" (Levin, 2016, p. 441). However, "today, the need for visual literacy has spread to other disciplines.

Margin Memo

Belief #3: Technologies provide new ways to consume and produce texts. *What it means to consume and produce texts is changing as digital technologies offer new opportunities to read, write, listen, view, record, compose, and interact with both the texts themselves and with other people.* Technologies most assuredly allow for new ways of consuming and producing texts. Students can "read" by listening to a podcast, watching an online video, or reading a digital copy of the text. Instead of giving students a quiz or test at the end of a unit, technology can make assessment exciting as students showcase their skills and illustrate their learning.

Because so much information is communicated visually, it is more important than ever that our students learn what it means to be visually literate" (Baker, 2012, p. 44). As English teachers, it's even more imperative for us to address visual literacies in our classrooms so students are prepared to use those skills across the curriculum.

This chapter focused on three different types of visual texts—paintings, photographs, and graphic novels—in order to isolate visual literacies in the classroom. The two chapters that follow showcase two main learning activities supported by technologies that we believe can offer unique access to expanding student and teacher visual literacies: memes and infographics. Memes are presented primarily as an example of consuming/reading visual texts, while infographics are discussed as producing/creating visual texts.

But, just as a reminder, this is pretty complicated. All of these processes are recursive and overlap at multiple points in an experience. We are always shifting from one mode to another, sometimes instantaneously. Memes and infographics represent two models of visual texts that can, with the help of technology, build and strengthen our visual literacy skills.

Consuming Visual Texts: Memes

Chapter Four

Introduction

*I*mages can provide quick access to students' visual literacy skills. By combining texts and images into a single panel, memes provide another opportunity for learning about visual literacy. Technically defined, memes are a mashup of an image from popular culture with text superimposed that draws meaning from another context. Memes can range in content from cultural jokes to political satire; they are funny, critical, and often irreverent; and they have become a mainstay of social media such as Twitter, Instagram, Facebook, and TikTok. If you think about how quickly memes can be created, shared, spread, and remixed, the viral nature of memes makes sense! Individuals from children to grandparents can be found sharing and enjoying a quick laugh from a meme. In this chapter, we will apply FIMS to consuming and producing memes as visual texts.

Consider this example we share with future ELA teachers when we introduce memes as an example of visual literacy (see Figure 4.1). Yes, memes can poke fun at cultural and societal events, but they can also teach grammar. In this meme, the text focuses on a challenge that many students struggle with: the homophones *there*, *their*, and *they're*. Why is the English teacher sad? Because their students continue to struggle with these homophones!

FIGURE 4.1. Grammar meme.

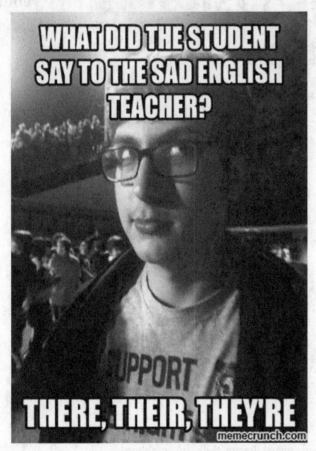

As we introduced in Chapter 1, FIMS offers a strategy for consuming texts that consists of four steps: identify, impact, influence, and imagine. Therefore, in analyzing this visual text, we would first *identify* that this is a meme that consists of an image of a secondary student with caption text. The *impact* of the visual is the facial expression and his eyes, as well as the bolded text emphasizing the homophones. We ascertain the *influence* of the meme when we consider the relationship between the question at the top and the answer at the bottom, playing on the words and the common expression meant to calm someone: "There, there, there." Using our imagination, we see "there, their, they're" but hear the comforting sound of "there, there, there," without distinguishing the homophones. We laugh because of the mix-up in meaning as it intersects with understanding grammatical concepts. Consider how many layers of literacy we have unpacked in this single, funny meme!

In this chapter, we share some strategies for teachers to capitalize on the succinct humor of memes by integrating them into their classroom practice as an example of visual literacy. We begin with some background on memes, what they are, why they are an important example of visual literacy, and why they are useful for teachers. We then move to a focus in our context, educating PSTs, where we invite students to use memes to explain their initial teaching philosophy. We embed the voices of preservice and current classroom teachers in the text below, but we also include QR codes that will take you to additional resources, for example, a podcast episode or, where applicable, teaching materials to accompany the lesson or activity we're discussing.

Memes, while funny and irreverent, are also a unique way to share and communicate meaning visually that is particularly accessible to our students. As Julie, one of our HS teacher participants, said, "a meme gets the students' attention and gets them hooked into the class." In what follows, we push teachers' thinking to consider how memes can go beyond accents on a classroom wall.

Matthew: I have multiple group chats in a variety of apps and other modalities that represent the most important group memberships throughout my life. My immediate family pepper those chats with messages about family happenings, videos of funny and momentous events from my niece and nephews, and a good number of memes. There are at least four other group message chains I am actively involved in that include friends from graduate school, colleagues from previous jobs, and friends from all over the world. I would wager that at least 50% of our messages are devoted to the sharing of and commentary about various memes that have significance for our group. Some message group threads are completely devoted to memes. And, some of the richest and funniest meme sharing happens in my ongoing text chat with my co-teaching colleague and coauthor, Pauline!

Pauline: In Year One of our class, I remember observing a student teacher and noticing a bulletin board at the back of the classroom with a collection of memes arranged in a collage. From far away, I wasn't sure what the bulletin board was all about, but as I got closer, I realized that it was a visual set of class rules for the students (see Figures 4.2 and 4.3). The student teacher and her mentor explained that they had invited the students to give their input on the guidelines for their class. The student teacher took it upon herself to find memes that correlated with those guidelines. I wondered at the time, why use memes instead of a list of class rules?

What is it about memes—their humor, their visual component, or something else—that both appeals to and also informs students? In this case, the student teacher chose memes that embedded the popular culture of Beyoncé and Harry Potter to communicate the class rules. That experience gave me something to ponder. What if more of us brought memes into our classrooms and applied them to content, beyond just thinking about them in terms of class rules? Moreover, what if we were to use memes to help us critically reflect on our beliefs about teaching and learning and about ourselves as teachers? I knew I needed to do more research at that point in order to situate memes in classroom contexts.

FIGURE 4.2. Meme on grading.

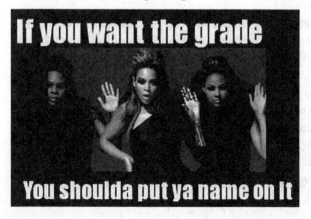

FIGURE 4.3. Meme on class preparedness.

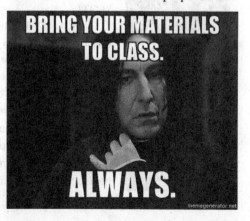

Memes as Visual Texts

Memes have become so popular that even scholarly researchers are now discussing and debating the significance of them as topics of academic study. One question for scholars is whether or not memes should be considered as a stand-alone genre, such as nonfiction or mystery. A recent recommendation from new media research argues that we should consider memes as an artifact of "participatory digital culture" (Wiggins & Bowers, 2014). We agree that memes are an important part of how students and teachers are engaging and existing in their day-to-day lives. What we fail to notice is that memes can be approached as an example of a *visual* text worthy of deeper reflection and analysis in the classroom. For that reason, we think memes should be taken from the screens of our smartphones and brought into the classroom.

As cultural artifacts, memes are packed with meaning and are perfect examples of visual texts that can be utilized in the ELA classroom. What is more, "students can learn to use the tools [of literacy] first with visual texts, which are highly accessible and easy to manage" (Bryan, 2019, p. 3). While we may think that memes and other visual texts are relevant only for a quick laugh outside of the

---

FIGURE 4.4. Excerpt of meme analysis from Wiggins and Bowers (2014, pp. 1886–1888).

In 1735, French artist Joseph Ducreux was born. Known for his portraits, Ducreux was made a baron and appointed first painter to Queen Marie Antoinette. In 1793, Ducreux finished his self-portrait *Portrait de l'artiste sous les traits d'un moqueur (Self-portrait of the artist in the guise of a mockingbird)*. The portrait shows Ducreux, a French aristocrat, dressed in a brown coat and black hat, smugly grinning, and pointing at the viewer.

Fast forward nearly 300 years to find Ducreux's painting on Reddit and Facebook pages as an image macro with one major alteration (an *image macro* is understood within popular culture as an image with captioned text). The portrait now included popular rap lyrics—lyrics which were altered to fit a more archaic form of speech. For instance, overlaid on top of the portrait are the words, "Gentlemen, I inquire who hath released the hounds?" which is a transformation of the popular lyrics, "Who let the dogs out?" Since its first appearance as an image macro in 2009 (Knowyourmeme.com, 2013), hundreds of these transformations have occurred and have been distributed through social media.

classroom, they may actually provide alternative pathways to teaching the power of literacy to our students.

For example, consider Wiggins and Bowers's (2014) brief deconstruction and analysis of a popular meme.

If only Ducreux could see how his painting has been adopted and transformed in the age of the meme! The analysis conducted by Wiggins and Bowers (2014) could be replicated with other memes.

We should not ignore the power of these visual texts, not only because of their cultural significance but also because of their ability to serve as sample texts for PSTs. We agree with Bryan (2019), who argued that "by teaching students to engage meaningfully with visual texts, we are better positioned to help them to engage with written texts, both when they read and when they write" (p. 4). What is more, by demonstrating this for our PSTs, we hope that they will carry this skill set into their future secondary ELA classrooms.

Educating Preservice Teachers

In this section, we describe one of our introductory activities where we ask our PSTs to select three memes that describe who they think they are or will be as educators. We then share examples of their memes and their ideas about how they might use a meme activity with their future students. Specifically, this includes exploring PST identities through memes, along with other scaffolding activities to help them draft an initial teaching philosophy and digital video, which is the subject of Chapter 11.

> **Margin Memo**
>
> **Belief #2: Consider literacies before technologies.** *New technologies should be considered only when it is clear how they can enhance, expand, and/or deepen engaging and sound practices related to literacy instruction.* As you can see from this chapter and the last, we recognize the importance of literacies before technologies. Visual literacy occurs in both traditional ways (e.g., artwork and photography) and in technologically infused ways, and memes are a great example of this. You can find memes on your phone and on the computer, but they can also exist as pieces of paper on classroom bulletin boards. In this way, we invite teachers to think about visual literacy strategies and use these skills to inform and center the use of memes, rather than just focusing first (and perhaps solely) on the technologies involved.

Here is how we typically introduce the meme assignment in the first week of our course:

- THINK - Who are you as a teacher? What's your teacher identity?
- SELECT - Browse the internet and/or create your original memes that capture how you see yourself as an educator.
- WRITE - Explain, describe, and connect your choices on a cohesive statement (about one to two pages should suffice).

We then step back and let them search. Some students are really quiet and search independently. Meanwhile, others informally group up with friends and share their memes.

Pauline: So, welcome to WRH 325, everyone. This class will help you think about technology as a PST. In this class, we will regularly be asking you to complete an assignment as a student but to then reflect on that same assignment as a teacher. Our icebreaker is going to seem a little different to you. First, I want you to consider the following slide.

Pauline: Dr. Kruger-Ross and I have already done ours. So, let's start by giving you an example. This is one of my three, and this will give you a sense of who I am as an educator. I am the advocacy chair for PA Council of Teachers of English Language Arts (PCTELA), and I've traveled to Washington, DC, several times to speak with our US senators and representatives about the funding streams for the National Writing Project and higher education. What is always frustrating to me, as a 27-year veteran teacher, is that policy decisions are left up to folks who have little to no experience teaching a class at any level. Willy Wonka's facial expression in the following meme truly represents how I sometimes feel on Capitol Hill.

Matthew: One of my memes captures a moment in time from my experience as a middle school teacher attempting to "manage" a class of disinterested students. I thought that "I'll just wait right here until it's quiet" would surely work as an effective classroom management technique. Of course, and this is what makes this meme of the skeleton so funny, I ended up waiting for over fifteen minutes for my students to settle and quiet down. Fifteen minutes! Think of the educational journeys we could have taken if I had just followed my gut and hollered: "Come on everyone! Quiet down now!"

Pauline: So, everyone, take out your phone or computer, whatever device you have with you today, and look for "teacher memes." It may help if you respond to that prompt in your notebook first so you have a sense of what you are trying to find.

FIGURE 4.6 (LEFT). Pauline's sample meme using Willy Wonka.

FIGURE 4.7 (RIGHT). Matthew's sample meme highlighting classroom management.

After about ten to fifteen minutes, we ask if anyone is comfortable sharing with the class. Usually, there are a few brave souls who step forward and share. The expectation is set that this is a class where participation is valued and expected. The next time the class meets, all the students share their memes in small groups, which also helps them get to know one another. In Year Five, when we taught remotely, we used breakout rooms in Zoom as a way to support student sharing and collaboration. We then gathered again as a whole class to share our progress. The goal of the activity is to encourage these PSTs to explicitly name and reflect on themselves as future teachers.

One of the reasons we start with memes is that almost always the PST's teaching philosophy statements (that are traditionally required) are framed as written statements drafted to meet a teacher preparation program's requirement. Students write what they think we *want to hear*. Or, they string together quotes from "experts" that don't reveal their unique personalities. Spanke (2007) describes this kind of assignment in *English Journal*, stating, "without exception, each of my pre-service teachers conceived of the assignment in the same, predictable way" (p. 85).

We strive to help our PSTs cultivate their own unique teacher voice at this point in their program; that is, before student teaching. We approach and conduct our course as a critical inflection point marking the transition from being a university student to preparing to enter the profession of teaching. The teaching philosophy statement, we believe, provides the necessary impetus and motivation for this transitional phase. "We recognize . . . that changes in the digital age have not only influenced composition and products for digital literacies such as the Web or e-books, but the use of images in traditional texts has dramatically increased as well" (Miller & McVee, 2012, p. 6). But, how can they *know* what their philosophy is *before* they've stepped in front of a classroom? They can only predict it at that point, so we try to guide them through this creative and challenging process by starting with memes.

The three memes our PSTs select are accompanied by a reflective statement describing their selection processes and reasoning. By writing this reflection, they've essentially written the first draft of their teaching philosophy statement. The difference now is that their own individual voices and opinions are centered in the document. Consider this example: Megan, a PST in Year Five of our course, chose the meme in Figure 4.8 as one of her memes. Paired with her reflective statement, it becomes clear that Megan is developing her philosophy of teaching and pushing the boundaries of traditional understandings of curriculum and assessment.

FIGURE 4.8. Megan's chosen meme on assessment.

Using FIMS to analyze her response, we first *identify* that this image is a meme, the composite of a photograph from a traditional exam question with captions at the top. The *impact* of the meme is the recognition that the student in question is thinking outside the box. The composition of this meme *influences* the future teacher to ponder the question: what do we do with this response from a student as a teacher? The PST now must imagine what she will do in this scenario, how she will respond. In her reflective statement, Megan writes:

Traditionally, the answer given in this meme would not suffice, nor would it be given points because it could be considered "incorrect" or a "joke." However, not every student learns traditionally and not every student will be good at certain core curricula, but allowing them to occasionally flex their creative muscles even on a test or in the classroom pushes them to be who they are.

She continues to express her beliefs about how she will support her students in their creativity by finding ways for them to be "freethinkers." These reflective pieces "signal a new and developing epistemological literacy where we are reading images not solely as narratives and icons, but as identity performances and representations" (Nicosia, 2013, p. 40). Further, this component of the assignment serves several purposes: it builds our class as a community of learners, it helps us get to know one another, and it embeds visual literacies into a traditionally text-based assignment. After we taught this introductory lesson in Year Four of the class, we asked two of our students, Jen and Sophie, to stay after class to share their experiences with the meme project. Jen revealed:

This assignment was actually surprisingly more difficult than I thought it would be because it required a lot of self-reflection from a teacher perspective, which I haven't done much of yet. I did like the assignment, however, because once I found appropriate memes to use for myself, it made me think in new ways about the classes I have been in as a student and how I will go about preparing to be in the classroom as a teacher. It was overall a nice, light introduction assignment that set up the premise for this course nicely.

Listen to a clip from our interview with Jen and Sophie.

Sophie explained:

I enjoyed completing this assignment as it allowed me to connect experiences and thoughts that were relevant to me into my perspectives on education, as well as use technology in an enjoyable way. I found it useful in reflecting on what key ideas are important to me as a future teacher and inside the classroom . . . Not only did they relate to ideas on content and subject area, but also classroom management that I thought were both significant pieces of education. Lastly, I think this would be an interesting way to get students involved with learned material in class.

As teacher educators who have used memes and meme-centered activities for many years, there does come a time when existing memes do not adequately summarize or represent the necessary meaning we are interested in accessing. We have watched our PSTs bump up against this challenge, too. They find a meme that *mostly* gets at what they're trying to share, but not quite. Then the question becomes: why can't we just make our own memes?

If we think of typical engagement with memes, sharing existing images with others and not wondering about where they've come from or how they were put together, we can think of this as the beginner mode of meme activities and use. As we transition from beginner to intermediate, we find that memes don't always accurately portray what we're trying to communicate. From intermediate to advanced, we find the meme generators—those individuals who make their own meaning by creating memes themselves or adapting existing memes to fit the intended purpose. Whole websites and communities have developed online to support these advanced users, such as imgflip's meme generator and MakeaMeme.org. Having our PSTs create their own memes remains a growing edge for us, but we have learned a great deal from some master secondary ELA teachers who are utilizing memes in this creative way.

As a model for their future middle and secondary students, the meme project encourages these PSTs to explore, identify, and experiment with defining themselves and their beliefs in a non-threatening and low-stakes way. The project also provides them with an opportunity to analyze memes as a visual text. We model the conversation around memes so that our students see one way of studying visual literacy.

Margin Memo

Belief #2: Consider literacies before technologies. *New technologies should be considered only when it is clear how they can enhance, expand, and/or deepen engaging and sound practices related to literacy instruction.* Remember, as the NCTE Position Statement shows us, whatever technology you use is secondary to the underlying literacies, in this case the literacies surrounding visual texts. We have seen that as some of our students transition into becoming classroom teachers, they may take the focus on visual literacies toward memes but they also find other creative ways to apply it to other visual texts. The annotated bibliography contains additional resources of this kind.

From the University to the Secondary Classroom

Our ultimate and overarching goal as teachers of future teachers is to equip them with the skills, knowledge, and attitudes they need to be able to walk confidently into their secondary ELA classrooms and integrate technologies effectively. Therefore, it is only fitting that we discuss the ways that memes and meme activities can show up in the secondary ELA classroom. We hope that our PSTs can build on the meme project that we use in *their* future classroom context and see it as connected to their content or classroom procedure. As Justin reflected here:

> I pictured an assignment almost exactly like this but with the memes being based around a character analysis or plot points in a novel we read in class. It also helped me sort out my subconscious expectations toward teaching and be a little funny with them.

In this section, we meet Katy, who blends memes and pop culture with the study of literature, and Hailey, who uses memes to teach grammar and as a basis for students to write their own myths. We highlight these colleagues' activities as examples of both consuming and producing memes as visual texts.

We have seen memes being integrated into classroom use through a novel study in which students explore how memes can represent and synthesize key plot moments or character decisions. Katy, a ninth-grade HS teacher, and also one of our previous PSTs, describes an activity where she integrates memes into her students' study of *To Kill a Mockingbird*. In this activity, memes become the way students can represent

---

FIGURE 4.9. Katy's instructions for her meme assignment.

Assignment Instructions:

Learning Target: I can connect pop culture to *To Kill a Mockingbird*.

Directions: Make a meme for *To Kill a Mockingbird*! In order to earn credit for this assignment, you must meet all of the requirements listed below.

1. Your meme must be 100% school appropriate.

2. You may use any TV show or movie as inspiration. The dialogue should be 95% the same—only change a few words if you need to, like a name.

3. You must include a caption, just like the SparkNotes examples attached.

4. In the same document as your meme, you must type up at least a paragraph that explains the relationship between the image/dialogue you chose and *To Kill a Mockingbird*, with a quote from the novel to support your explanation. Your paragraph should be at least 5–7 sentences.

To Submit: Upload a Google Doc that includes your meme and your written explanation. I recommend using Google Drawings for your meme and then inserting that image into the Google Doc.

their understanding of an event or a sentence from the book. Her instructions explicitly describe what her expectations are for her students to receive credit. After sharing a number of sample memes related to Shakespeare's *Romeo and Juliet* as mentor texts, Katy then sets up the activity as shown in Figure 4.9.

Listen to more of our interview with Katy here.

Katy also references SparkNotes, a company/website that in the age of social media and the meme has encouraged the creation and sharing of memes to represent an understanding of texts. We only thought of SparkNotes as books that provide quick summaries of major pieces of literature alongside themes and character notes, among other textual analyses. Without Katy's insight, we would have never realized SparkNotes was, at least at present, sharing memes in this way. A key difference in the meme activity that Katy introduces is the purposeful production of a meme. In our work with PSTs, we have learners choose from existing memes. Katy encourages her secondary students to take this one step further by requiring them to find and select an image and then draft the captioned text to ultimately create a new meme. Moreover, she has her students connect their newly created meme with a quote from the source text, *To Kill a Mockingbird*, providing further evidence of the depth of understanding. See Figure 4.10 for a student example that mixes *To Kill a Mockingbird* with Pixar's *Finding Nemo*, representing the moment Jem touches Boo Radley's house.

FIGURE 4.10. Sample student-created meme from *To Kill a Mockingbird* unit.

Rather than using the FIMS *consuming* practices, Katy's students showcase the *producing* strategies that invert the consuming order: imagine, influence, impact, and identify. Students use their imagination to connect *To Kill a Mockingbird* with another well-known plot from pop culture. Katy has given the parameter for *influence*—the image needs to be in a meme format, so she has focused their attention in the creation process. The students have chosen this critical moment from *Finding Nemo* to make an impact on the viewer, to encapsulate the meaning by making the parallel with Scout, Jem, and Dill: the three characters from *Finding Nemo* literally mirror the scene from the novel. By sharing the meme with their peers, they can *identify* their success by making this rhetorical argument. For example, if the person viewing the meme chuckles at the thought of the line, "Whoa. He touched the butt [boat]," within the context of *To Kill a Mockingbird*, then the students have met the learning target. If a person looks at this meme and thinks it does not sufficiently connect the two texts, then the student has not been successful with this activity.

Within visual literacies, students who complete this activity begin with a traditional text, explore existing memes, create their own meme, and return to written text to chronicle their decision-making process and analysis. In this activity, and in Katy's classroom, memes are more than fun images to share with peers—they are helpful in connecting to literature in new and unique ways.

Listen to a clip of Hailey describing these activities.

Another fantastic teacher, Hailey, shared two activities with us about how she uses memes in her ELA classroom. In the first activity (Figure 4.11), her students worked with preexisting memes to storyboard a myth project, while in the second (Figured 4.12 and 4.13), Hailey required her students to create memes about comma rules and usage in student writing. The memes were not only created by students to help them learn the rules but also ended up being critical to assessing their learning as well.

The first activity Hailey described was inviting students to use memes within the context of a larger unit where students were studying myths and mythology. However, Hailey did something a little different. She invited her students to storyboard or sketch out the key moments by using memes, almost like a comic strip. We have had our PSTs complete a similar storyboarding exercise when drafting assignments, but with this example that uses memes, Hailey pushed our thinking further.

Storyboarding with memes is a new way of approaching the writing process that had never occurred to us before. Students sometimes chose memes that included the same characters or theme, and others decided to select memes for their meaning regardless of the theme. Given that this was in support of the storyboarding experience, which is often seen as drafting and malleable, this decision to leave the kind of meme up to the students makes sense. Hailey's students progress through the FIMS producing steps of *imagination* by applying key myth elements to popular memes.

FIGURE 4.11. Meme from Hailey's student on Pandora's Box.

PANDORA'S BOX... AS TOLD BY MEMES

Then they move to *impact* by being able to translate the key plot points from the myth into the meme genre. Further, once they share these storyboards with the class, they can assess whether or not they were successful by the reaction of the viewers. Hailey illustrates how she values student autonomy, voice, and choice, and this activity shows how she honors these values in her classroom. Hailey also has students create their own memes, but in a way that is different from Katy's classroom and students.

Hailey has her students use memes to learn, understand, and teach each other grammar concepts correctly in their writing. By selecting memes to engage students in this activity, Hailey is not only providing a visual representation to demonstrate the importance of grammar rules but is also encouraging students to use and play within the boundaries of grammar—a sometimes overlooked aspect of language study.

View the storyboard of the entire myth of Pandora.

Students create memes for this class activity by first selecting whatever image they want as their background and then drafting a caption that includes the correct usage of a rule. After students create the memes, they share them during class time to create a game of who can analyze the meme to uncover the humor behind

FIGURE 4.12. Sample grammar meme.   **FIGURE 4.13.** Sample grammar meme.

Hey Girl,

I saw the way you explained there, their, and they're to that couple.

You're right, our love is greater than **their** love. **They're** hoping to be like you and me, babe. They'll never get to that level, babe. No, they will never get **there**.

See you tonight.

GERUNDS...
When -ing verbs go rogue.

the grammar rule. In Figure 4.12, students would first *identify* an image with text on the left half and the image of Ryan Gosling on the right. The *impact* of his image and the largest text, "Hey Girl," would strike them and likely remind them of the viral series of other similar memes. The *influence* is to remove the confusion that still exists among high schoolers with the homophones *their, they're, and there*. For the full meaning of the visual text to make sense, students would have to *imagine* reading the text to themselves within their minds. From the fun of the classroom, Hailey then selects a number of student-generated memes to build a study guide for the students. This multilayered and multipurpose use of memes in one activity is impressive!

Not only is Hailey honoring her belief in helping students create their own voice, she is actively reminding students of the true purpose of language—to enable us to communicate with one another. What is more, she is demonstrating that the rules of grammar are useful, not as a set of meaningless rules but as keys to unlocking meaning that can often have hilarious results! Within visual literacy, Hailey believes that by having students create their own memes to graphically and textually represent grammar rules, students will be able to better recall what can often be abstract, disconnected knowledge. We would agree. Hailey is building her students' capacity for visual literacies by integrating memes in this way into her classroom.

Concluding Thoughts

We are constantly learning from our peers and our colleagues in the secondary ELA classroom. Based on the examples provided by Katy and Hailey in their ELA classrooms, we are excited to see how we might adapt their lessons in our future classes. We hope it's the same for you and that this chapter has given

Margin Memo

Belief #3. Technologies provide new ways to consume and produce texts. *What it means to consume and produce texts is changing as digital technologies offer new opportunities to read, write, listen, view, record, compose, and interact with both the texts themselves and with other people.* The activities in this chapter have focused primarily on consuming memes, but there are a few examples described that highlight creating memes. A few decades ago, reading memes as a visual text wouldn't even make sense! After teaching students to deconstruct and analyze a meme, urging them to use digital technologies to produce their own pushes them to use their prior knowledge to create their own text sets that can both inform and entertain.

you reason to pause and consider how memes might make their way into your own classroom as a pathway to experimenting with visual literacies. Please do not forget to visit the annotated bibliography at the end of this text to locate additional tools and technologies that can be utilized for using and creating memes in the classroom. In the next chapter, we present another access point to visual literacies: infographics.

Reflection Box

How do these examples make you think about your own classrooms? How might you use memes in creating classroom communities, teaching literature, and teaching writing?

Other Ways to Use Memes
to Support Visual Literacies in the Classroom

- **Consuming:** Have students create a weekly or monthly wall of memes to chronicle the viral nature of memes and the shifting interpretations embedded within the media itself. Every quarter, take the best memes and collect them into a portfolio that is cultivated by the students.
- **Consuming:** In groups, students can access and follow the SparkNotes Twitter account to locate memes aligned with traditional ELA texts. Have students discuss, list, and then rank the best/worst/funniest/ most accurate memes shared.
- **Producing:** Assign students a particular character from a text being studied. Have the students create three to five memes that the character might post on social media.
- **Producing:** To extend traditional vocabulary activities, encourage students to create memes to offer humorous and irreverent definitions.

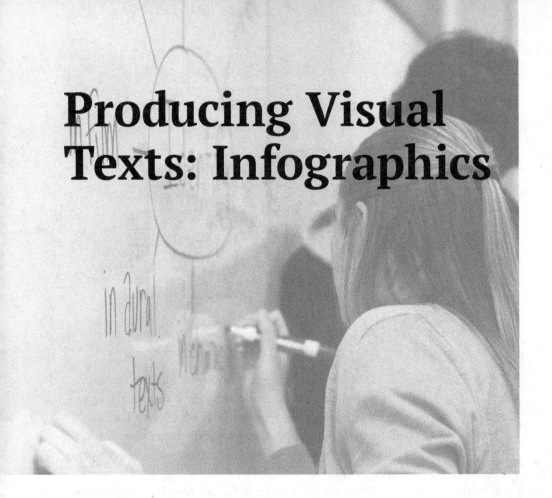

Producing Visual Texts: Infographics

Chapter Five

Introduction

Infographics are not new, but the word infographic and our access to tools to create them are. With the increased accessibility of web-based tools, the creation of these visual images combining information and graphics is easier than ever. In this chapter, we discuss examples of how infographics can be used in the secondary ELA classroom and specifically highlight free, online tools, such as Canva, Piktochart, and Google Apps, that help students create and evaluate infographics. We also revisit FIMS through the lens of creating/producing info-graphics. We are surrounded by infographics, and we don't have to look too far to encounter them. Consider this example: The two of us are both active citizens who regularly use news media to keep up to date, and we were particularly immersed in the 2020 election cycle while writing this book. During that time, everyone was inundated with polling, predictions, and even conspiracies before and after Election Day. And so we were fascinated by the multiple visual representations of the United States Electoral College and how some fulfilled the promise of infographics more than others.

FIGURE 5.1. Electoral College map of the 2012 US presidential election.

One way to represent the Electoral College is through a traditional map (see Figure 5.1). But this traditional image misrepresents the actual weighting of Electoral College votes. For example, taken together, Nebraska, North Dakota, and South Dakota appear geographically larger than Texas. However, they only get 11 electoral votes combined as compared to Texas's 38.

We typically view Figure 5.1 as a map, but we might also think of it as an infographic. What happens when we see the information included in the map represented n a different way, like this alternative from *Financial Times* that gives one block for one vote, thus transforming the map of the United States into an infographic (see Figure 5.2).

As the article's author writes: "The tile grid cartogram shows each state as a number of shapes equal to their votes in the electoral college. This allows the states to approximate their shape and borders, and makes it easier to compare states' sizes." Take a second look now at the original Electoral College map, and you can see the difference in what is communicated by this alternative map!

This example focuses on consuming infographics, but given the access that teachers and students have to tools to easily design, create, and share infographics, one way to expand on this might be to challenge students to reimagine their own electoral maps in a way that might better communicate the information.

Read the entire *Financial Times* article here.

Explore the Daily Infographic here.

FIGURE 5.2. Tile grid cartogram of the 2012 US presidential election.

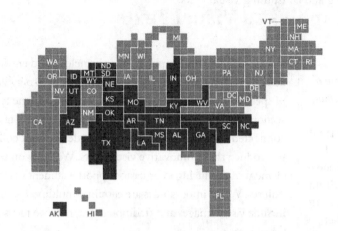

For teachers and students who really appreciate infographics, there is even a website called Daily Infographic that, once you sign up with your email address, will send an infographic a day straight to your inbox! We believe that this shift toward

Matthew: I appreciate the attempts made to reimagine the Electoral College map because of the dramatic inaccuracies conveyed by simply using the US geographical map. Historians and statisticians have long asserted that the Electoral College is skewed and biased toward smaller districts with smaller populations, and the use of maps as infographics glosses over and misrepresents the actual numbers. We teach the fifty states and require elementary students to memorize the state capitals; in many ways, one of the most memorable infographics in young people's minds might be the US geographical map. But when students see this familiar infographic without digging further into the deeper meanings embedded, it can often lead to dramatic misunderstandings.

Pauline: Exactly. Fast forward to 2020, when a teacher friend of mine shared that a student in his class was fully convinced that the recounting efforts in Maricopa County, AZ, would completely change the results of the presidential election. This obviously puts the teacher in an awkward position, but more importantly, it points to the importance of visual literacy. With a strong visual literacy, that student should be able to assess just how small that county is within the context of the entire country.

Reflection Box

Think about a recent infographic that you have seen. How might you use that infographic to teach your students how to read and critique these visual texts?

access represents a wonderful opportunity to build on secondary ELA students' skills in producing and consuming visual texts.

Infographics as Visual Texts

Margin Memo

Belief #1: Literacy means literacies. *Literacy is more than reading, writing, speaking, listening, and viewing as traditionally defined.* It is more useful to think of literacies, which are social practices that transcend individual modes of communication. Within the first belief statement, we are reminded that English teacher educators, alongside preservice and inservice teachers, should "critically evaluate a variety of texts (across genres and media) using a variety of theoretical perspectives" as well as "model classroom use of literacy practices for creating and critiquing texts." Infographics, as visual texts, can serve as useful examples of visual texts to meet these goals.

Visual texts like infographics not only include and encompass the ability to tell stories and reframe meanings but also include the use of specific strategies to represent, analyze, and critique texts. In this section, we discuss infographics and describe how new technologies connected to infographics can help students work collaboratively to produce these innovative visual texts. We focus on the FIMS element of producing in order to support a student's visual literacy skill set. While infographics are certainly multimodal, since they include visual images and traditional text, here we focus on their visual aspect.

All teachers use visuals and visual aids in their classrooms. When we are discussing the setting of a scene in a novel, we often sketch a map or layout for students. Or, when introducing a new topic, we quickly draw out a KWL chart (i.e., know, want to know, learned) on the board. What these two examples have in common is that while they are visual texts, they remain simple substitutions (recall the SAMR terminology we introduced in Chapter 2) relying on physical items like paper and pens or whiteboards and markers. Although these visual activities are useful and can be enlightening for students, they are static and immobile, and collaboration can be limited. Infographics, when integrated into classroom instruction, can nudge learners toward a more dynamic understanding of concepts.

Given the ease of access to free digital tools like Canva and Google Drawings in recent years, we can transition from simply substituting to modifying and redefining using technologies to expand students' visual literacies. With these tools, students now have access to editing and authoring images and graphics at a scale and quality unknown to users in the past. Given the prevalence of visual media that surround students today, teaching students to create their own examples of these visuals, such as memes and infographics, can help to demystify visually attractive and alluring graphics and help students focus on the substance.

With infographic authoring tools, such as Canva or Piktochart, the use of templates can blur the line between an image created for an educational purpose or a professional infographic shared to communicate vital information or data to a public audience. In short, the ease of access to and use of professionally designed templates means visual literacy now includes and requires critical literacy skills, such as determining authorship, evaluating for bias, and differences between facts and opinions.

Consider, for example, this mentor text to explore the inequities within the publishing industry in 2019 (see Figure 5.3). Lee & Low Books created the infographic below to illustrate current statistics in a compelling and easily accessible manner. While the content is jarring, as it demonstrates problems in the industry, our focus would be to

FIGURE 5.3. Infographic illustrating publishing demographics data.

DIVERSITY IN PUBLISHING 2019 • DIVERSITY BASELINE SURVEY BY LEE & LOW BOOKS

INDUSTRY OVERALL

RACE: 79% White/Caucasian
GENDER: 78% Woman/Cis-woman
ORIENTATION: 88% Straight/Heterosexual
DISABILITY: 92% Nondisabled

- 79% White/Caucasian
- 4% Black/African-American
- <1% Native American/Alaskan Native
- 7% Asian/Native Hawaiian or other Pacific Islander
- 6% Hispanic/Latino/Mexican
- 1% Middle Eastern
- 5% Biracial/Multiracial

- 21% Man/Cis-man
- 78% Woman/Cis-woman
- <1% Trans-man
- <1% Trans-woman
- <1% Intersex
- 1% Gender nonconforming

- 88% Straight/Heterosexual
- 7% Lesbian/Gay
- 4% Bisexual/Pansexual
- 1% Asexual

- 8% Yes
- 92% No

Diversity in Publishing 2015 *Diversity Baseline Study* by Lee & Low Books blog.leeandlow.com — LEE & LOW BOOKS

EXECUTIVE LEVEL

RACE: 86% White/Caucasian
GENDER: 59% Woman/Cis-woman, 40% Man/Cis-man
ORIENTATION: 89% Straight/Heterosexual
DISABILITY: 96% Nondisabled

- 86% White/Caucasian
- 2% Black/African-American
- 1% Native American/Alaskan Native
- 7% Asian/Native Hawaiian or other Pacific Islander
- 2% Hispanic/Latino/Mexican
- 1% Middle Eastern
- 1% Biracial/Multiracial

- 40% Man/Cis-man
- 59% Woman/Cis-woman
- <1% Trans-men
- <1% Trans-women
- 0% Intersex
- 0% Gender nonconforming

- 89% Straight/Heterosexual
- 9% Lesbian/Gay
- 1% Bisexual/Pansexual
- 1% Asexual

- 4% Yes
- 96% No

Diversity in Publishing 2015 *Diversity Baseline Study* by Lee & Low Books blog.leeandlow.com — LEE & LOW BOOKS

EDITORIAL DEPT.

RACE: 82% White/Caucasian
GENDER: 84% Woman/Cis-woman
ORIENTATION: 86% Straight/Heterosexual
DISABILITY: 92% Nondisabled

- 82% White/Caucasian
- 2% Black/African-American
- 1% Native American/Alaskan Native
- 7% Asian/Native Hawaiian or other Pacific Islander
- 4% Hispanic/Latino/Mexican
- 1% Middle Eastern
- 3% Biracial/Multiracial

- 15% Man/Cis-man
- 84% Woman/Cis-woman
- 0% Trans-man
- 0% Trans-woman
- 0% Intersex
- 1% Gender nonconforming

- 86% Straight/Heterosexual
- 6% Lesbian/Gay
- 8% Bisexual/Pansexual
- <1% Asexual

- 8% Yes
- 92% No

Diversity in Publishing 2015 *Diversity Baseline Study* by Lee & Low Books blog.leeandlow.com — LEE & LOW BOOKS

BOOK REVIEWERS

RACE: 89% White/Caucasian
GENDER: 87% Woman/Cis-woman
ORIENTATION: 91% Straight/Heterosexual
DISABILITY: 88% Nondisabled

- 89% White/Caucasian
- 1% Black/African-American
- 1% Native American/Alaskan Native
- 3% Asian/Native Hawaiian or other Pacific Islander
- 3% Hispanic/Latino/Mexican
- 1% Middle Eastern
- 2% Biracial/Multiracial

- 12% Man/Cis-man
- 87% Woman/Cis-woman
- 0% Trans-man
- 0% Trans-woman
- 0% Intersex
- 1% Gender nonconforming

- 91% Straight/Heterosexual
- 8% Lesbian/Gay
- 1% Bisexual/Pansexual
- 0% Asexual

- 12% Yes
- 88% No

Diversity in Publishing 2015 *Diversity Baseline Study* by Lee & Low Books blog.leeandlow.com — LEE & LOW BOOKS

use this infographic as inspiration for students to produce a visual text of their own. How might you use infographics like this in a school setting?

For this analysis activity, we would ask students to focus on consuming the image critically, seeing the infographic as a mentor text and using the FIMS process to better understand the creation of this visual text. For example, we would ask students to imagine what the authors were thinking as they reflected on how they could best communicate

Margin Memo

Belief #4: Technologies and their associated literacies are not neutral. *While access to technology and the internet has the potential to lessen issues of inequity, they can also perpetuate and even accelerate discrimination based on gender, race, socio-economic status, and other factors.* Technologies and their associated literacies are not neutral. As the publication infographic above shows, technologies can also be used to highlight and draw attention to areas of inequity, but students need the critical literacy skills to understand the source and the data that is being presented. Now more than ever, students need these skills to evaluate the validity of information being shared while also determining the source and understanding how the information is presented.

these data. Who are the authors trying to *influence* by choosing an infographic for this representation? Consider the specific colors, the pie charts, the bolded text, as well as the demographic breakdown underneath. What *impact* did the authors want this to have on the viewer? How can the authors *identify* whether they have been successful in conveying their message? While guiding students through the consuming process, teachers can remind students that they are reading like writers, and in this case, consuming with producing in mind.

The final thing we would like to emphasize is the key role that visual literacies play in the production and evaluation of infographics. When students work with and create graphic representations of their learning through the use of infographics, they are not just "designing" or being "creative." Students are practicing and exercising an important literacy that is often overlooked as we rush to focus on writing or reading in more traditional ways. In the sections that follow here, we share examples of using infographics in the classroom in ways that demonstrate the robust work of visual literacies.

Educating Preservice Teachers

In this section, we describe how our PSTs use infographics during their book club assignment, which was discussed earlier in Chapter 1. Once our PSTs have had a few weeks to read their paired books, we have them complete is an infographic activity. Not only are we able to quickly check their understanding of the two books, but we are also able to examine their visual literacy skills. Following at the top of the next page is the introduction to this assignment from Year Four.

During this discussion time, the questions that we read aloud remain displayed on the screen and we circulate around the room to get a feel for how the book club groups are working together, ensure everyone has completed the reading assignment, and take the temperature of the group dynamic. Once the initial buzz of conversation has passed, we gather everyone's attention as a class and have a ten- to fifteen-minute discussion about what they shared in their groups. We ask about any conflicts that may have bubbled up during discussion or what modality they chose to read their books. We end with the overarching theme of the day by asking them to share their observations about the connection between their books and the canonical text, *Romeo and Juliet*, which the entire class read. Having taught together

Matthew: Hello everyone! We hope you enjoyed wrapping up the reading of your two books. Remember that you were to have finished reading *Romeo and Juliet* a few weeks ago on MyShakespeare.com; by today, you should have finished reading your contemporary texts.

Pauline: If you're not already in your groups, go ahead and take a moment to gather your things and move into your book club groups.

Matthew: As you're transitioning, be thinking about this first conversation you're going to have with your group about your contemporary book. What did you think? How did it align or not with *Romeo and Juliet*? Did each of your group members read the book in the same way, time, or place?

Pauline: Take five minutes to connect and share within your group about your initial reactions.

for many years, a quick look between the two of us signals it is time to introduce the infographic activity.

To quickly recap, we are asking our PSTs to, as a group, draw on visual literacies to create an infographic that focuses on one text or that compares and contrasts two texts. First, we give them time to discuss their texts. To support the discussion, we provide a number of prompts to get them started. By providing this time in class, we are communicating to them that their ideas matter. We do not tell them what to think about the books, but we want to hear how they connected (or didn't connect) to the modern young adult texts and/or classic works. First, they need to consider these texts as readers, and then we push their thinking to consider the texts as future teachers. Following we include examples from

Pauline: As we introduce this next activity, we want you to go ahead and start practicing the switch in your minds we presented earlier in the semester. You're going to be completing this activity with your book club groups as our university students, as PSTs in class, right? But we also want you to start thinking about how you might integrate and use this activity as a future teacher at the same time. Some questions for you to consider might be: "How will I adapt this activity for my future students?" and "How might I introduce or evaluate this activity with secondary students?"

Matthew: So, what we want you to do is create an infographic together as a book club group, something that could be used as either an advertisement for the book or a book talk. You have a bit of a choice to make here. The first is what kind of infographic you will make and what technology you will choose to create your infographic. These two choices are actually connected: you can choose to create a "one-pager" or a Netflix landing page. If you choose the one-pager, you will use either Canva, Piktochart, or Google Drawings to share something about the themes, characters, or another main component of your contemporary text. If your group chooses the Netflix landing page, you will be using a template that can be accessed and edited in Google Slides or Microsoft PowerPoint.

Pauline: If you choose the one-pager, another option is creating a comparison between *Romeo and Juliet* and your contemporary book. With the Netflix landing page, you're going to want to focus on just your contemporary text. We'll give you a couple of minutes to check in with your groups to see which infographic you're thinking of making, and then we can check for understanding and answer questions.

groups who read *All the Bright Places* by Jennifer Niven and *Love, Hate, and Other Filters* by Samira Ahmed. In Year Four, the groups read these more recent books alongside *Romeo and Juliet* and used their infographics to share quotes and symbols from the novels. Specifically, we encourage them to offer visual summaries without spoilers.

If we look at the one-pager example for *All the Bright Places* (see Figure 5.4), we can use FIMS to retrace the producing choices that our students made. To begin, they started with their *imaginations* by considering what they were trying to create. They decided to communicate elements of the plot in a one-pager format. In terms of *influence*, they decided that the one-pager was the best response to our prompt to create an info-graphic that could be used as an advertisement for their book or as a book talk and as a way to present their text to others without any spoilers. They chose to use a magazine cutout or collage to incorporate the element of the story that was told on sticky notes. They *identified* their success by presenting this to their colleagues during class time, reflecting on their design choices as it connected to the book.

One of our PSTs, Hana, worked with her book club group on a one-pager info-graphic for *Love, Hate, & Other Filters* (see Figure 5.5). After completing the activity,

FIGURE 5.4. *All the Bright Places* one-pager.

FIGURE 5.5. *Love, Hate, & Other Filters* one-pager.

she shared that she appreciated having the opportunity to use an infographic to bring the novel to life. Hana liked how her group was able to make visual connections through the use of symbols and other visual aspects. She was aware that other book club groups chose an alternative mode, the Netflix landing page, and did wonder if her group's work was limited in a way that other groups' work was not since her group had chosen the one-pager. She reported that she loved the visual aspect of the infographic but wanted more space to develop, possibly even using a symbol as a design tool for the infographic, as can be found sometimes with poetry.

Access larger versions of these infographics here.

In Year Three of the infographic activity, we encouraged our PSTs to create a visual comparison of two books. As examples, we include three infographics from

FIGURE 5.6. Three infographics created by PSTs from paired books groups.

groups that read the following pairings: *Diary of a Young Girl* and *The Hate U Give*, *Lord of the Flies* and *Beauty Queens*, and *1984* and *The Handmaid's Tale* (Figure 5.6). In the comparing/contrasting option, groups chose to highlight particular themes. The *Diary of a Young Girl/The Hate U Give* group chose to focus on the oppression of young girls in historical contexts, the *Lord of the Flies/Beauty Queens* group used their infographic to share thematic parallels between the texts, and the *1984* and *The Handmaid's Tale* group created their infographic within the framework of censorship and banned books.

In all of these examples you can see how each group focused on the second and third practice of the FIMS producing steps: *influence* and *impact*. While it manifested in different ways, it is clear that each group applied the same strategies. For example, when considering influence (Who are you trying to communicate to? What do you want to say?), the PSTs were communicating with future secondary students. When turning to *impact* (How can you best convey the intent of your text?), they all carefully chose the color scheme and symbols that were appropriate for their texts.

In Years Four and Five, as described earlier, we challenged the PSTs to create a Netflix landing page for their contemporary text. A quick Google search for "Netflix landing page template" will provide access to multiple templates created in Google Slides or Microsoft PowerPoint that mimic the popular streaming app's landing page or home screen. When given this option, the PSTs are encouraged to think about how they would transfer their contemporary texts into this different format to visually convey their book. What is more, they can then take this activity to the next level because they must figure out how to convert their book into an episodic format—the standard for the template is ten episodes. In addition, the groups must select images, draft one-sentence summaries, and determine keywords to represent their adaptation. By selecting this activity for their infographic, the book club groups exercise their visual literacy skills as well as key components of the FIMS producing strategy.

Explore the Netflix template here.

Justin, whose book club group read *Eleanor & Park*, enjoyed creating the Netflix landing page with his group. (Figure 5.7) His group liked the challenge of thinking through their book and how it would be organized as a show. Converting the plotline of the book into an episodic format required particular creativity because so many important plot points in *Eleanor & Park* occur toward the end of the text. This forced the group to reflect on *influence* when creating this specific visual text. Justin wondered aloud, along with us as his instructors, in what ways the Netflix landing page was or was not an infographic. He considered the *impact* of this format on the reader. Ultimately, he helped us see how the activity had helped him and his group members exercise their visual literacy skills, including, for example, in selecting the graphics and images for the pages, as well as selecting the episode titles. The size, placement, and type of images selected mirrored what his other classmates had shared while working on their one-pager infographics.

Interestingly, Aliza, Justin's fellow group member in the *Eleanor & Park* book club group, echoed many of Justin's points but went in a different direction during a lesson planning activity later in the course. When she drafted her sample lesson plan, she used the one-pager infographic model rather than the Netflix landing page. Aliza designed an activity where her future secondary students would use Canva to create comic strip-like panels of key moments in *Eleanor & Park*. She selected Canva as her technology tool because of its ease of use, free access for users, and previous experience with its templates that she found aesthetically pleasing.

Aliza reflected back to us when processing her thinking about creating this activity that it might be easier for students to sketch out this activity by hand but noted that she wanted her students to gain more experience with the aesthetics of creating professional-looking infographics, especially since many secondary students today live in an "Instagram world" where a single image is meant to tell a story. The ability to create and decode images for their narrative impact is a key component of visual literacy for Aliza, and the aim of her lesson plan was to place a focus on this.

Listen to our full conversation with Aliza here.

FIGURE 5.7. Netflix landing page created by PSTs for *Eleanor & Park*.

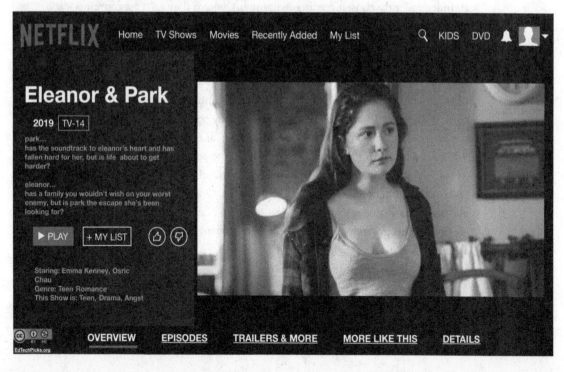

As teachers, we also regularly reflect on our pedagogy before and after class. While we are proud to share examples from the higher education context, we are also equally excited to share the ways that our secondary teacher colleagues are utilizing infographics in their classrooms.

From the University to the Secondary Classroom

When doing our research for this book, we were thrilled to find many of our colleagues in the secondary ELA classroom also using infographics in their varied forms to exercise and expand their secondary students' visual literacies. Some teachers shared with us that even some popular curriculum frameworks are now integrating infographics as an option for students to create. Below we meet Abigail, who has her students create an infographic depicting an archetype in literature, and then we encounter Brett, who has not only included infographics in his classroom but has also published articles online about his work with his students. We are excited to see infographics incorporated in more curriculum and classroom settings.

Abigail teaches in a suburban high school outside of Philadelphia and uses technology in a variety of ways; specifically, we were impressed with her use of infographics in the classroom. Abigail teaches her students about archetypes while reading canonical texts. After reading the canonical texts, the students follow up with an independently chosen reading assignment, where they select a contemporary young adult text. She draws on the novel study to parallel an assignment for their individual books. She has her students create their own infographics showing how one of their characters is an archetype. Abigail isn't strict about the characters students use—she is most interested in having her students use their *imagination* to convey their understanding of the text and communicating this understanding in a visually meaningful way. Students must seriously consider the *influence* and *impact* of the image they create to meet the requirements of this assignment.

All of this prior scaffolding work within the activity is in service of building and strengthening students' visual literacy skills so that they can complete their ultimate task: the creation of an infographic using Canva. One of the conversations that Abigail inevitably has with her students involves the use of color. Abigail shares the following about how this prior work helps support her students in completing the culminating activity of the unit:

I think it really shows students the different ways we take in
information visually all the time without thinking about it. One of
the things that stands out for me is color. Kids immediately gravitate
towards color meanings that we have already impressed in ourselves

within a community. For example: red as meaning stop or bad. We look at anti-smoking ads and find that some of those richer, bolder colors are meant to say "alert!" And then other ads that are about pleasurable experiences often have softer colors.

What we love most is that her students were driving their own project and could choose *any* young adult book for the infographic assignment. We know that when students are given choices, they are more engaged in the learning *and* metacognitive work that follows. What Abigail built into the assignment was a limit on the words they could use, thus forcing them to create a persuasive advertisement using their visual literacy skills. The students had to consider which visual image or representation would have the greatest *impact* on a viewer, then they also had to

Explore samples of Abigail's students' work here.

carefully select the limited words to convey their idea. They enact the FIMS strategy for producing by creating these rich, visual texts.

Another teacher who has championed the impact of infographics on visual literacies for many years is Brett, a ninth-grade ELA teacher. When we asked Brett to reflect on his work with infographics and his students, he shared that he first became interested in infographics outside of the classroom while flipping through magazines. His eye would be drawn to the graphic, and after studying the information he would find himself motivated to read the article associated with the infographic. Brett has taken this personal inspiration and translated it into his grade 9 classroom.

Infographics have become a staple in Brett's classroom, particularly within his yearly research project. Rather than having his students complete the typical research paper writing process, Brett has his students select a research topic, do the essential research, and then develop an infographic about that topic. He acknowledges that infographics are powerful because they can communicate so much meaning in one graphic, and this seemed the perfect fit for the research project. Students design an infographic from scratch that they use to communicate something about their topic, and then they have to develop a one-page argumentative piece of writing to support and expand on the information presented in the infographic. In this way, he draws on and challenges his students' visual literacy skills in a manner that mirrors the traditional writing process itself.

Rather than having his students immediately jump to using Canva or Piktochart, Brett encourages his students to create their infographics in PowerPoint. We were surprised because of the ease of use of websites such as Canva, but Brett assured us that PowerPoint offers its own benefits. Key among these benefits is the ability to resize and change the orientation of the traditional slide format, which creates a large, blank canvas for his students to create their graphics. When using Canva, for example, you typically must select a template and find a way to fit your ideas within that template. PowerPoint gives students a blank space so they can create from

Read more of Brett's work here.

FIGURE 5.8. Infographic created by one of Brett's students on school suspensions.

SCHOOL SUSPENSIONS

By CHRISTIAN K.

In 1975 (*Goss v. Lopez*), the Supreme Court ruled that it was illegal for a school to suspend a without giving them a hearing and a chance to tell his/her side of the story first. You would think that because of this the amount of students suspended each year would decrease. Well you'd be surprised to know that you're wrong.

In the U.S

3.3 Million Students Suspended Each Year

Since 1974

x2 The rate at which American schools suspend students has almost DOUBLED.

Effects on Freshman

According to a series of reports released from the UCLA Civil Rights Project, a student suspended once in ninth grade is less likely to graduate from high school than his/her peers who never got in trouble

After a student's first suspension the chance of Graduating decreased by **23%**

1 in 4 High School Students have been suspended more than once

Image Credit: Christian K.

scratch as the producer. Moreover, in recent years, many features (such as objects and clip art images) have been built into the application and can be accessed easily by students. Brett noted that his students were already fluent in using PowerPoint from creating presentation slides, and this comfort with the application made the activity that much more accessible.

Before letting students unleash their creativity in PowerPoint, however, Brett spends time showing his students a number of infographics as mentor texts. Students can quickly identify which are well-designed infographics and which are not. Brett reflected that he was surprised at how little technology teaching he had to provide for students, while he found that he had to teach them a great deal more about the elements of design. Students also had trouble designing their infographics because they tried to include too much information or selected odd colors and multiple fonts. Brett relies on a marketing quote when advising his students: "Data is king, color is queen." The use of mentor texts calls back the notion of "reading like a writer," and in this case, we consume infographics like a producer, as students get ready to create their own.

One of Brett's students chose school suspensions for their research topic and created the infographic shown in Figure 5.8 as a part of their project. If we consider the student's creative process via FIMS, the student used their *imagination* as they gathered research, knowing that delivering the information in an info-graphic would be most *impactful*. The student then made a choice about the specific information they wanted to communicate, as illustrated by the large number 3.3, blue 23%, and the one in four blue sad faces. They made the choice that the size and color was going to draw the consumer's eye to these key points. In their one-page written reflection, the student *identified* the reasoning behind their design choices and what they learned through the process of creating the infographic.

Not only is Brett stretching and expanding upon his students' visual literacy skills, he is also actively encouraging his students to present information in a visual text. What is more, he is demonstrating that visual texts must not only be carefully read but also critically produced by pairing the creation of infographics within a research project. Within visual literacy, Brett believes that by having students create their own infographics to graphically and textually represent the research that they have completed, students will better be able to critique and analyze other visual texts. We were impressed with Brett and his students—Brett is building his students' capacity for visual literacies by integrating infographics into his classroom.

Concluding Thoughts

Using images and graphics to communicate a message is nothing new, but the accessibility of technologies to aid in the creation of these visuals is. In this chapter, we present infographics as a pedagogical strategy to stretch and strengthen students' visual literacy skills. However, there are other tools and strategies available for infographics, and we share more of these in the annotated bibliography.

Given the increased visual culture that we all live in, infographics are here to stay, and we should focus on teaching our students not just how to create them, but also how to evaluate them for their truth, value, or ability to sway opinion. This echoes Eisner's (2002) argument for the importance of visual literacy: "reading images as texts in order to reveal their political and often covert purposes is one form of reading" (p. 29). In the next chapter, we shift to a different modality for exploring literacies: the aural.

Margin Memo

Belief #3: Technologies provide new ways to consume and produce texts. *What it means to consume and produce texts is changing as digital technologies offer new opportunities to read, write, listen, view, record, compose, and interact with both the texts themselves and with other people.* Abigail's use of Canva is an excellent example of students producing a text using visual literacy skills. Her lessons guide students to consume infographics as mentor texts that prepare them for this task. Thinking critically about infographics in this way is an innovative means of analyzing and thinking about existing texts. By limiting the word input, students are encouraged to think about their argument visually rather than relying solely on the written word.

Other Ways to Use Infographics
to Support Visual Literacies in the Classroom

- **Consuming:** Have students search through recent and relevant infographics found online and have them critique them for visual appeal and factual accuracy.
- **Consuming:** In groups, encourage students to seek out infographics from popular news sources (e.g., *The New York Times* and *The Washington Post*) and require them to check the sources of the data. In what ways does the infographic support or challenge the journalist's message?
- **Producing:** Building on Brett's example, allow students to select their own topics aligned with their interests and create effective and meaningful infographics to exemplify an argumentative text.
- **Producing:** Challenge students to create infographics of the plots of traditional texts to visually communicate the stories and characters in the text.

Part III
Aural Literacies

Focusing on Aural Literacies

Chapter Six

Introduction

To continue our journey into literacies and technology, we now turn to aural literacy. Think for a moment about the significance of sound in our lives. The first way that we engage with language is through hearing and speaking. Parents and guardians delight in young babies and children experimenting with making sounds as they begin to recognize the meaning of words, including their names, and ultimately speak for the first time. We learn our first languages and dialects from a very young age, learn to read the tone and mood behind words and phrases, and realize very soon that words spoken aloud have immense power, can create and destroy, offer love and care, and bind our families and communities together.

Aurality is the word we use to describe this type of literacy and includes (but is not limited to) speaking, singing, listening, and hearing. Typically, aurality takes a back seat at around age four or five as students enter compulsory schooling and more fully develop their skills in letters and words—those skills associated with visual literacy and the reading of visual texts (understood here as the traditional literacy of words and characters). Isn't it fascinating that we do not focus as much on sound and aurality within our teaching and the classroom when so much of our work as teachers is done through speaking and listening to our students? We ask students to listen, of course, but what does that really mean? And, do we actually teach them how to listen effectively?

Unfortunately, when students enter school, the educational system pressures students to master reading and writing, which inevitably causes teachers and parents to forget the importance of aurality. This is ironic, since aurality informs our ability to read and write in a myriad of ways and remains the predominant means of communicating both inside and outside of school with teachers, family, and friends. Despite this, we too often overlook our students' ears! So, we ask how we can help shift both teachers' and students' thinking about both reading the world and representing their learning through different aural modes. By exploring how sounds and spoken words, specifically, can be seen as texts, students and teachers gain a new appreciation for aural literacies beyond the traditional text. In this focus chapter, we introduce aural literacies and the scholarship that supports our approach.

Interest in the aural (and the oral) has grown in intensity over the past two decades in the public and academic realms. Researchers have even created a discipline to house the study of aurality: sound studies (e.g., Rubery, 2011; Sterne, 2003, 2012). To contextualize and provide a foundation for our work with aural literacies, we begin by explaining what we mean by "aural text" and "reading aural texts." We consider an "aural text" as any combination of sounds and spoken words, either recorded or heard synchronously. Because as a culture we are not used to talking and writing about oral (speaking) and aural (listening) experiences, you might find yourself stumbling at first over some of the words and phrases we use in this chapter, as well as struggling to understand some of our thoughts on what aural literacies might sound like in the classroom. This may not have been the case as you read our earlier chapters about visual literacies, probably because of their prominence in our daily lives and experiences. As we wrote this book, though, we began to realize that it is useful to spend time unpacking these ideas and vocabularies further to help ground and bound this important and underappreciated literacy.

The value of aural literacies remains contentious within school culture and can easily be demonstrated in the status of the audiobook within popular culture and educational settings. When someone tells you they just read a book on Audible, how do you respond—positively or negatively? Do you think listening to an audiobook is

---

Reflection Box

How do students learn to listen in your classroom? Identify three lessons where you could easily add an aural literacy component.

cheating, or do you think listening to an audiobook can be considered "reading?" What if it's one of your students? How would you react?

We argue here that listening to an audiobook is reading and it is not cheating. The recording is an aural text, and "reading an aural text" would mean listening, experiencing, and understanding the recording in ways that are similar to reading a visual text. Reading an aural text is most traditionally understood as listening to a recorded spoken word or sound, which is an inherently asynchronous activity where the text was recorded at a previous time. Understanding what an aural text is and learning how to read an aural text are the basic components of aural literacy. (We will delve more fully into audiobooks in Chapter 7.)

By singling out our sonic or acoustic experience, or what we refer to as aural, we are specifically drawing attention to the too often ignored capacities of student hearing and speaking. Over a decade ago, Diane Penrod (2008) defined aural literacy as "the ability to code, de-code, and/or re-code sound or music as message" (p. 51). In the examples we present in this chapter, we push beyond this initial definition provided by Penrod to align with the expanded focus on literacies provided by the NCTE Belief Statement that suggests we must consider literacies rather than literacy and literacies before technologies. The next section explores how we can use aural texts to help us access and support students' aural literacies in the classroom.

Distinguishing Aural Literacies in the Classroom

Before considering how digital technologies have modified and redefined aural texts, we want to first explore the very concrete, analog ways that secondary ELA teachers draw on speaking and listening. Then, in the next two chapters, we look first at what digital technologies have made possible for experiencing texts aurally via audiobooks (Chapter 7), and then how technologies inspire the creation of texts with podcasts and podcasting (Chapter 8). Remember that there is an interplay with consuming and producing, however, so there are examples of both in the chapters to come. Here, though, we want to focus on the everyday practices we and other teachers utilize to stretch and expand our students' aural literacies: through classroom discussions, read-alouds, and the intersection of music, lyrics, and poetry.

Margin Memo

Belief #2: Consider literacies before technologies. *New technologies should be considered only when it is clear how they can enhance, expand, and/or deepen engaging and sound practices related to literacy instruction.* We can easily turn to the popularity of aural texts, such as audiobooks and podcasts, because of the access provided by the new technologies that make them possible. We should not focus on technological efficiency but rather ask how aurality can be expanded and explored based on the availability provided by the technologies. In this focus chapter, we present more traditional ways that aural literacy occurs in the classroom. We think that it is important to focus on these examples prior to jumping to technologies because it helps teachers understand the strategies behind the literacies that can be missed when trying to incorporate new and emerging technologies. The Position Statement reminds us that literacies come before technologies, and in focusing on these examples first, we honor the spirit of this guidance.

Classroom Discussions

Although the first activity that might come to mind when teachers think about exercising student aurality might be helping students to learn to listen to directions or even a lecture, we think an even better activity might be to help students understand how critical discussions are to a lively, supportive, and meaningful classroom space. Learning how to participate in a discussion—from whole-class exercises to small-group work—is a lifelong skill that needs attention and practice. Put differently, class discussions are a wonderful opportunity to highlight and focus on the ways in which we "read" with our ears as well as our eyes. Teachers must reframe the discussions we have with students as aural texts.

In order to start distinguishing this with students, we can begin by teaching them about the absence of sound: silence. In the same way we would begin to approach a visual text by asking students to *identify* the text as a whole, we ask students to consider the noise behind all of our speaking and between the gaps in our words and phrases. This can be as simple as inviting students to listen for and *identify* those gaps of silence while a person is speaking, such as the space that opens up in our listening while someone is

FIGURE 6.1. Levels of listening.

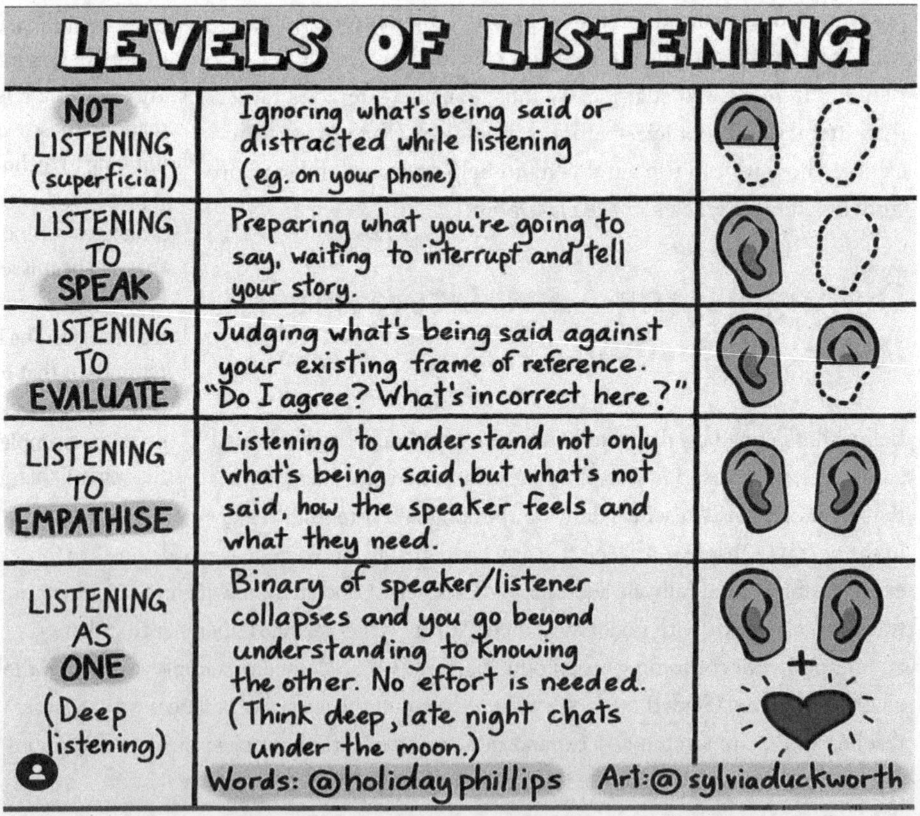

NOT LISTENING (superficial)	Ignoring what's being said or distracted while listening (eg. on your phone)	
LISTENING TO SPEAK	Preparing what you're going to say, waiting to interrupt and tell your story.	
LISTENING TO EVALUATE	Judging what's being said against your existing frame of reference. "Do I agree? What's incorrect here?"	
LISTENING TO EMPATHISE	Listening to understand not only what's being said, but what's not said, how the speaker feels and what they need.	
LISTENING AS ONE (Deep listening)	Binary of speaker/listener collapses and you go beyond understanding to knowing the other. No effort is needed. (Think deep, late night chats under the moon.)	

Words: @holidayphillips   Art: @sylviaduckworth

thinking and says, "Um . . ." or when they ask for agreement at the end of a sentence by saying, "you know?" What is the *impact* of these spaces? Are they spaces for emphasis or introspection? Are they spaces to hold the floor? Are they something else? When we are truly listening to others speak, we can begin to hear those spaces between the words. We can also test our students' comfort levels with shared silence as can often happen during a class discussion. How long are students (and teachers) comfortable with letting silence continue before jumping in to say something or ask another question (see Figure 6.1)?

These activities are done in order to scaffold the importance of listening within class discussions. In recent years, strategies of listening labeled "active listening" have become popular tools for teachers to draw on. One key binary associated with active listening is listening to respond versus listening to understand. The difference lies in how we listen: if we are listening to another speaker only to affirm what we think they are saying while planning our rebuttal, we are listening to respond. If we quiet our minds and focus only on grasping the meaning behind what someone is sharing aloud, we are listening to understand. We can take time to formulate a response after we pause in our listening, but taking this sort of time to pause and think before responding is typically not our go-to way of behaving in discussions.

To demonstrate this skill set, that of listening to understand, teachers can set new ground rules for a discussion during class time to incorporate the response, "What I'm hearing you say is X. Is that right?" before students are allowed to respond. This serves to slow down the pace of discussions but clearly and quickly showcases the difference made when we listen to understand rather than simply to respond. Here's what this dialogue might look like:

Teacher: So, what did everyone think of last night's reading? Whom did you align with more, the hero or the villain?

Armand: I loved the chapter, but I couldn't decide which character I liked more. I think the villain was really funny, so maybe the villain?

Albert: What I'm hearing you say, Armand, is that you liked the reading, and the villain was your favorite because they were funny. Is that right?

Armand: Well, not my favorite! But yeah, I guess I aligned with them more.

Albert: Okay, so I actually agree with you, but I don't think it has to do with being funny. The villain was actually being ironic in the way they . . .

This discussion method would continue for the average length of class discussion time given the culture and context created by teachers and students. Or, and maybe more likely, teachers would try to support this method of discussion for as long as the students can maintain their discipline by asking "check for understanding" follow-ups before responding. Not all class discussions can be carried out according to this method, but every once in a while, when a group of students needs to tune up their listening skills, this could be a useful tool in the teaching toolbox. Guided reflection questions, or

Margin Memo

Belief #2: Consider literacies before technologies. *New technologies should be considered only when it is clear how they can enhance, expand, and/or deepen engaging and sound practices related to literacy instruction.* Writing, as we are, from the perspective of being in the middle of an unprecedented year filled with heightened political rhetoric, a global pandemic, and millions of students learning through remote instruction, the aural literacy skills surrounding listening to others could not be more important. Students notice and see how many of the adults on television, the media, and the internet speak without listening or specifically engage in active non-listening practices in public discourse. The secondary ELA classroom can be one of the spaces in students' lives where listening to understand is not only preached but also practiced.

time to journal about the feelings and insights associated with the activity, would be an excellent way to chronicle and support the development of students' aural literacy. This activity could also be repeated within small groups for those students who prefer not to share in a whole-class discussion space.

A final practice to help students approach classroom discussions as spoken texts—and to encourage their listening skills—is to host a metadiscussion about the quality of discussions in class. For example, as a teacher, we urge you to ask and reflect on the following questions:

- Who are the students who speak the most often?
- Who are the students who do not speak that often?
- Do you leave enough "wait time" to allow students to think before responding to a question they've been asked?
- Do students feel as if they are being heard by you and by their fellow students?

If, upon reflection, you identify some startling answers to those questions, you could make plans to adjust or compensate for the next class discussion. For example, you could purposefully indicate and ask that you want someone who doesn't typically share to speak, or you could use a random name generator to mix things up. Or, in small groups, you could encourage group members to nominate a student who doesn't normally speak during class discussions to report on behalf of the group. We acknowledge that some of our more active or engaged students might feel the sting of this activity, but we are aiming for equity across classroom discussion where everyone has an opportunity to be heard.

While some teachers may have overlooked the aural literacy skills of their students before, thinking carefully through the everyday discussion practices they engage in should give them pause. When we consider the back and forth of questions, answers, rebuttals, and agreements that happens on a daily basis, it should be clear that students are experiencing, consuming, and creating aural texts all the time.

Read-aloud

One of our earliest memories is our parents, siblings, and other family members reading to us, as well as us reading to and with our friends. Many of you may also remember doing the same and may also have fond memories of read-alouds playing a central role in your kindergarten through grade 6 schooling. Educationalist Kieran Egan (1986) sketched out a heuristic for teaching and preparing lessons in *Teaching as Storytelling* that was grounded in imagination, emotions, and, ultimately, stories and storytelling. In some cases, and with remarkable teachers, read-alouds remain a key feature all the way into post-secondary education! Further,

> if we see reading aloud as central not only to the curriculum but also to the needs of students both as individual readers and as members of a literary community, then we are not finding time for something extra; we are simply choosing to value something that we know has a powerful impact on their reading lives and development. (Bellingham, 2020, p. 142)

We both have fond memories of being read to and reading aloud to others in all of the above scenarios and embrace the notion that you are never too old to be read to. The term *read-aloud* is actually a fancier synonym for a more basic word and concept: storytelling.

Stories are at the core of who we are as human beings. Our affinity to hearing, listening, and being told stories draws on this innate and almost automatic ability we have to understand ourselves and our lives as situated within an overarching narrative. Ancient Greek philosophers recognized the human proclivity for oral storytelling thousands of years ago, yet we seem to need reminding of this powerful tool for teaching even after students have sufficiently mastered their letters and words for us to focus primarily on written literacy in all subject areas. Reading aloud to our students models literary elements like audience, tone, and mood in a way that will help our students understand the *impact* of a story and situate themselves within the narrative using their *imagination*. What is more, it is not just the story form that grips us and our students; there is something different and altogether captivating about a story that is *told* rather than read alone in silence.

Matthew: One of the fondest memories I have from elementary school were the read-alouds by my teachers, a special time carved out during the school day. For Mrs. Enoch in grade 5, it was right after lunch when we were all tired from eating and socializing. She would turn off the overhead lights, read the last few sentences of the previous chapter, and then simply read to us. Mrs. Enoch didn't really do voices, but you knew (somehow) that a different character was speaking. For ten-year-old Matthew, reading was just okay. I read when I needed to and maybe an occasional magazine article. But when Mrs. Enoch read *The Bridge to Terabithia* aloud to us, I was absolutely enraptured. I can still remember feeling frustrated when she stopped reading at the end of a chapter to transition to our next subject. I needed to know what happened next!

Teachers reading to students is the most familiar type of read-aloud. But read-alouds also include students taking turns to read aloud, one paragraph at a time. This method of reading aloud has been criticized and for good reason, in some cases. Whereas the narration is driven by only one person and voice in the teacher-led read-aloud, the same is not true when allowing students to share in the read-aloud. It can also be quite stressful for students. Although some students might excel at reading aloud, their peers might experience extreme anxiety at the thought of making a mistake in front of their friends. Fearing public embarrassment is not limited to elementary or middle-school students, it can also be a real fear for secondary students as well.

The texts read in the secondary ELA classroom can be filled with unfamiliar vocabulary, especially as students encounter books within the canon that were, we must remember, originally written for the adult reader. Still, we think that students should be encouraged to participate in shared or group read-aloud experiences as it allows them to tap into their aural literacy skills. Consider the FIMS strategy for experiencing/creating an aural text during a student's read-aloud. Before a student reads aloud, they must *imagine* themselves reading aloud the assigned portion of the text.

- Is the text narration?
- Does it include dialogue between characters?
- What about how the sentences look on the page—are they longer with little punctuation, or are they short and portioned off?

Here the student begins to consider the *impact* of what must be read aloud—what is the text trying to say, and how must it be said? The thinking moves rapidly now. How can the student, in their read-aloud, *influence* the audience or *impact* the meaning? As they begin reading, can they *identify* whether their read-aloud is successful in the moment? Are their peers following along and engaged? By pausing to consider the steps through which students progress when engaging in this aural manner with a written text, we can see FIMS clearly on display. If a reader is inexperienced or has anxiety about reading out loud, they might be so preoccupied with their own reading that they aren't actually listening to their classmates. We think that with practice this skill can be mastered.

This strategy will be best showcased during the study of dramas. It is common-place now to recommend that students dedicate a portion of their time spent studying a play to acting out (both staged and read aloud) whole acts and scenes. What is less appreciated is the utilization of students' aural literacy skills during and throughout this process. Students must constantly engage each of the four I's—*imagine, influence, impact, and identify*—when conducting read-alouds. And in the process of acting out a scene, the students' "acting" is also an ongoing demonstration of their aural literacy capabilities.

In another example, teachers can use reading poetry aloud so that their students learn to honor dialects and relevant enunciation, cadence, and rhythm of language. Poetry is an essential genre for English classrooms and can be integrated into class lessons and activities in a variety of ways. Some teachers encourage students to not only recite but also memorize an assigned poem. There is certainly value in these activities, but we would encourage our teacher colleagues to consider the use of poetry, lyrics, and music to help students understand the concepts of voice, tone, and mood. When we discuss these terms solely within the context of writing (and visual literacy), we ignore the obvious connection to aurality.

There are some current trends right now to teach "living poets" in classrooms. The obvious benefit is that students can find audio files of the actual poet reading their work aloud. These poets are pushing beyond traditional assumptions surrounding poetry in ways that can honor the focus on aural literacy. Poetry is not simply a standalone genre that includes the study of poems and poets from centuries ago. As an example, consider that the two most recent National Ambassadors for Young People's Literature, Jacqueline Woodson (2018–2019) and Jason Reynolds (2020–2021), both published novels in verse. These texts can, of course, be read traditionally—as silent reading conducted in solitude. Or, and this actively draws on aural literacy, they can be read as aural texts. Reading these texts in this manner echoes the read-aloud strategy but also takes the experience of the text to another level when students can access audio recordings of the author reading their own work.

Jacqueline Woodson's memoir, *Brown Girl Dreaming* (2016), is composed of a series of poems that trace her personal story, sharing what it was like to grow up as a "brown girl" in the 1960s and 1970s. Silently reading the words of the text lacks nuance that is gained by listening to the author read those same words aloud. One activity that teachers might consider when teaching their students about tone and mood within an aural text is to listen to Woodson's reading together. By focusing on their listening, students can hear the *influence* through the tone and mood of her words, inflection, intonation, and cadence. Students can *imagine* what it feels like to be Miss Bell and the Marchers in this piece. What is more, they can read the words on the page as they listen in order to grasp how Woodson pauses and breaks at punctuation and not at the end of the line. The particular excerpt linked above comes from about a quarter of the way through the book, and students can allow Woodson's voice to carry them through the story and experience how her way of speaking impacts their understanding and emotions simultaneously.

Listen to Jacqueline Woodson reading an excerpt from *Brown Girl Dreaming* (2016).

Another helpful example for this listening activity comes from the work of Eric Gansworth. At a recent conference, Gansworth (2020) unpacks the complexities in his latest work, a memoir in verse and visual art called *Apple (Skin to the Core)*. Students can connect with the narrator just by hearing the author read the lines as

Listen to Eric Gansworth unpack the complexities in his latest work, a memoir in verse and visual art, *Apple (Skin to the Core)* (2020).

he embeds popular culture and musical references throughout the work. If a student reader approaches the text visually, upon first glance, they might *identify* the page as being mostly empty, except for a column of text (see an example below in Figure 6.2). They might also *identify* the play on Beatles' lyrics, and they might even question the *influence* of the narrator's tone. But once students are able to hear the page read aloud, they are able to more fully appreciate the impact of the words and their meanings. The depth and insight of this memoir is revealed as Gansworth reclaims the slur of "apple" and fights against the stereotypes of the American Indian to share his story of growing up as part of the Tuscarora Nation in the 1960s and '70s.

FIGURE 6.2. Sample page from Gansworth's *Apple (Skin to the Core)* (2020).

APPLE RECORDS
We say we want a revolution,
well, we know, you all want to change
the world.

We tell you that it's evolution,
well, we know, you all want to change
the world,

but when we talk about reconstruction,
don't I know that I can count you out.

View the warm and cool feedback protocol we use with our students.

Read-alouds can not only help our understanding and appreciation of literature, they can also help us through the process of writing and revising our own work. In our co-taught class for PSTs, we require each student to read aloud a piece of their writing to a peer for editing at least once during the semester using the warm and cool feedback protocol. This activity comes after a different peer has conducted a silent read-through of the assignment and provided written feedback. In this aural iteration, the student author gets the opportunity to wrap their lips and tongues around the words that previously swam within their heads or on paper in order to discover what works and what doesn't, or what feels "right" and what phrases fall flat. We have used this same read-aloud strategy in our coauthoring too; each piece that we collaborate on (including this book) gets read aloud, paragraph by paragraph, at least twice by each of us. In this way we, too, catch similar errors and make the same kinds of necessary edits that we know our students experience as well. What is more, we find this strategy critical in continuously capturing, refining, and polishing our shared voice as writers.

Music and Lyrics

Throughout this chapter, we have presented and discussed traditional ways that aural literacy can be identified and exercised. The first sections focused on two specific classroom exercises that are common in the ELA classroom: discussions and read-alouds. This final example creates a bridge from poetry to music and lyrics that showcases ways that aurality can be highlighted in the classroom.

One of our recommendations for other teachers interested in conducting a similar activity with their students is for them to be thoughtful about the choices they make surrounding music. It helps if students aren't familiar with the song or music so they are really capturing their initial impressions and not just reacting to a popular song or artist whom they already know. The power of listening to music is further explored when listening to an instrumental piece, or any piece of music without words or lyrics. Our go-to composer and artist are Bach and Yo-Yo Ma, but this can be done with any piece of classical or instrumental music. For example, our students have also responded positively to selections from Disney's *Fantasia*. We begin by lowering the lights in the classroom and asking students to close their eyes. We play just a few minutes of "Clair de Lune" for them and watch as the stress seems to leave their bodies. They sit still, relaxed to the sounds of the gentle piano playing.

Once they have finished listening, we talk about what they heard, drawing on FIMS. What sounds can students *identify*? Piano, yes, but what about other instruments? We

Listen to the song "The Sleepy Giant" sung by Natalie Merchant at the very beginning of her TED Talk.

Pauline: An example of song lyrics that I have used with students to focus on listening also attends to assumptions we may make about someone simply based on a description. In one lesson, I use "The Sleepy Giant," originally written as a poem by Charles Carryl and reimagined as a song by Natalie Merchant in her *Leave Your Sleep* (2012) collection. I start by reading the poem aloud to students. And, just as we modeled in the previous section, I invite students to sketch or write what they think they know about the giant based on the poem. After sharing their initial thoughts, we listen to the song sung by Natalie Merchant at the very beginning of her TED Talk. Immediately, I notice students returning to what they wrote to add or delete descriptions without my prompting. Once the song finishes, I ask them to write and share again. Consistently, students initially identify the giant as male. But when they hear Merchant's rendition, they begin to wonder whether the giant could be a woman. The final phase of this activity is to show the illustration in the text, which shows a very regal, female giant. There is no right answer here, but the rich discussion that takes place shows how students can focus on one aspect at a time.

talk about how the music made them feel or the *impact* the melodies had on them. We encourage our students to consider how the composer *influences* us with the composition and what meaning they were trying to convey. Finally, we ask what they pictured in their heads as they listened, what they *imagined*—for example, where might this music show up in a movie? If time allows, we show them the clip from the film *Fantasia* and ask them to compare it to their own musings in their journals.

To extend the example to apply to songs with lyrics in the classroom, we like to pair different versions of the same song for students to analyze. One of our favorites is "I Want to Hold Your Hand," originally sung by the Beatles in 1963, paired with the

Listen to "Found Tonight," featuring *Hamilton*'s creator Lin-Manuel Miranda and *Dear Evan Hansen*'s Ben Platt.

version performed by the character Kurt from the television series *Glee* in 2010. The songs are identical in lyrics and basic structure but vastly different in other important ways, including tempo (the speed of the music), voice, tone, and orchestration. Students quickly *identify* the shift from the playful and fun tone of the Beatles' original with the wistful and solemn tone of the remake in *Glee*. We ask students specifically to reflect—both aloud in discussion and in their reflective writing—on the interplay between the lyrics and music and how they combine to *impact* the moods and tones of the different versions of the song.

A final and timely example for students to analyze is the mashup song, "Found Tonight," featuring *Hamilton*'s creator, Lin-Manuel Miranda, and the star of *Dear Evan Hansen*, Ben Platt. Students may know these songs as "You Will Be Found" and "The Story of Tonight," from their respective musicals, but they may not know that the two artists collaborated and performed this version to benefit the March for Our Lives initiative in 2018. In this example, we ask students to consider the *impact* of how these two songs, from very different musicals, come together as one. Unlike the two previous examples, we have these artists performing each other's songs, and the original meaning and *influence* is altered simply by the shift in voices. Because the mashup was created intentionally within a particular context (in response to gun violence), Miranda and Platt's *impact* is particularly saturated with meaning. Because of their heightened aural skills, students who are familiar with the original versions of both songs will experience a mixture of emotions and appreciation that would not exist without this particular creative expression.

While the connections between lyrics, poetry, and music are obvious and well-known, these modalities can be misunderstood or underappreciated as avenues for identifying and strengthening students' aural literacy skills. The focus on audiobooks and podcasts in the following chapters highlights how technologies can push our understandings of aurality even further.

Conclusion—
Now, Let's Shift to Application:
Audiobooks and Podcasts

This focus chapter identified how aural literacy is already present within the secondary ELA classroom in everyday and common ways. In a time that seems to be increasingly defined by listening to respond rather than listening to understand, we think the focus on aural literacies is long overdue, and thus we have highlighted some ways that these skills can be actively emphasized and exercised. The following two chapters offer examples of two aural modalities that have been supported by digital technologies: audiobooks and podcasts. We know that these examples can create new ways of understanding, experiencing, and creating aural texts, as well as new ways of exploring students' and teachers' aural literacies.

Margin Memo

Belief #3: Technologies provide new ways to consume and produce texts. *What it means to consume and produce texts is changing as digital technologies offer new opportunities to read, write, listen, view, record, compose, and interact with both the texts themselves and with other people.* Returning to the third point in the NCTE Belief Statement, technologies allow for new ways of accessing and creating texts. Audiobooks and podcasts are two examples of aural texts that can, with the help of technology, build and strengthen students' aural literacy skills.

Consuming
Aural Texts:
Audiobooks

Introduction

*I*n this chapter, we sketch the importance of reading with our ears and the power
of utilizing audiobooks to distinguish and develop secondary students' aural
literacy. As we begin this discussion, you might notice how words start to sound
a bit funny when we use the word *read* when talking about listening to audiobooks. But
we agree with Moyer, who writes:

> listening is in fact "real" reading and . . . listeners can engage with audiobooks
> in much the same way as they can engage with printed or electronic texts.
> Therefore, theories of engaged and motivated reading based on printed or
> digital texts can certainly be applied to audiobooks. (2011, p. 254)

Audiobooks are increasingly popular as aural texts. For example, every year the
American Library Association recognizes several categories of award-winning books,
media, and research and announces them during the Youth Media Awards ceremony.

In 2008, the Young Adult Library Services Association announced a new category of awards specifically for audiobooks called "The Odyssey Award." This award, named after the Homeric epic poem of the same name, reminds us of the ancient tradition of oral storytelling. It seems strange in many ways that an ancient form of storytelling is new to the awards circuit, given that the Newbery Medal has been awarded since the 1920s and the Caldecott has been awarded since the 1930s. What's also interesting is that the list of honorees and winners includes a combination of new books read by authors and voice actors and older classic novels read by popular actors and actresses.

Audiobooks as aural texts have a longer history than you might realize. In many ways, the development and growth of audiobooks is directly related to advancements made in technology. From the beginning, recording technologies have been used to enshrine the human voice. One of the very first recordings was actually of Thomas Edison reading "Mary Had a Little Lamb" in 1877. But Edison's photographic cylinders only had a capacity of four minutes; and Mark Twain "gave up recording his novel, *The American Claimant*, on a rented phonograph after filling four dozen cylinders in 1891" (Rubery, 2010, p. 5). Think of how many audiobooks your smartphone or tablet can hold now. As technology advanced, so did the availability and efficiency of audiobooks. But from the beginning, as we alluded to above, there were challenges around what to call these newfangled things. For many years, they were called "talking books," in an obvious nod to their relationship to the physical book (i.e., to books that had been read aloud and recorded).

There is more to this story. It is commonly accepted within sound studies that audiobooks as we understand them today became popularized by their increased availability for blind service members in Great Britain returning from WWI (Rubery, 2010). The technology rose to the occasion, and suddenly there was a viable option to help people with visual disabilities maintain and expand their literacies. As the public saw and experienced the increased availability of audiobooks, production companies and governments supported their further expansion. Around fifty to sixty years ago, we started calling them audiobooks, and the name has stuck.

Some educators have been advocating for audiobooks for decades. For example, citing the 1985 US Department of Education report *Becoming a Nation of Readers*, Beers (1998) argues that "the single most important activity for building the knowledge required for eventual success in reading is reading aloud to children" (p. 33). This is still true today, and yet, there are some in our profession who continue to push back and question the legitimacy of audiobooks. Audiobooks are not a new technology, but perhaps the ways in which we can access them are. Whereas we were once mostly stationary in the 1980s, forced to sit still with our headphones and a cassette or CD player in order to read and listen, now we can take audiobooks with us anywhere and listen on our phones, in our cars, and outside of the classroom or library setting.

We know that "children's listening vocabulary usually is larger than their reading vocabulary" (Chen, 2004, p. 22), and so we wonder why educators continue to overlook audiobooks in their classrooms. "Audiobooks," according to Wolfson, "may be used with adolescent readers to improve fluency, expand vocabulary, activate prior knowledge, develop comprehension, and increase motivation to interact with books" (2008, p. 110). Struggling readers and English language learners can benefit from audiobooks as they "act as a scaffold that allows students to read above their actual reading level" (Beers, 1998, p. 33). With all this praise and research, you might still be wondering why there is resistance to the use of audiobooks: "U.S. audiobook sales in 2019 totaled 1.2 billion dollars, up 16% from the previous year, with a corresponding increase in units. This continues the EIGHT-year trend of double-digit revenue growth" (Audio Publishers Association, 2020). So, if sales are up, and adults use them outside of classrooms, why shouldn't we let kids use them inside classrooms as well?

Since the practice of listening to audiobooks is typically one done in solitude while wearing headphones or earphones, it is often experienced as personally and intimately significant. Consider our own individual experiences with audiobooks:

Pauline: For me, the love of the audiobook occurred when I listened to all seven *Harry Potter* books read by actor Jim Dale as I drove around my area to observe student teachers. Usually, I was in the car alone, but occasionally, my kids would be in the car with me. When we planned longer road trips, we made sure we had *Harry Potter* along for the ride. At the beginning of my journey, I only knew Dale's work as the villain in the original *Pete's Dragon* movie. I thought I knew the type of character actor he was, but it turns out I was wrong. Now, Jim Dale isn't a voice actor in the way that Robin Williams was a "voice" actor, but through nuanced accents and shifts in tone and pitch, he captured all of the characters in those books. In fact, the final book in the series was honored in The Odyssey Award's first year, and the American Library Association's website says, "Jim Dale masters and maintains voices for all genders, ages, species, and emotions created by author J. K. Rowling in this final *Harry Potter* adventure." After this experience, I went on to read other audiobooks—some independently, some with my family. I've also encouraged my PSTs to consider audiobooks for some of our course readings.

Matthew: I started listening to audiobooks during long drives as well but didn't get into them truly until the past few years, with the increased popularity of Audible. I typically have five or six books that I'm reading at a time, and now I have included a number of audiobooks into my rotation. Most recently, however, I have been experimenting with my own literacy practices as an adult reader. A number of my graduate students taught me about how they have been reading books for class while listening to them at the same time—reading with their eyes and listening simultaneously. The only time I ever did this was in college when I had to read James Joyce's Ulysses and barely made it through! My first experiment with this new way of reading was listening to former President Barack Obama's *A Promised Land* while reading the physical book simultaneously. I was initially frustrated with the experience, as Obama's voice was too slow for me; my eyes kept pulling me further down the page as my brain tried to race ahead of my ears. I took a deep breath and tried to lean into his reading and my listening, and I have since embraced the slower pace. I rekindled reading for the pleasure of the experience, being read to, and enjoying learning new things.

Building from popular demand through our own personal experiences with audiobooks, we turn to how audiobooks can be a key component of a student's aural literacy development. We look first at aural literacy and its connections to audiobooks before reflecting on our work in the university classroom with our PSTs. We then share more about what our innovative colleagues in secondary classrooms are doing with audiobooks to support their students and engage their aural literacy.

Audiobooks as Aural Literacy

Often overlooked, aural literacies can be as critical as visual literacies. In this chapter, we refocus and connect our definition of aural literacies to not only narrative studies but also to the oral tradition of storytelling chronicled throughout human history. The power of story, and in particular the story as *heard*, is best accessed via aural literacy and has been brought into the twenty-first century through audiobooks. Consider the amount of time that goes into the production of an audiobook as an aural text. Consider also that these texts are rarely consumed in one setting. The reader develops a relationship with a narrator that is similar to, but also slightly different than, the relationship they develop with an author. When students and teachers read silently and to themselves, they listen to the tiny voice in their minds. But, when they read an audiobook, the narrator's voice fills their ears and heads, and this relationship becomes ever more prominent and important. Cahill and Moore consider the narrator's role:

> A narrator's decision about tone, voice, and emphasis can be the determining factor in a listener becoming engrossed in or disengaged from the listening experience. Just as meaning is conveyed through voice, so too is it communicated through pace. The narrator's pauses convey meaning just as the words do. (2017, p. 24)

We know some students and colleagues who have strong preferences regarding the narrators of the audiobooks they choose to listen to. Some people debate whether an author should narrate their book themselves or if a trained voice actor should do it instead. Either way, the narrator of the audiobook becomes an important figure in the reader's relationship with aural texts.

An example of an author reading their own work is Elizabeth Acevedo's reading of *The Poet X*. Where Beers (1998) argues that audiobooks could help English language learners learn English, we would argue that listening to the musicality and rhythm of Acevedo's voice reading her verse novel could also help students unfamiliar with Spanish get a better feel for the language. Another example is Jason Reynolds' reading of his award-winning verse novel, *Long Way Down*.

Listen to an excerpt of Elizabeth Acevedo's *The Poet X*.

Pauline: When I read the hardcover text of *Long Way Down*, I read it at a breakneck pace, knowing that the entire story took place in one elevator ride. I felt Will's adrenaline rush as the elevator descended to the first floor and a different ghostly encounter took place every time the elevator door opened. I flipped through the pages, hoping to find a positive resolution for the protagonist. But then, when I listen to Reynolds read that same story, I *identify* a marked change in the pace of the story. He slows it down for the listener. He pauses for silence and emphasis. For example, when the narrator is talking about his brother Shawn, he says, "Shawn's [pause] dead," almost as if there's a period after his brother's name. The *impact* of this pause can confuse the reader, increasing suspense. There are also moments when the audio clears up a possible confusion. For example, there's a line that says "know me know me," which visually looks like a typo, but in the audio, the listener immediately understands the *influence* of the author/narrator. It is not a typo but an example of repetition for emphasis.

Audiobooks are now readily available on multiple platforms, including popular options such as Audible and iTunes, and promoted in many ways. Public libraries, for example, offer access to an enormous collection of audiobooks that can be accessed from home. In fact, we owe a lot to librarians and school librarians who have helped advocate for using audiobooks as aural texts (Beers, 1998; Chen, 2004). Librarians have long been connected directly to the everyday reading practices observed throughout communities (Gander, 2013; Moyer, 2011), and the promotion of audiobooks both reflects and expands those practices.

Watch Jason Reynolds read an excerpt from *Long Way Down*.

Beyond the work of libraries and librarians, new technologies have changed the availability of audiobooks and aural texts even further. For example, during the pandemic, a large number of authors and publishers uploaded audiobooks to YouTube and Spotify for free. Since so many children and adults were spending their days staring at screens, these authors and publishers expanded our concept of reading by offering aural options to complement the increased screen time we all were experiencing. Just one example is Spotify offering Ibram X. Kendi's *Stamped from the Beginning: The Definitive History of Racist Ideas in America* as an audiobook for free as protests

Access Ibram X. Kendi's *Stamped from the Beginning: The Definitive History of Racist Ideas in America* audiobook on Spotify.

erupted across the US after the death of George Floyd in May 2020. We do not yet know what the staying power of these availabilities will be in the long term since we are not sure how copyright issues might be addressed with these types of recordings. However, we are happy to see the increased access and availability of audiobooks, especially books that are important for the consciousness-raising that is happening within US culture surrounding race and police violence.

As we transition to exploring the use of audiobooks as aural texts in the postsecondary and secondary classroom, we note how audiobooks make literacy accessible in a different mode for people who are blind and as a mode of differentiation and modification for learners with differing abilities. However, we also want to acknowledge that audiobooks and aural texts are for everyone—not just struggling readers but for all readers. Learners of languages can experience texts in completely new ways when the words are heard rather than read, adults can enhance and deepen their reading practices, and students' imaginations can be ignited in new ways thanks to the aural contextual clues and multiple voices embedded in audiobooks.

Educating Preservice Teachers

This section highlights the power of reflexive practice in preparing future teachers; it was, in fact, our students who first introduced us to the possibilities that audiobooks present. We focus in this section on sharing the insights we have gleaned from our students about integrating audiobooks not only into their college coursework but also into their teacher preparation courses. Our PSTs have helped us to transform our thinking about literacies and have pushed us to ask questions about our own personal literacy practices, as well as the role of aural texts in preparing future teachers.

Matthew: My initial encounter with aurality was actually through my graduate student PSTs, students who were returning to receive their master's degrees with a teaching certification. One day in class, a student asked me if I could provide a cleaner copy of an article or book chapter I had quickly scanned and asked them to read. At first, I was taken aback, but then I asked for more information. And I am glad I did! The student shared that they used a program to read documents aloud to them, and the PDF of the reading I had provided could not be read by their software. By this point, other students were listening and weighing in. They asked their colleague for the name of the software, and then they asked me for a cleaner copy of the PDF as well! I knew something was there that spurred me to continue to explore adult aurality and literacies.

As mentioned previously, our PSTs work together in book groups that pair a young adult book with another canonical text (see the QR code in Chapter 1). In Years Four and Five, this included a Shakespearean play such as *Romeo and Juliet* or *Hamlet*. Many PSTs already own copies of the play, but we encourage them to consider aural literacy in their reading practices by listening to the plays read aloud. While there are official audiobook versions of *Hamlet* available online, we provide students with nonprofessional and podcast-based versions to utilize in their reading. LibriVox is one option that recently published a read-aloud of *Hamlet* as a podcast.

Access the *Hamlet* podcast series on Apple.

Once each group learns about their pairing, they can begin reading the play while securing a copy of the young adult texts. When we make these assignments, we generally assume that these young adult texts will be read visually. In Year Four, however, Pauline casually mentioned that the audiobook of *Aristotle and Dante Discover the Secrets of the Universe* was read by Lin-Manuel Miranda. As the semester progressed, some students shared that they selected that audiobook specifically because of the narrator.

Haley was one of those students; she shared with us that she had frequently relied on audiobooks as she was a slow reader who struggled. As a young reader, she would put the CD in a boom box and listen to the book in her school's library as she followed along with a physical copy. For our class, she listened to *Aristotle and Dante* while she was at work and on her commute. She did acknowledge that it is a "different kind of learning. When you are listening, you have to be more absorbed in the text." We were fascinated by her experiences, especially as she reflected on her reading as a learner and then on how that might impact her as a future teacher. She wants to actively include audiobooks in her classrooms, but she also wants to "make sure students have a physical book in front of them. They will more likely pay attention as the book is being read to them." Judging from her own experience, where she was distracted while listening, she reflected and then came up with a suggestion to mitigate distraction that we would also endorse.

Thinking of audiobooks as a way to differentiate learning, Aliza, who is a dual English/special education major, sees them as effective tools for her students. She describes herself as a fast reader, so audiobooks frustrate her because of the pacing and feelings of redundancy that can arise when listening to someone else read. While she holds these personal feelings about audiobooks, she acknowledges that she could still use them in her future classroom: "As far as comprehension goes, I think it is a really great resource for special education students. Kids who struggle will comprehend the book much better when they listen to the audiobook." We would hope that all teachers would be like Aliza, able to distinguish between their own experiences and what might or might not work for their students. Maybe questioning the legitimacy of audiobooks is unintentionally impacted by a teacher's personal opinions on audiobooks as aural texts, leading them to discount them as valuable resources for their students.

One of the Year Five book club groups read *Hamlet* and *Hey, Kiddo*, a memoir told through a graphic novel format. As we researched audiobooks in our writing of this chapter, we learned that in 2020, *Hey Kiddo* won The Odyssey Award. But how could a graphic novel win an audiobook award? This concept fascinated us as we tried to understand how a graphic novel could be experienced as an aural text.

We listened to the first few minutes as we looked at the opening pages of the print text. So much extra context was provided by the audio that was merely drawn within the graphic novel. For example, while listening to the aural text and looking simultaneously at the first pages of the graphic novel version, we started to feel that *identifying* the basic core elements of the story became complicated. If a reader has already read the physical novel and then returns to reread along with the audiobook, the same opening page is transformed. You can *identify* the cemetery and see the car rolling through the gates while a narrator explains a key plot point: learning to drive in a cemetery. The *impact* and *influence* of the graphic novel's opening pages is muted compared to the audiobook at this juncture. The graphic novel on its own somehow seems slightly less powerful, while in the audiobook, the narrator provides greater context and details about the setting. The added sound effects of wind and leaves then catapults the *imagination* into the action of the story.

We were so moved by this experience of interpreting the aural versus the graphic text that we encouraged the book club group to listen to the audiobook as well and take notes as they did. The group reported varied experiences of layering the audiobook on the graphic novel reading. Some of them loved the audiobook and said it gave them a whole new appreciation for the story, whereas others still preferred the novel in its original form. However, they agreed that they would share both options with their own students and let them decide which one is better. They envision a lively debate about this particular text ensuing.

When we initially read Moyer's (2011) claims about audiobooks and advocating for student choice and leisure reading, we didn't immediately consider a choice of genre, mode, or even delivery. The explosion of technology has impacted our thinking with the reality of different kinds of texts and different kinds of reading. What we have learned here, though, is that with the transformation of kinds of texts, we move beyond simple choices for students. With the example of *Hey, Kiddo*, that might mean merging genres or even reading them side-by-side. If the goal is for all kids to read, then we need to embrace all genres and all forms.

From the University to the Secondary Classroom

In this section we share how early career teachers are utilizing audiobooks as they discuss their own strategies for accessing and building on their students' aural literacy. They also identify some of the challenges they have faced in pushing the boundaries of accepted definitions of literacy to include audiobooks within their classrooms. Julie finds examples and samples of authors narrating their own texts on YouTube to share with her students, while Hailey creates structured listening activities to support her students' aural literacy skills. We also encounter Ashley, who actively encourages her secondary students to seek out and utilize audio versions of the texts they read in class.

A ninth-grade cyberschool teacher, Julie, spoke to us about the unique experience of teaching a young adult literature course. In her class, students are mailed the hard copies of the books they need, but she found that many of them preferred to listen to the audiobook format. Julie engages her students' aural and multimodal literacies even before they begin reading. As educators who regularly attend NCTE's annual conference, we have been fortunate to see, hear, and even meet many authors of young adult books, but students don't usually have that experience. So, as a prereading exercise, Julie finds clips of authors on YouTube so that her students can put a face to the name and the books they are reading.

She shared some of her tips for finding audiobooks on YouTube that she initially learned from her students. Sometimes this involves downloading the audio to share with her students via the learning management system that the cyberschool uses. She also works closely with the school's librarian to obtain audiobooks for her students; she is fortunate that the librarian has included audiobooks in her budget. If as a teacher you do not have this luxury, you can reach out to your local library/librarian to see what is in their inventory. Her students rave about the accessibility of audiobooks and their impact on their reading comprehension. She has shared that no matter *how* the students are reading, they are ultimately reading and engaged in the texts she is teaching.

Hailey, another secondary ELA teacher, also sees the value in having students use audiobooks both to contribute to instructional time and to support students' literacy practices. One example she shared was when her students used audiobooks during the state standardized testing season to pass the time while sitting quietly for several hours after completing these assessments. While her main goal was to provide her students with a brain break, she also engaged her students in informal discussions about the audiobook modality. Here's what some of Hailey's students had to say about audiobooks:

Ron: I could concentrate longer.
Leslie: I didn't have to worry about running out of class time while reading/not being able to keep up because I am a slow reader.
Donna: I could sketch out the plot while listening to help me better understand character dynamics.
Tom: Audiobooks helped me focus more on the text's figurative language.

Ultimately, this reflective discussion gave the students the confidence to realize what mode of delivery worked best for them as readers.

In her classroom, Hailey also uses clips from audiobooks as mentor texts for her students' writing. For example, when teaching about characterization in their own writings, she plays a clip from one of the *Harry Potter* audiobooks and asks students what they can identify. The narrator of an audiobook plays a special and unique role in determining and developing these characterizations. Jim Dale, the narrator of the *Harry Potter* books, reflects:

> When you listen to a book what you're doing is you're being given another dimension to that character . . . . Suddenly, the character in the written word is coming to life because they are speaking the words that the author wants you to hear in the dialect that the author wants you to listen to.

Watch Jim Dale read an excerpt from *Harry Potter* on YouTube.

In a YouTube clip, Dale begins with this quote and then starts to read aloud. The listener hears the shift in the pitch of his voice when he is embodying Professor McGonagall, and then again hears a different shift in his voice when he voices the "Sorting Hat" song. These subtle shifts help the reader *identify* that another character is speaking; the *impact* of the higher register signals Professor McGonagall's entrance in the story. The *influence* of the element of mystery when the Sorting Hat appears is clear by Harry's reaction to seeing it for the first time. All this unfolds in the *imagination* of the listener, who is carried away by the voiced narration. Dale even voices Harry's internal monologue in a slightly different tonality to indicate changes in narration.

Hailey and her class also complete a lesson where they listen together to the first two pages of *Harry Potter and the Order of the Phoenix* and then identify specific examples of imagery. Hailey structures this listening activity to support her students' understanding of the audiobook. Then, students listen to pages three to five independently, with access to printed copies to follow along with if they want and to refer to the text when completing the activity. Students choose between examining the setting, relationships (in this case Harry and Uncle Vernon's relationship), and mood as they listen independently for further examples of imagery. They use the examples of imagery in the first few pages of the book to help them understand how imagery is more than just making a book interesting. Students also explore how imagery contributes to how the reader views the setting, helps depict character relationships, and reveals the mood. Once students establish their selection, they work in groups to collaborate and then finally jigsaw the whole activity together.

Our final example is provided by Ashley, a passionate ELA teacher at a charter school. She actively advocates for audiobooks in her classroom because of research she encountered while studying for her master's in reading specialist. She initially embarked on this quest for knowledge to help her support her struggling readers, but she found that listening to audiobooks helps all learners. Ashley learned about fluency and the parts of the brain that are activated when someone is listening to an aural text and realized the impact of choosing high-interest texts with teens that engage them in ways she hadn't observed before. Tackling such texts as *The Kite Runner* and *The Hate U Give*, she has trained her students to yell "pause" if they need to stop the action to ask a question or ponder something in the text. She scaffolds and empowers her students to take charge of the learning by examining a particular literary lens with them, arguing that when the students are at the center, they will pause and do the same from their own perspective.

In our conversation, she detailed some of the tech tools she uses to access audiobooks, such as Audible, and how she innovated and adapted to remote teaching using the Chrome extension to play audiobooks on Google Meet. She mentioned her school library's access to vast resources, including ebooks and audiobooks, but also highlighted that some special education students with individualized education programs need to make use of those resources as well. She works closely with the school's librarian to get as many licenses for these aural texts as possible.

Concluding Thoughts

While it is important to adhere to laws and policies related to accessibility and access, we would urge teachers to see audiobooks as aural texts that expand and extend all students' literacy practices. We were intrigued that many of our secondary ELA colleagues had turned to audiobooks as an alternative mode of reading during a time of heavy remote instruction with increasing screen time. We hope that other teachers and teacher educators will consider aurality and aural literacy more and more, not just as an escape from the screen but also as a legitimate reading practice on its own. Beginning in Chapter 9, we will start to look at how aurality can be highlighted even further as one mode among many in an exploration of multimodality.

This first chapter in the aural literacy section explored audiobooks as an example of a robust aural text. The power of story and narrative, which are truly keys to literacy as a whole, is too often

Margin Memo

Belief #1: Literacy means literacies. *Literacy is more than reading, writing, speaking, listening, and viewing as traditionally defined.* It is more useful to think of literacies, which are social practices that transcend individual modes of communication. Some teachers still insist that audiobooks are somehow cheating at reading, but the first bullet point of the belief statement clearly states that "literacy means literacies." More specifically, reading does not just refer to the activity that students do while seated silently in a chair with a physical book and their eyes scanning the text on the page. It also includes the book being read to them through their earbuds while sitting in the back seat on the way to a grandparent's house or while on the bus/subway on the way to and from school. Audiobooks are reading, too!

overlooked in a visually saturated modern world. Next, we turn to the connections between aurality and production to examine the storytelling potential of podcasts.

Other Ways to Use Audiobooks to Support Aural Literacies in the Classroom

- **Consuming:** Have students create their own book clubs that utilize aural versions of traditional texts. Students can visit a resource like Lit2Go to find aural texts that are freely available.
- **Consuming:** Students can interview adults in their lives to find out how they use audiobooks to expand their literacy practices. Parents and students can also share in reading aural texts together.
- **Producing:** When a piece of literature transitions into the public domain, it can be recreated in an aural format without any copyright concerns. Have students create their own aural text versions of literature and texts to be studied.
- **Producing:** Within student groups, have students write, create, and produce aural stories or scenes from texts, including sound effects, character voices, and impactful music. Build a library of classroom aural texts to share with future students!

Producing Aural Texts: Podcasts

Chapter Eight

Introduction

*B*uilding from the previous chapter and the exploration of audiobooks as aural texts that students can read and consume, the aim of this chapter is to look at podcasts and podcasting (used as a verb to describe the writing, creation, and publishing of a podcast episode or series) from the perspective of writing and creating aural texts. But before we turn to this aim, we think it might be helpful to consider the ways that podcasts are pushing the boundaries of literacy right now beyond the classroom. We start with two examples: the storytelling power of a podcast series and the explosion of podcasting within the news and journalistic worlds. It is no secret that technologies and technological advancements move at a rapid pace. As soon as we learn how to use this tool or that new app, another *must*-have or *must*-see tool or app is already waiting in the wings for us to consider. However, the staying power of the podcast is intriguing. Podcasts have been around since the early 2000s, when every new technical advancement was considered *Web 2.0*. Podcasts are technically based on very simple technological means, and this may be why their popularity has exploded since about 2015.

Two podcasts that have taken the general public by storm are *This American Life* and *Serial*. Many teachers will be familiar with these podcast series as powerful examples of aural storytelling. *This American Life* was a popular radio show that had to be listened to at specific times of the day and week that, with the rise in technical ability and popular interest, shifted into the podcast space. Because of its background as a public radio show, *This American Life* maintains the tone, tenor, and makeup of the radio show in its podcast form. The individual podcast episodes are told in three acts, often connected by a theme chosen or identified by the producers. The podcasts are primarily voice based and rely little on musical elements or background noise for further context.

Serial, a podcast series that is a spin-off of *This American Life,* was created to make space for telling longer stories that required multiple and episodic treatment. *Serial* is immensely popular for its unique ability to craft an aural narrative. From the beginning, the program was intended to be heard in podcast form. It is also an example of a type of true crime series. We will see later in this chapter how *Serial* has been used by ELA teachers as an aural text in their classrooms. In a manner that has captured audiences and defined the podcasting experience, *Serial* has set the standard for the structure and tone of this genre of storytelling. There is always a primary narrator who guides the listener along a journey. Sound effects, music, and noises from the real lived experience of the narrator are included to provide the full context for the listener. There are silences and pauses that are purposefully left in the podcasts because they create a space for the listener that the narrator and producers want to be held open for suspense, further reflection, or to allow the emotional weight of what has just been said to be experienced and felt.

Let's think back for a moment to tease out the connections between podcasts and FIMS. In particular, consider this example of the purposeful silence described above. When there is a large and regular amount of noise heard throughout the podcast, the moments of experienced silence cause us to listen differently. We *identify* the silence, are struck by the *impact* of the quiet, and immediately jump to wonder how this lack of noise *influences* us in the story. The *imagination* kicks into high gear to figure out what to think and feel in the moment. And all of this happens in seconds, or possibly milliseconds.

This American Life and *Serial* represent examples of modern, technologically supported aural storytelling but they are only two instances found in the podcasting arena. Since 2015, the number of podcasts and podcast series has exploded, so much so that they are fast becoming a required feature of major news organizations across various news media platforms. Newspapers (e.g., *The New York Times* and *The Washington Post*), radio stations (e.g., NPR and SiriusXM), and magazines (e.g., *Slate* and *The Atlantic*) have each in their own way transformed their offerings to include podcast options of their news reporting. What is even more intriguing is that for an industry so concerned with its long-term economic viability, these daily podcasts are for the most part offered to the public for free.

Matthew: I am a podcast-aholic. I am obsessed and cannot get enough. My whole day is punctuated by podcasts. I even have a structured order and routine for what I listen to depending on the time of the day, and this applies to listening to weekly podcast series as well. My day begins with NPR's *Up First* and is immediately followed by *The New York Times' The Daily*. This gives me roughly thirty minutes of news to prepare me for my day because I listen to my podcasts at 1.5x speed and have for as long as I can remember. From here, I turn to either *Slate's What's Next* or *The Washington Post's Post Reports* to round out my news intake for the first part of the day. Then, I splurge and check to see if there is an *On the Media* or *Radiolab* episode (both produced by WNYC), or 538 (now owned by ABC News) to get a nerdy and numerical take on politics. I also subscribe to other podcasts that reveal my true and lasting dork interests, such as *The West Wing Weekly*, a variety of shows on the US Supreme Court, such as 5-4, and technology and science podcasts. Finally, I have actively tried to diversify my personal podcast feed by seeking out shows with voices and stories I wouldn't normally come into contact with, including *Our Body Politic* (which highlights political news from underrepresented voices and includes women of color), *Throughline* (which situates current news in a historical context), and *Scene on Radio* (a documentary-style series that focuses on whiteness and masculinity), for example. Podcasts are a huge part of my literate life and are one of my favorite things to talk and think about as a teacher as well.

Pauline: While I may not be as big a podcast person as Matthew, I have found some podcasts that align with my hobbies and passions that have been really enjoyable. For example, when I found *Potterless: The Harry Potter Podcast*, I was in love. Since my son and I read all of the books and saw all of the movies, we were intrigued at the premise that the host, twenty-eight-year-old Mike Schubert, had never read any of the *Harry Potter* books. To prepare for each episode, he reads a chunk of the books and then shares a metacognitive reflection of that section. Beyond that one, Matthew got me hooked on *West Wing Weekly*, which similarly follows a pattern of the hosts watching and deconstructing each episode of the beloved series. I think what appeals to me is that both of these series are aural "close reading" of texts. The hosts think deeply about the nuanced dialogue, characterization, and plots of the book and television series, respectively. From a teacher's standpoint, these could make for excellent mentor texts for students to analyze a text by using a podcast format.

Podcasts are still growing in popularity. Podcast Insights (2022) has collected and synthesized the data on podcasting from a variety of trusted sources, including Nielson and Apple Podcasts. They report that as of 2021, over 55% of the US population has listened to a podcast! For perspective, that's about the same number of people who voted in the 2020 US election (approximately 155 million). Not only are news organizations pumping out new podcast series left and right, but authors, celebrities, and musicians are creating podcasts as well. Podcasts are also being created to approach, highlight, and report on particularly sensitive and important topics within the broader US culture, including sexual violence and assault (e.g., *Canary* by *The Washington Post* and *Believed* by NPR), US democracy and the impact of slavery, gerrymandering, and authoritarianism

---

Reflection Box

We shared some of our favorite podcasts—what are yours? Take time to ask your students about their favorites, too.

View a list of all the podcasts we mention here.

(e.g., *The Land That Never Has Been Yet* by *Scene on Radio*), and Native American tribal sovereignty (e.g., *This Land* by *Crooked Media*). We are even excited to see podcasts like *Hysteria!* focus on news but from a specific demographic and perspective; in this case, primarily feminist. There really is an explosion of aural texts being created and consumed at present.

The dramatic increase in the number and variety of podcasts now available in the world echoes and increases the ease with which the everyday person can, with little to no monetary investment, set up, host, and record a podcast. In the wake of the COVID-19 global pandemic, many people have taken to recording their home-grown podcasts using the popular Zoom video conferencing software and simply uploading the video to YouTube. As human beings, we seem to be gravitating toward this not-so-new modality of creating and writing texts, and we believe that ELA teachers should take notice of the phenomenon. In this chapter, we build upon the popularity of podcasts to explore how they can become a permanent feature in the secondary ELA classroom, not only as texts to be read but as a form for students to use to tell their own stories and share their voices with the world.

Podcasts as Aural Texts

Podcasting can be used in many ways to stretch and enhance students' aural literacies, which is something we will explore in depth in this chapter. We begin by considering how podcasting can be used to enhance how students both consume and produce aural texts. While the previous chapter on audiobooks focused on awakening an awareness of aural literacies, and specifically consuming audiobooks as aural texts, now we want to consider how podcasts and podcasting can be used to consume and produce aural texts.

Podcasts are unique aural texts and differ from audiobooks. Whereas audiobooks are typically versions of physical books being read aloud, podcasts are often not correlated with a physical text. We make the distinction between audiobooks and podcasts as follows: audiobooks are, most of the time, read-alouds of books that were probably meant to be read silently; and podcasts are typically recordings of conversations specifically scripted to be read aloud, to be heard by the reader rather than read silently. Podcasts do often offer transcripts of their content, but this typically follows the release of the aural text itself—the podcast episode—and is seen as supplementary to or derivative of the aural text rather than the primary or mentor text in the way of the audiobook.

The aural texts created by daily news podcasts, such as NPR's *The Daily*, are intended to be heard by the reader; transcripts are made available for accessibility purposes, which is important, but the intended audience is the listener. To return to FIMS, podcast hosts and producers must always *imagine* how their content can best be communicated. They must continuously understand their *influence* in producing an aural text—a version not meant to be read silently but rather listened to. By considering the creation of aural texts, we encounter a new and exciting territory with literacies: reflecting on how best to communicate using our ears rather than just our eyes. To be sure, audiobooks can capture our imaginations and stir our emotions, but how can we prepare students to create and produce podcast episodes that are meant to communicate only via sound? What an exciting challenge!

Educating Preservice Teachers

In this section, we share the narrative of a transformed podcast assignment in the methods course that we co-teach. In short, a simple podcasting activity became the backbone of a thorough study of aural literacy utilizing podcasting as a venue for book talks or a transformation of the traditional book report. We specifically make the case that podcasting is not only a useful tool for teaching secondary students but is also useful for educators and co-teachers alike.

When we first received the syllabus for the course that we have now co-taught for five years, it included a group podcast activity. The podcast assignment was framed as a localized version of *This American Life* and asked students to work in groups to produce an episode of *This University Life*, with episodes focused on their lived experiences as undergraduate students. Being new to the course and simply trying to keep our heads above water, the first time we taught the course, we simply performed the syllabus as written—and then we received the final drafts of the podcast episodes!

There was an episode on how to get into local bars, the history of an old restaurant-bar that used to be on the edge of campus, and dorm hall ghost stories. We had a hunch

> ## Margin Memo
> **Belief #1: Literacy means literacies.** *Literacy is more than reading, writing, speaking, listening, and viewing as traditionally defined.* It is more useful to think of literacies, which are social practices that transcend individual modes of communication. Perhaps the podcast is the most significant signal thus far in this text as an embodiment of the first belief statement: "literacy means literacies." With the podcast, and the audiobook too, we fully embrace the fact that literacy includes speaking and listening. Creating and producing aural texts that are meant to engage the listener is a skill set that is not often developed in the secondary ELA classroom as much as it could be. Enacting this aural literacy is a direct evolution from understanding literacy as literacies.

that these maybe weren't the best examples of podcast episodes, but it wasn't until we started asking students to put their podcast episodes on their final teaching portfolio websites that we realized we had a problem. It was probably not a great idea to include a podcast about the best bars in town on your portfolio as a technological artifact when trying to get a teaching job. We took the insight and knowledge gained from our first time teaching the class and the work our students produced and transformed the podcast assignment for the next iteration the following year.

While the podcast *This American Life* is an iconic example of an aural text, we realized we needed to reframe the podcast assignment as something that our PSTs could actually use in their future classrooms. Within the book club context (see Chapter 1), the podcast episodes found a new purpose: the PSTs would be required to record an episode discussing their books and the special connections that they had identified (or not) between the books. We encourage our students to progress through the typical writing process while preparing their aural text by brainstorming, outlining, and scripting/storyboarding their episodes before sitting down to record them, but then another challenge arose. We found that the quality of the group's podcast episodes was mixed, and many groups, despite engaging in the planning and mind mapping process before recording, submitted aural texts that were not up to the standards we had set.

Access the *Notorious Pedagogues* podcast on Anchor here.

By Year Three, we finally hit our stride in implementing the podcast assignment with our PSTs. We realized that our PSTs needed a bit more structure in their podcasts and therefore decided to create our own podcast series, *Notorious Pedagogue*s. Instead of creating stand-alone episodes discussing their book pairings, our PSTs would be a part of our podcast series, contributing an episode to an already existing structure. The challenge then became very personal: we had to put ourselves into our students' shoes and learn to become podcasts hosts and producers as well! Just over three years ago, we set up a single microphone in Pauline's office for the first time, hit record, and started recording our pre- and post-class reflections with one another. This made us consider FIMS long before we had distinguished the steps.

We had to *imagine* our audience: who would want to listen to the two of us ramble on about our teaching woes and successes? What was our *impact* in the podcast episodes? Yes, we wanted to create something for our students to contribute to, but what else did we have to offer? When people listened, how would we *influence* their thinking and feeling? Could we *identify* whether or not we'd been successful?

When we introduce the podcast assignment now, we tell our students more about the history of the assignment and encourage them to listen to past episodes— not only of the book club episodes created by former PSTs but of our own solo episodes as well. We point out how the quality of the episodes changes and is mixed as we have learned more and more about the medium. The quality of our earlier episodes reflects our never-ending search for quiet places to record our episodes.

Explore our setup and the specific products we used.

We recorded our first episodes in the concrete cinder-blocked and tiled echo chamber of Pauline's office, and the amount of noise reduction filters we had to use to clean up the audio rendered the final audio tinny and hollow. When we later went back to listen to those episodes and recognized their poor quality, we knew we had to do something about it.

We reached out to other colleagues on campus and found out that there was a recording booth provided by our technology services department that was rarely used. While the recording booth was freely available for booking, it was created for only one person to use. We quickly booked the studio every other week for the remainder of the term, and the two of us squeezed into the tiny booth to record our episodes. The audio quality dramatically improved as a result. We were so impressed that we then struggled to find a quiet and soundproof room elsewhere on campus that could accommodate our book club groups to record their episodes. We were able to find a somewhat quiet office, but it definitely did not offer a soundproof experience comparable to that of the recording booth.

We share all of this to encourage other ELA teachers and teacher educators to explore the physical spaces in their schools and on their campuses as possible recording spaces. You may be unaware that such spaces already exist in your school; and if they're not available, there are cost-effective work-arounds. When our university transitioned to remote learning, we had to record our *Notorious Pedagogues* podcast episodes separately, and then Matthew had to mix the audio together using a software application. Many popular news podcasters have shared stories about recording their own podcast episodes under blankets in closets at home during COVID-19 and when working remotely.

We hope that our secondary and university colleagues can learn something from our journey and the lessons learned during remote work and teaching to overcome the barriers to engaging in podcasting work. On the following page is how we set up the podcast assignment for our PSTs in Year Five.

In Year Five, we tried to remedy some of the stumbling blocks by asking fewer questions and reminding students that when they come in for their recording time, we are truly looking for genuine conversations about their books rather than asking the same perfunctory set of questions of each group. On the next page is the list of questions that currently guide our interviews.

Having our PSTs create podcast episodes has created challenges for the PSTs and for us as teachers. One challenge for us is keeping our own pedagogical and content

Pauline: We hope that you are as excited as we are to get started on the podcast project! You have been working in your book club groups for a while now, and you have other assignments that you're working on together as well. But the highlight of the next part of class is working together to contribute to our podcast, *Notorious Pedagogues*.

Matthew: You've listened to some of the episodes before, including some older episodes where the sound quality was not as good. But you can hopefully get a feel for what our podcast series is all about. *Notorious Pedagogues* is all about sharing our thinking as we plan and teach this course and capturing insights into the blessings and bumps in the road related to co-teaching.

Pauline: Right. So, with your groups, you will be coming in to record an episode about your book pairing with us as your interviewers. We've blocked off a large portion of the next two weeks of class time so that you can come in as groups to record with us, and the groups that aren't recording can be working on the lesson plan assignments. We will be interviewing you, but not like a job interview! We want the episode to present a genuine and enjoyable discussion. A conversation, if you will.

Matthew: The main thing we want to drive home is that this must be conversational, or feel conversational, when you produce your final product. Each group will come in and sit with us for a thirty-minute recording session, but your group will need to edit your episode down to approximately twenty minutes. That means you will have to cut and remove at least ten minutes of the original recording. This is a challenge, and we know it is. I'll help you with the technical aspects of cutting, editing, and producing, but your whole group will need to think about how to best produce your podcast episode as an aural text. You'll be chopping out more than just "ums" and extraneous noises—you'll also cut out parts of questions or sentences that just don't fit. Think of this editing like editing a paper or an essay. It's the same thing, but you'll be editing an audio file, not a word processing file.

Pauline: Now, this is the blessing of co-teaching. If you have questions about your books and the pairings, let me know. If you have questions about the technology and the audio editing, you'll be bugging Dr. Kruger-Ross! You'll have about a week to finalize your episodes, but know this: we have returned episodes that were either too long or did not make the cut. Your episodes are a contribution to our public series and we want to put the best content out there. Your future audience includes past students, yes, but also practicing ELA teachers—who knows what they might gain or learn from listening to your episodes!

Matthew: And, I'll just reiterate that we will be providing additional technical support with videos and PDFs to help you learn more about processing and editing the audio files. There will be one point person for each group who connects with me to share and upload your audio, so remember that. Be sure to go back and listen to past episodes from the book club podcast series; you have at least 20 to choose from! There are even episodes where we did a director's cut version where we provide commentary on what past groups have done well and where they've stumbled.

choices up-to-date when public artifacts of our previous podcast assignments are so readily available. In practice, this has meant updating the book pairings each term we teach the course so that the PSTs (and our listeners) have a fresh series of episodes and books to learn more about each year that we teach the course. Even though we finally hit the sweet spot with the technology and the assignment's format, we still have to keep

> ## Guiding Questions for Interviews
> - When you think about teaching your young adult literature book, what type of literacy skill set best fits with your novel (i.e., visual, aural, or multimodal)?
> - Describe the connections you've made between the canonical/mentor text and your book? (In Year Five, the canonical text was Hamlet.)
> - Share a lesson or activity from the lesson plans you are drafting that you are proud of.
> - What kinds of lessons have you and your group learned from pandemic times about technology and the use of class time for a/synchronous activities, and how will this impact you as a future teacher?

our content fresh and engaging. This has been an unexpected bump in the road that we want other teachers to be aware of if they choose to have students create podcasts episodes across multiple years.

At the time of writing this book, we are processing and producing our third iteration of the book club podcast series and have been impressed with the responses and feedback we have received thus far from our PSTs. They are in the unique position of having to record their podcast episodes over Zoom due to the pandemic, so this adds an extra layer of complexity to the audio work to be done. Uniquely, and unlike other assignments in our course, our students engage with their podcast episodes as aural texts by creating their own episodes and also by referring back to and listening/reading previous students' episodes. The podcast assignment has grown and transformed into a pillar of our co-teaching, and students often refer to it as a memorable component of our course.

Bobby, one of our PSTs from Year Two, who is now a practicing secondary ELA teacher, reflected back on his experience in our course while completing the podcast assignment. Bobby took our course before our podcast series *Notorious Pedagogues* began, when the book club groups simply created an episode on their own. Bobby's group was assigned Nathaniel Hawthorne's *The Scarlet Letter* and *Speak* by Laurie Halse Anderson. Bobby noted that his group approached the recording of their podcast episode as a recorded book talk presentation. His group focused on working together to identify similarities and helpful components as they thought through teaching their books and built out unit plans to teach the books. His group

Listen to Episode 109, "Sample Book Club Podcast: *Scarlet Letter & Speak*" here.

did multiple takes or recordings of their episode rather than edit a final draft, and he noted how they enjoyed working with the technology and the fun they had as a group. *The Scarlet Letter/Speak* group was actually one episode we, as the *Notorious Pedagogues*, recorded as we annotated.

As he reflected on his group's experience with creating their podcast episode, Bobby also noted how podcasts had been integrated into his daily life as a PST/early career teacher. He now listens to a lot of podcasts while on walks and prefers a podcast series with a strong plot, often favoring mysteries. Bobby's personal connection to podcasts has encouraged him to consider podcasts as a genre within his secondary ELA classroom as well:

> I want my students to see and hear something new and different. It is one thing to read a [physical] book and another to listen to something and experiment it [via your imagination] with sights and sounds. For example, it is cool to hear a conversation in one headphone, and in the other headphone there's another sound, almost in a different part of your head!

Bobby's description of his aural reading experience is similar to what we've heard from our other PSTs and what we have experienced ourselves.

One point we would like to emphasize is that while we embrace and focus on aural literacy, it takes time and practice to fully activate this skill set in students. For example, to engage our PSTs with a podcast episode for the first time as a class, we suggest talking about podcasts with students to gain a greater understanding of what their comfort level is with the medium. Are they new to podcasts? Are they avid listeners? Then, we encourage them to reflect on and share their own listening practices. Have they ever reflected on their ability to listen and make meaning over a longer and sustained period of time? After posing these questions, and possibly after some journaling and discussion, find a ten- to fifteen-minute podcast episode and listen to it together as a class. At the end, ask for volunteers to share aloud about their listening experience, focusing on these prompts:

This activity would then lead to engaging with longer aural texts, explaining and modeling for students the need to practice our listening, giving them time to adjust and build up their listening stamina. The ultimate goal, of course, is for our PSTs to embody this listening practice as they transition into thinking about planning for their secondary ELA students.

- Did you take any notes?
- What did your mind do while listening?
- Did you find your attention wandering?
- What can you remember from the podcast episode?
- How might you think about preparing a practice listening exercise like this for your future students?

From the University to the Secondary Classroom

Podcasting is not only useful for professionals or PSTs but also for inservice teachers and their students. In this section, we highlight examples of secondary teachers who have integrated podcasts into their classrooms. We introduce you to some teachers who integrate podcasts as aural texts and others who have their students record and produce their own podcast episodes and series. We meet Molly who uses *Serial* as an entire unit in her ELA classroom. We also hear from Tim, who has his students create short podcasts on characterization, and close with Erin's multistep unit that builds from student-created podcasts focused on American values. All of the examples demonstrate the power of podcasting to enhance and strengthen aural literacy as well as a foundational technological skill set.

If teachers are ready for a longer, unit-length study, they might learn from Molly's example. Molly's favorite unit to teach in her ninth-grade ELA classroom draws on the first season of the popular *Serial* podcast as the core text. The first season of *Serial* tells the story of Adnan Syed, who was convicted of murdering Hae Min Lee, one of his classmates, in 1999. Prior to introducing the podcast, however, Molly introduces the Innocence Project to her students. They learn about the project and its goal of advocating and fighting for freeing innocent people from jail. She has each of her students research a different person from the Innocence Project website, learn more about why they were imprisoned, what happened, and the general details around their incarceration. With her students' minds on fire, she then introduces them to the *Serial* podcast series.

Molly's goal is for her students to listen to and understand podcasts as aural texts. She teaches them to analyze what they are hearing, to maintain their attention while listening to longer episodes, and to interpret these podcasts as texts. Her district provides transcripts of each episode so that students can read along and mark up a physical text while listening synchronously. Molly's students become swept up in the aural story, taking on the role of detective as they try to evaluate whether or not Adnan Syed is guilty of the crime for which he is serving a prison sentence. They become angry when they realize that there is no one correct answer, and Molly notes that for many of her students, this is the first time they've encountered injustice in the criminal justice system. Her students' connection with the Innocence Project puts names and faces to real injustices, just as they are learning about the same in the *Serial* podcast series.

As we have argued, pulling these literacies apart for students is necessary because they need practice listening to these longer episodes. The episodes range in length from thirty to sixty minutes each, and Molly has her students listen to all twelve episodes of the podcast. She engages her students during their reading through:
- discussion-based exercises,
- four corners debates on Fridays,

- reenactments of one of the episodes where the hosts drive and time themselves trying to retrace Syed's movements via cell phone tower data and a map.

With these and other activities, Molly demonstrates our point about practicing students' listening/aurality skills. Students can use the discussions and debates, for example, to *identify* if they are understanding the podcast episodes and ultimately grasping the *impact* intended by the show's producers. By reenacting the cell phone mapping exercise, students realize the *influence* of this episode on the listener as they *imagine* not only the host's movements but also those of the main protagonist, Syed.

While we are excited to share how our secondary ELA colleagues are integrating podcasts into their classrooms as aural texts to listen to and analyze, we are also intrigued by other teachers who are having their students create and produce their own podcasts. In pre-pandemic times, Tim, an eleventh- and twelfth-grade ELA teacher, uses podcasts to help his students develop and share their opinions. Each student selects a movie to watch and then records a two- to three-minute podcast episode reviewing the movie with another student. Tim purposefully requires his students not to prepare any notes or scripts in advance because he wants the students to sound natural, bouncing ideas off one another in their reviews. Tim also encourages student choice in their movie selections and allows them to determine what to watch and review because he finds the recording stilted and choppy when he is the one to assign the movie for his students to review. He's also been open to his students selecting TV series to review because he wants to capture his students' natural conversation and opinions in the moment, which is why he has turned to podcasts as an aural text for this activity. Being in the moment is a feature of the medium.

Tim often finds that students often go over his two- to three-minute requirement because they get so involved and invested in their podcast recordings. He has even had a few students who have chosen to create and produce a podcast series for their final project. One student group recorded four, one-hour-long episodes on *Avatar*, where the students picked apart the characters and fully unpacked the movie. The students used GarageBand to create their own theme song and used the voice memo feature on their phones to record their portions of the episodes. Tim reflected that they could have used the learning management system recording feature or a built-in tool on their school-issued Chromebooks, too. Tim is also considering having his students host a class podcast that includes weekly episodes created by students. We hope that Tim moves forward with this project and we welcome him and his students to the podcasting world!

Erin, a twelfth-grade teacher in Michigan, introduced us to a full-fledged podcasting unit. Along with her second-semester seniors and her brother, who contributed his expertise in educational technology and podcasting, Erin crafted a unit called The Hero's Journey. She readily shared that the germ of the idea came from her brother and that the connection to her Writing Explorations class was almost like kismet. When thinking back on the most important things she learned from teaching this lesson, she offered two pieces of advice: (a) give students choice, and (b) focus on the transferable skills between writing and podcasting.

Listen to Erin's complete podcast.

Here's how the unit worked. Students were challenged to identify an American value that they wanted to study, write about, and create a thirty-minute podcast about. Some students chose freedom or independence. One even chose baseball, and Erin acquiesced to the student by acknowledging that while baseball wasn't exactly a value, they could explore it anyway. Erin, who likes to complete the assignments she gives her students alongside them, chose individuality for her value. If we analyze Erin's podcast episode where she interviewed her colleague Coach Foy, we see that she *imagines* this project and its future audience, knowing that her students will benefit from a teacher-made mentor text. She interviews a teacher in the hopes of *impacting* her students so that they can *identify* with her chosen value of individuality.

Erin had students complete a number of activities and brainstorming writing exercises in the first half of the unit to help them connect with and unpack their chosen American value. One activity included an analysis of the lyrics of two popular folk songs, "This Land is Your Land" and "America the Beautiful," to *identify* how students' chosen values showed up in the songs. She led discussions to push her students' thinking, asking such questions as "What do we, as Americans, share as values?" These discussions were always paralleled with writing prompts as Erin repeatedly noted the connections between creating a podcast and writing.

Part of the success of the unit, Erin acknowledges, was the commitment of and collaboration with her brother Bruce, who was able to bring connections to the technical requirements of producing a podcast. They utilized Soundtrap to help record, mix, and produce their final podcast episodes, and every week, Bruce would come visit her class to help advise and support the students. Erin found benefits for all students, in part because they chose their own value to pursue. While some students took the project more seriously than others, they all did really well and created amazing episodes. Erin,

Listen to Erin and Bruce's episode on Soundtrap.

Bruce, and her students even took selections from the podcasts and submitted them to NPR for a competition. They also took a few of the podcasts and presented them at conferences such as NCTE and ISTE.

Erin noted that the writing emphasis was heavier in the beginning but then shifted into a different modality as students learned the ropes of the technology and all that goes into creating and recording an aural text like a podcast, pointing out the parallels between writing and podcasting. How do you get better at writing?

You practice it. The goal of all writing instruction is that students will continue to write long after they have left the formal classroom setting. The same is true with podcasting and practice. Yes, there is a learning curve, but the more you practice splicing audio and cutting segments, the better you get. As Erin says, "When you think of it, anything you do can be thought of as a writing process."

While this isn't always the most important feature of a unit, Erin did share that the podcasting experience fit into the Michigan standards nicely and this, in part, has encouraged her to consider repeating the unit in the future. She is even thinking of pitching a stand-alone podcasting course.

Listen to us reflect on our writing process in September 2020.

Margin Memo

Belief #3: Technologies provide new ways to consume and produce texts. *What it means to consume and produce texts is changing as digital technologies offer new opportunities to read, write, listen, view, record, compose, and interact with both the texts themselves and with other people.* Just like the infographic in the chapter on visual literacies, the podcast is a popular medium that teachers and students are using to share and convey knowledge.

Concluding Thoughts

Podcasting holds a place near and dear to our hearts, not just because of our connections to podcasts as aural texts in the secondary and university classroom but because we host our own podcast series. What grew organically from our teaching was not only the need to find a home for our students' podcast episodes but also the appearance of a space that suddenly opened up for us to share our thoughts and woes about our own teaching, planning, and practice. We have even recorded podcasts about our writing process for this book!

As a separate arm of research and scholarship, we have continued to explore how producing and editing a podcast series can serve as an aural text recording our professional praxis. When we started our podcast, we had no idea who would listen. Who would want to hear us complain about a lesson that flopped, or that we were experiencing writer's block? But as the adage says, "if you build it, they will come," and if you record a podcast, your listeners will appear!

In this chapter, we highlighted some of the best moments related to consuming and producing podcasts from our PSTs as well as our secondary ELA colleagues. We remain optimistic about the power of podcasting as a way of creating and reading aural texts and hope that this chapter has encouraged you to get out your microphones and start experimenting.

Other Ways to Use Podcasts
to Support Aural Literacies in the Classroom

- **Consuming:** Incorporate a daily podcasting practice into the classroom or encourage students to incorporate one into their daily literacy practices. Choose from one of the national or regional news sources that has an established presence in the podcasting space.
- **Consuming:** Encourage students to expand their interests by finding a podcast series that pushes the limits of their thinking. A quick search for "ghost story podcasts" or "true crime podcast series" will provide many options to choose from!
- **Producing:** Task students with embracing the aural storytelling format and have them convert creative writing into aural stories in podcast form.
- **Producing:** Transform the traditional research paper into podcast format! Use the Radiolab model and have students create segments devoted to particular references, and so on.

Part IV
Multimodal Literacies

Focusing on Multimodal Literacies

Chapter
Nine

Introduction

*I*n this third and final focus chapter, we turn to multimodal literacies. To be sure, the way that we live our lives day-to-day is typically multimodal. As water is to fish, multimodality is to human beings, and it can sometimes be hard to fully appreciate how subsumed and surrounded we are within multimodal life. We can gain a quick understanding by breaking down the word into its parts: *multi* and *modal*. Multi, of course, means many. And modal is the manner in which something is expressed (for our purposes, things such as written language, visuals, and gestures). In short, multimodality is about how we use multiple modes to make meaning in our lives. In the first two focus chapters of this book, we looked at two modes of multimodality: visual and aural.

Researchers have been thinking and writing about multimodality since the 1990s, and educators are still working to fully unpack and embrace these ideas within K–16 classrooms. Kress and van Leeuwen (2001) and Kress (2010) are fundamental sources of multimodal scholarship if you are interested in learning more about the background of multimodal theory. While this theoretical knowledge informs our work, we focus here on its practical use and application.

For the purposes of this book, and as a means of helping you think about teaching in multimodal ways, we purposefully broke multimodality down into visual and aural literacies in Parts II and III. We believe that this breakdown—even if it was a bit artificial—allowed us to take a step back to unpack and analyze the component parts of literacies and demonstrate how you as a teacher might begin to consider teaching literacies in new ways. Our hope is that by first considering the visual and then the aural, you are now able to appreciate multimodal literacies—really, the full expression of literacies in their multimodal synergy. In particular, we share how FIMS can be used to help support teaching and student learning surrounding the multimodal. After reviewing more traditional ways of accessing and highlighting multimodal literacies, we then turn to exploring and consuming multimodal texts through augmented and virtual reality technologies (Chapter 10) and consuming/producing multimodal texts via digital videos (Chapter 11).

Again, human beings typically live multimodal lives without always being aware that they are doing so. If you glanced at a newspaper at some point today, you immersed yourself in a multimodal text, albeit a paper-based one. The newspaper had a large title, smaller text, images to enhance a story, and possibly even a graphic forecasting the weather. If children are in your homes, they might have watched digital animations on TV during breakfast—animations that include visuals, colors, sounds, songs, and likely written language appearing on-screen as well. Consider that this book in your hands is a type of multimodal text, combining written language, graphics, and video/audio clips (via QR codes) into one text.

We take for granted that we are constantly taking in multiple streams of information and meaning via our senses. Jennifer Rowsell, in *Working with Multimodality: Rethinking Literacy in a Digital Age,* describes this eloquently:

> We are constantly in the flow of multimodality from what to wear, what
> and when to Tweet, what register to apply to a given situation, when
> to use caps versus lowercase letters; there are so many choices when we
> communicate. Yet, there remains a veil of secrecy around what experts in
> production, design, and multimodality know and do and a discrepancy
> between that and the conventions that we teach students when they
> produce texts in school. (2013, p. 1)

Why is this focus on the multimodal important for us to consider and understand? Our students are surrounded by multimodal texts. Because they bring multimodal experiences from their daily lives into our classrooms, we have a duty to help them consider, analyze, and critique the impact of those texts on their lives.

To truly embrace multimodal literacy in the twenty-first-century classroom, we (and our students) need to understand (a) what a multimodal text actually is, (b)

Reflection Box

Set a timer for five minutes and sit quietly observing all of the multimodal things around you. What are you taking in aurally, visually, multimodally?

---

how to read a multimodal text, and (c) how to create or produce a multimodal text. Takayoshi and Selfe (2007) describe multimodal texts as "texts that exceed the alphabetic and may include still and moving images, animations, color, words, music and sound" (p. 1). We see a multimodal text as any combination of visuals (still or moving), sounds, spoken words—either recorded or viewed synchronously—and bodily gestures such as dance or performance.

Learning to read multimodal texts is something our students (and we) do over and over again, all day long! Consider a typical, face-to-face class period. As the students enter the room, they may notice there is writing already on the board at the front. There are other students talking and reconnecting with one another before class begins. The TV is playing a continuous loop of announcements about school events and upcoming sports games while the overhead speaker system alerts students about the pep rally later that afternoon. The teacher may already be projecting the slides for the lesson that day as students quickly glance at their phones to see messages from parents, updates from social media, and alerts from news outlets. The typical secondary student navigates this overwhelming multimodal world all the time. They have to cut through that noise and all of those images to *identify* what is important to them in both short- and long-term contexts; they have to consider the *impact* of the information being lobbed at them in multiple ways.

While consuming the world around them multimodally, our students are simultaneously composing and producing multimodal texts throughout their day. Consider that typical middle school and high school students move through their day being asked to create a sculpture or painting in art class, respond to literature in writing, follow sheet music and play an instrument in music class, experiment with chemicals in a science laboratory, and solve complex equations in math class—and that's just their academic life! Much to the chagrin of educators, students are also texting or Snapchatting with their friends throughout the day and planning their after-school and extracurricular activities through group chats or apps as well. Some may even be composing TikTok videos that may go viral.

Consider how the student's multimodal world challenges them when writing a traditional research paper. Today, a student's initial search for information begins by consulting a search engine such as Google or Bing rather than a physical book or text like an encyclopedia. In this way, students must be fluent in accessing, reading, and evaluating websites and web-based resources as multimodal texts. The primary challenge for the student as they review their search results in terms of FIMS is *influence*. Students need to ask themselves:

- What modes are being used on the webpage to communicate meaning?
- Who is putting the information out there? Why?
- How can this source be fact-checked for accuracy?
- How can the site be evaluated as a reliable, unbiased source?
- Are there discrepancies among the headline, the text-based article, the images/graphics, and the (possible) video embedded in the article?

Then, the teacher has to consider the following:

- How can the tools of multimodal literacy support a student's ability to evaluate resources online?
- How can red flags in unreliable or biased sources be taught to students?
- How can a student who is relying on a source that is inappropriate be handled?

A recent graduate student who teaches at the undergraduate level at a peer institution recently shared with us that one of her students referenced a LiveJournal entry from 2007 in a research paper. Our colleague, after a chuckle, had to redirect the student to consider whether this source was credible or legitimate. Websites often are filled with text, images, ads, embedded videos, and possibly audio; the savvy student must learn to read multimodal texts with a critical eye in order to determine fact from fiction.

Margin Memo

Belief #4: Technologies and their associated literacies are not neutral. *While access to technology and the internet has the potential to lessen issues of inequity, they can also perpetuate and even accelerate discrimination based on gender, race, socioeconomic status, and other factors.* We argue that multimodality does not only include the use of technologies. The fourth belief statement reminds us to consider students' ability to access technology. Multimodality can include embodied practices, such as dance and performance, and arts-based strategies including drawing and sketching, for example. Multimodality exists separately from technology while simultaneously being spurred on by it, as evidenced in the structuring of the chapters in this book. But we must remember that the riches of multimodality are not dependent on technology; rather, they are a gift of literacies.

Distinguishing Multimodal Literacies in the Classroom

Before considering how technologies have modified and redefined multimodal texts, we want to first explore the very concrete ways that secondary ELA teachers already use multimodal texts. In the next two chapters, we look first at what digital technologies have made possible for experiencing virtual and augmented worlds as multimodal texts (Chapter 10) and then how technologies inspire the creation of texts with digital videos (Chapter 11). Here we want to focus on the everyday ways we and other teachers utilize multimodal texts to stretch and expand our students' multimodal literacies through films and movies, dramatization, and the creation of professional teaching portfolios. As we have suggested in our introductions to other parts of the book, we believe that by exploring these more common and everyday practices, you will be better prepared to explore the impact of technology on consuming and producing multimodal texts.

Movies and Music Videos

Movies are frequently used in the secondary ELA classroom, and we want to consider the ways in which they can be appreciated as multimodal texts and as powerful learning tools for students. As teacher educators, we often urge our PSTs to consider how teachers are portrayed in movies or television shows. We are inspired by the work of Shoffner (2016), who points out that "teachers—real and representational—are everywhere, so embedded in our daily lives that we learn as much about teachers from the fictional as the factual" (p. 2). And so, we challenge our students to reflect on how they are consuming these fictional tales of educators via these multimodal texts. We think there is value in viewing teacher movies with PSTs as they are constructing their own teacher identities; there is much to learn about teacher portrayals, and the assumptions we make, based on those multimodal representations.

One of the most iconic images of an English teacher is Robin Williams's character Mr. Keating in *Dead Poets Society* (1989). Many PSTs identify his style as a charismatic teacher as one for them to emulate. With our students, we could analyze the most memorable moment in the movie using FIMS to explore how meaning is written into the movie as a multimodal text. The moment we explore is when all of the students slowly, one by one, climb onto their desks and call out "O Captain! My Captain!" to Mr. Keating. We walk the PSTs through *identifying* the swell of music and the impact of the emotion as Keating packs up his belongings and the students climb on top of their desks one by one. We experience the *influence* of Keating on his students, even though their parents forced him out of the school. We can *imagine* ourselves as either Keating or the young male students feeling a deep student–teacher connection—one that we should want to embody as future teachers.

But how can this movie, as a multimodal text, help our PSTs critique this supposedly exemplary example of teaching? To embed this fictional example within the actual context of the film and how it would unfold in lived reality, FIMS could help us problematize this simple and deceptive understanding of teacher identity. As teacher educators, we would never want to see one of our PSTs misunderstood or fired for a student's suicide. We might even reposition Dead Poets Society as a cautionary tale for future teachers as we see the prominent families in this elite setting with more power and efficacy than the teacher possesses. By zooming in to focus on this context, we can appreciate the greater nuance allowed by the film's narrative and characterizations. While we have chosen to use a teacher movie to explore how FIMS can be integrated into evaluating a film as a multimodal text, ultimately FIMS can be applied to any movie, regardless of topic. For even more specific examples to consider with PSTs, we defer to Shoffner's *Exploring Teachers in Fiction and Film* (2016).

Building a thematic text set can also provide a way for teachers to incorporate movies and clips alongside other texts such as poetry and nonfiction; for us, we stretch that boundary to include audio, video, and other multimodal texts. We recently published a chapter that focused on the theme of gender identity. As our main texts, we paired *A Midsummer Night's Dream* and *Simon vs. the Homo Sapiens Agenda* and provided strategies to read them using a gender theory lens (Schmidt & Kruger-Ross, 2021). In our chapter, we explore both the written and movie versions of both texts. Our ultimate goal was to have students understand and challenge the gender binary that dominates society.

In another effort to build a multimodal text set to explore assumptions about gender, we consider a clip from the TV show *Lip Sync Battle*, where celebrities mouth the words and

dance along to pop songs to battle for recognition and bragging rights. This particular show features the actor Tom Holland, performing a mashup of "Singin' in the Rain" (iconically performed by Gene Kelly) and "Umbrella" by Rihanna, and the actress Zendaya, performing "24K Magic" by Bruno Mars. Students might recognize these two performers from the Spiderman movies, but here they appear in costumes that challenge gender stereotypes.

Watch this particular performance of *Lip Sync Battle* on YouTube.

We could ask students a variety of questions to analyze this multimodal text: What do you *identify* that is inherently masculine/ feminine? Why? What is the *impact* when you see Tom Holland dressed as Rihanna and Zendaya dressed as Bruno Mars? How do some of the hypersexualized costuming choices *influence* viewers? Using your *imagination*, why is this significant? The beauty of a show like *Lip Sync Battle* is that the contestants frequently imitate a film clip or a well-known music video. While some of us are old enough to remember when MTV played music videos twenty-four hours a day, seven days a week, our students might need a quick history lesson on some of the iconic videos of the past. If we think back to the music component in Chapter 6 that was focused on aurality, our students have the tools to consider a multimodal text like a music video. When students have the confidence to analyze the sounds, teachers can add the visual to that and have them examine short movie clips or music videos.

While there is no longer a channel on TV that is completely dedicated to music videos, music videos are released on YouTube and spread like wildfire on social media. Three powerful videos that we would offer up as examples in the last few years are "Lemonade" (2016)

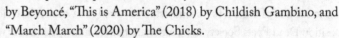

by Beyoncé, "This is America" (2018) by Childish Gambino, and "March March" (2020) by The Chicks.

A music video that might not have been on everyone's radar is "Shine" (2018) by Stoneman Douglas Students, so we included it in the YouTube playlist. They channeled their collective grief and had to use

their *imaginations* to build upon the traumatic experience of the mass shooting at their high school to create this powerful multimodal text. When the video is brought up on iTunes and YouTube, the image you see first is the entrance wall to their school covered in flowers, protest signs, religious artifacts, and stuffed animals. As the video begins, you

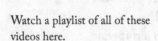

Watch a playlist of all of these videos here.

see the school classrooms, hallways, and gym all abandoned. In addition to the visual mode, we can consider the lyrics and music as well. We hear a single voice sing "You're not going to knock us down, we'll get back up again. . . . We're putting up a fight." The instrumentation starts with only a piano and single string instrument. The tempo is slow and somber. As more students start to enter the scenes of the video, the tempo increases and the number of voices multiplies. We consider the signal that these students are not going anywhere and they will not go silently; as we know, some of these students have become activists and try to *influence* the powerful gun lobby. The students knew that the creation of this music video would have an *impact* on classrooms, families, communities, and, hopefully, the federal government. At the four-minute mark, they even give specific directions on how to reach out to representatives in Congress. We *identify* the effectiveness of this text because we were emotionally moved by the combination of the visual, aural, and multimodal elements of this significant text.

Many multimodal texts contain a combination of powerful images, music, and lyrics that reflect a particular moment in time and tackle a variety of injustices in the world. Consuming these multimodal texts with a critical eye can allow them to serve as mentor texts for students producing digital videos of their own, as we will see in Chapter 11.

Dramatization

One way our instruction has changed includes integrating the use of MyShakespeare.com. We share our introduction to the use of this multimodal text in our co-taught class in Year Five.

Pauline: As we begin to read *Hamlet* this semester, you'll notice that we have asked you not to purchase a physical copy or critical edition of the text. We want to introduce you to a resource and website that you'll use to read *Hamlet*, but it has a unique twist.

Matthew: Yes, take a look. If you go to MyShakespeare.com or simply Google "my Shakespeare," you'll land on this page. Take a moment to create an account, because there are a number of interesting and helpful features that become available to you once you have done that.

Pauline: When I was in high school, I actually remember listening to Shakespeare played on a tape recorder in a classroom with my peers. Then, as a teacher, I didn't rely on the audio as much because of my background in drama. I did use film clips, though. This is one of the highlights and benefits of using MyShakespeare.com—it is a truly multimodal, hyperlinked text. The text of the play is there, first and foremost, with textual annotations that can help you unpack complicated words and phrases by clicking on or hovering over the text.

Matthew: But there are also video clips of dramatizations, and this is part of the point of us encouraging you to use this text—you can have the play read aloud to you line-by-line while you read along. Experiment with reading this way, either by reading simultaneously along with the narration or reading silently first and then listening to the recording. What do you notice about yourself as a reader? How might this shift how you think about your students as readers?

Pauline: To be clear, we are not claiming one is better than the other, but the site provides options for all learners. With the account you've just created, you can annotate the text, highlighting and making notes that will stay there as you move from this reading with us as PSTs into your future classrooms. So, as you read, make notes not only as a reader but also as a teacher. Mark characterizations, unfamiliar vocabulary, and important and recurring themes—not only for yourself but to prepare future lessons on the text.

Another way to engage students' multimodal literacies is through dramatization. Like dance and other types of live performances, dramatizations are types of gestural, spatial, and embodied multimodal texts that can be underutilized in the ELA classroom. Dramatizations can be introduced in several different ways, through fictional characters, role-playing, and rewriting or creative writing of scripts. Each approach can impact valuable and powerful learning outcomes.

Typically, in an ELA class plays are seen as an opportunity to act out the story because we have the benefit of stage directions written right into the page. But, how can we take this idea and move it into other genres? One way might be for students to consider chapters or scenes in a novel or a poem as dramatic texts and then embody the characters as they are represented. Applying an arts-based pedagogy and process to drama has always felt like a comfortable approach for Pauline, so much so that she has even been known to engage in those activities in different ways in the secondary classroom, from dramatic read-alouds to adding costumes, props, and movement. This embodied practice reminds us that we also engage in the world multimodally with our bodies.

Pauline: For example, one year I invited my ninth-grade honors students to tell their lit circle book's story using any form or method of storytelling. We were doing an author study of Mark Twain (this was in the late 1990s and way before #DisruptTexts entered the curriculum conversation). They had the assignment description, timeline, and rubric; I provided them time and an opportunity to ask questions, but most worked independently of me. When it was time for the groups to share, the *Pudd'nhead Wilson* group did a dramatic reading of three key scenes, the *Connecticut Yankee in King Arthur's Court* group set up a puppet show to summarize the story, and the *Adventures of Huckleberry Finn* group built a LEGO model of the Mississippi River and then told the story using the model.

While the first two groups used their bodies as multimodal storytellers, the final group did a dramatization—not with their bodies, but with LEGO. All of them were amazing and so creative; I never would have thought to suggest using LEGO as a tool for telling a story, but these kids did. All three groups used their *imagination* in very different ways. The first group's intent was to highlight Twain's use of language and dialects; the second group focused on the *impact* of the juxtaposition of the Yankee in a medieval setting through a puppet show with simple costumes; and the LEGO group produced a multimodal text out of LEGO, *identifying* the setting of the Mississippi River as central to the story. Today, students might complete the same activity using technological tools and produce a multimodal text like a digital video, digital animation using emojis, or a piece of software like Minecraft. I think that's what I love about multimodality—it's open to interpretation!

Maybe students felt comfortable with their open-ended storytelling assignment because they were accustomed to the multimodal approach I take to most of my pedagogy. Months before that assignment, I had them out of their seats, the class rearranged, and they were acting out the prologue of *Romeo and Juliet* standing on desks and using "swords" crafted out of duct tape. For me, this was a natural and logical approach to engaging students with texts. It was ingrained in how I described my teacher identity.

Connecting this concept of teacher identity back to watching the teacher movies, we can even consider our PSTs producing or reworking a scene from one of the films. Shoffner (2016) claims that PSTs "see the outcome, not the process . . . and they want to replicate that outcome when they finally enter their own classroom" (p. 6). What if we had PSTs imagine the process? Take a scene where a teacher is engaging their students and pauses the movie, asking them the following:

- What is on that teacher's lesson plan right now?
- What is the goal of this lesson?
- How do you know?
- Provide evidence for your claim.

Once they've written out their answers, they could collaborate with others to dramatize the "lesson planning" scene and share it with the rest of the class. This could make for a lively debate but eventually would add another layer of understanding for the PST; they would have considered the *influence* of the teacher and the *impact* the scene from the movie carries. They wouldn't just see the outcome as portrayed in the movie; they would have considered all the possibilities that were embedded in the process. By taking the multimodal text of the movie, collaborating and using their imaginations to write an extra scene, and then dramatizing the newly written scene, the PSTs engage with the multimodal text as it morphs and transforms from one mode to another.

For example, think back specifically to the example of *Dead Poets Society* to see how this might play out in our classroom. We never see a scene where Mr. Keating gets to defend himself or even speak to the parents who have lost their son. We would put PSTs in groups and have them use their *imagination* to write a script to role-play all of those important parts. They would have to account for the following questions:

- What would you say as a parent?
- What might Mr. Keating say in response?
- Would it make a difference in terms of the outcome of the story?
- How might this play out in a different context, for example, in a Philadelphia public school?

As they write their script, they must consider the intent of the characters, the *influential* power of the wealthy parents and the teachers at the elite boarding school, and how this would ultimately *impact* these characters. These understandings would no doubt affect the words written in the script but also in the dramatization through their bodily positioning, gestures, and aural tone. While this could potentially be a challenge for PSTs, we think there is value in having them anticipate and dramatize some of the most critical and difficult conversations they may have as teachers.

In our example, we build the context for them to embrace their professional identity via multimodal texts. There are other ways to start with a multimodal text, such as a movie, and transition to another mode, such as creative writing—all of which opens up possibilities for exercising their multimodal literacies.

These role-playing activities can lead to better lessons and presentations, but our ultimate goal with PSTs is to increase their confidence. Once they can act like teachers, they will see their true teacher identity in multimodal ways. This will help them as they move through field experiences and student teaching, and it will even help them as they produce a variety of artifacts for their portfolios that we will be mentioning in the following chapters.

Teaching Portfolio

Portfolios have long been seen as a useful assessment strategy in education. Within ELA classrooms, portfolios of written work to show students' growth over time and have been standard practice for decades. In its simplest form, a portfolio is a collection of artifacts that represent a journey of growth and development and usually contains written reflective components to record learner growth—in the case of PSTs, this reflects growth in their practice, from writing to lesson plans to giving presentations. In this subsection, we want to advocate for rethinking the use of portfolios to embody multimodal texts for students and for teachers.

Portfolios, or the collection of artifacts into one cohesive unit, have existed for a long time but are generally associated with the authentic assessment movement within K–12 education. In this way, portfolios are seen as the polar opposite to standardized and quantified tests that focus on demonstrations of knowledge via giving correct answers to scripted questions and prompts. Portfolios are inherently personal and qualitative and focus on recorded individual student progression in a practice such as writing. Indeed, the history of portfolios as an effective assessment tool has been a central component of writing pedagogy (Atwell, 2014). For a process as personalized and individualized as writing, many believe that portfolios represent the best way to assess and evaluate students along this line.

Teacher educators have also adopted the portfolio as a way to record, encapsulate, and provide feedback on preservice and inservice teachers' practice. The portfolio has largely been embraced by the educational domain as accreditors have embraced the portfolio as a tool to evaluate student teachers. We teach at an institution that has used a rough portfolio-based model for many years, yet something occurred to us as we collaborated on this book project. The expectations for professional teaching portfolios have changed from when Pauline had her first experiences with portfolios to when Matthew had his, and what is now expected from PSTs is different still. We think that this difference can be addressed more effectively within the language of multimodality.

For example, when Pauline completed her teaching portfolio as a PST (in the mid-1990s), she was required to collect and combine her teaching artifacts, such as lesson plans, teaching materials, and videos of her teaching demonstrations, into a large, physical three-ring binder (the teaching video had to be saved on a VHS tape and included within the physical binder). Given the affordances and under-standings of the time, Pauline's portfolio was primarily paper based and also mostly written. There were some photographs, and of course her teaching video, but the overall portfolio was quite static and unidirectional. To read her portfolio, a person would simply flip through the pages of her binder, exploring the sections using the tabs she had created. In fact, we have some colleagues who still utilize the physical binder method!

When Matthew completed his teaching portfolio just a few years after Pauline at another university, he had to scan copies of his artifacts that he uploaded to a basic web portal. Since Matthew was one of the earliest cohorts at his university to work with the newly developed system, his teacher education professors simply required their students to scan printed copies of worksheets, lesson plans, and other teaching materials that were then organized into a rudimentary web portal that could be privately viewed by a student's student teaching supervisor or advisor. Readers/viewers of Matthew's teaching portfolio could click through hyperlinks of scanned copies of his artifacts, which included brief descriptions and also a few photographs uploaded to the portal, of significant moments in his student teaching experience. He still had to submit a CD/DVD of his teaching demonstration video in hard copy, however, given the technical limitations of the time (early 2000s).

As we work with our teacher educator colleagues to further embrace portfolio-based assessments of our PSTs, we see echoes of some of the same sorts of challenges and limitations of our own teaching portfolios as early career teachers. This is not insignificant, as technologies have shifted the capacities now available to our PSTs. In the remainder of this section, we foreshadow the following two chapters that focus exclusively on technologies and their impact on multimodal texts by recasting the portfolios that our PSTs complete as multimodal texts.

We teach our PSTs according to the same basic outline described thus far in this book by starting with visual and aural literacies before more fully embracing and unpacking multimodal literacies. We have them read and create all kinds of texts, and at the end of the course, we encourage them (from a stance that em-braces multimodality) to approach the creation of their first drafts of their teach-ing portfolios as multimodal texts. In this third-year methods course, and as the course that most directly introduces these students to educational technologies, the majority are working with digital or technology-/web-based portfolios for the very first time. We also approach the portfolio as an expression of their teacher selves; in other words, as a public representation of themselves as teachers. Our students' portfolios are not simple binders that are stacked in our offices but are multimodal texts for the world to see, hear, and read.

We require our students to select a web-based design tool, such as Google Sites, Wix, or Weebly, to house their portfolio and course artifacts. They then create a navigation and organizational structure that best fits their current situation as a PST who will soon be looking to apply for full-time positions as a teacher in the secondary ELA classroom. We also require a professional photograph and biographical statement that situates them as the author and owner of the portfolio and contextualizes components of the site for the viewers. Once these initial components are set up, we then encourage students to include the course assignments that they have completed in our course, including lesson plans, group activities that incorporate infographics into the classroom, and video-based projects about themselves as future teachers.

This activity becomes more than a simple development of a personal website when we reintroduce students to FIMS and challenge them to view their portfolio sites as texts that can (and must) be read and interpreted. To take this even further, we adapt the questions posed by Ball and colleagues (2018) to focus on the anticipated audience:

- Which mode is going to best represent this artifact to my audience?
- Should I restrict access to certain components of my portfolio for that audience?

Once they've gone through this and created their website, then they can adopt the role of the reader/viewer to *identify* what the portfolio is about and understand how the viewer will navigate the different parts. How might the reader be *impacted* by the color and font choices made on the portfolio landing page? Maybe, and perhaps most importantly, how will they *influence* the intended audience? Should their video-based components simply be videos embedded on the page or should they include additional contextual text or instructions? Does the graphic or activity described best reflect them as a future teacher?

All of these steps are, of course, an activity of the PST's *imagination* as they switch back and forth between FIMS as a reader and as a creator. At the level of multimodality, however, it is not just about choosing your words carefully; students must now embrace their role as multimodal author to include choices that are normally outside the context of the traditional author's role.

We share local educator Tricia Ebarvia's website with our students to offer them information and inspiration as a mentor text. We contextualize and explain that she is a veteran teacher who blogs, presents, and writes for teachers. We try to remind them not to get overwhelmed and compare their novice experiences with a master teacher, but we zoom in to examine her organization. We also look at her tone and consider how she appeals to her audience. We highlight her headings "Writer," "Teacher," and

Read more about Tricia Ebarvia on her website.

"Reader" and point out how she has embedded her Twitter feed and her Goodreads profile into the page.

Portfolio designing doesn't stop at the end of our course. When we were creating our portfolios, we wrote and produced them as evaluation tools that would only be seen by our university supervisors and possibly future employers. Now, as public multimodal texts, our PSTs must create and write for their peers, future employers, the general public, and parents. In this way, we hope that these public texts can present an alternative story about the very real lives of teachers. What is more, although creating their portfolios for our class is a moment in time that we evaluate, we encourage them to think about the long game and how they can continue to develop and add to their portfolios in different ways. For example:

- What other artifacts can be included on the site? A resume? A recommendation from a professor or supervisor?
- How might the portfolio site shift as a multimodal text from exemplifying the work of a PST to that of an early career teacher?

The site could then serve as a text representing the work of the teacher and their students as they engage with and produce multimodal projects in their own ELA classroom.

Ultimately, we hope that our PSTs will be able to take this process of developing their teacher portfolios and translate that knowledge into helping their future secondary students. We want our PSTs to look at how their students' learning can be chronicled via portfolios that extend the traditional writing portfolio to include all kinds of work, specifically multimodal texts. This could, we think, also draw inspiration from the incorporation of multigenre projects as well.

> **Margin Memo**
>
> **Belief #3: Technologies provide new ways to consume and produce texts.** *What it means to consume and produce texts is changing as digital technologies offer new opportunities to read, write, listen, view, record, compose, and interact with both the texts themselves and with other people.* The final section of this multimodal focus chapter provides a pointed example of how technology has impacted portfolios as texts. Whereas Pauline's portfolio was a physical binder that enabled one kind of document, the web-based portfolios we require from our PSTs and the affordances the technology offers truly exemplify the impact of technology on creating multimodal texts. From VHS tapes to embedded online video is indeed what is meant by "new ways!"

Conclusion—Now, Let's Shift to Application: Augmented Realities/Virtual Realities and Digital Video

With this focus chapter on multimodality, we have reached an important milestone in the book. We began by looking at visual and aural literacies individually, focusing first on each as literacies in our everyday and traditional lives before considering examples that have been infused with technologies (e.g., memes and podcasts). However, we typically move through and exist in our day-to-day lives as multimodal readers and producers, and in this chapter, we highlighted through films and dramatization how we can consider our everyday multimodal practices. In the following chapters, we turn to consider the impact that technologies have had on our ability to read and consume multimodal texts through augmented reality and virtual reality. Then we consider the creation and production of digital videos as powerful ways to view and create multimodal texts with our PSTs and secondary ELA students.

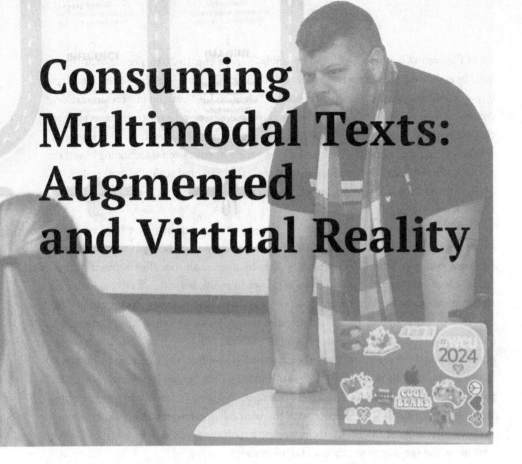

Consuming Multimodal Texts: Augmented and Virtual Reality

Introduction

Two new areas of technology that are stretching our understanding of multimodal literacies include augmented reality (AR) and virtual reality (VR). We think that in many ways this area is the most rapidly growing and innovative space at present. If you are reading this book while wearing a smartwatch, for example, you are, in a way, participating and engaging with the real/physical world in an augmented way. One of the more recent software updates on the Apple Watch (the most popular wearable as of 2021) can detect loud noises, sense if you have washed your hands long enough, and even call 911 if there is a sudden change in your heart rate or if the device detects a sudden movement that would indicate a fall. Yes, the wearer remains grounded in the physical world, but they are simultaneously engaged in an augmented way; reality is enhanced or modified beyond what would be provided by wearing a traditional wristwatch.

Notice how language starts to become cumbersome as we try and describe our experiences with AR/VR spaces. This is, we remind ourselves, quite normal as language evolves and adapts to help us name the world around us. Think of just a few years ago when Pokémon GO first burst onto the mobile app scene. In 2016, people of all ages quickly embraced the platform and started playing the game—the first of its kind in terms of blending the real and virtual worlds. Pokémon GO built on players' pre-existing connections to the Pokémon characters and offered a free and easy-to-use app platform that encouraged users to play. It takes time for our language to catch up to the pace of technological development. A recent call for papers in educational technology used the phrase *extended reality* to describe artificial reality, augmented reality, virtual reality, 360-degree photographs, and many more. Even scholars aren't quite sure what to call this new area of study.

In this chapter, we suggest that multimodal literacy can help give teachers and students a language to understand and unpack these new ways of being in a technologically mediated reality or world. As a lens for understanding, multimodality reminds us that we are constantly engaging in our everyday lives in multiple modes. Earbuds in our ears stream podcasts or the latest audiobook as we walk to complete our daily errands. Our eyes take in visual signals and messages from traffic signs and lights, advertisements and street signs (all combinations of images and alphabetic text), or other modes in our multimodal lives. Returning to the smartwatch example, the wearable technology tracks our path as we walk, measuring our heart rate and oxygen levels and alerting us to both nearby transit options and the opening and closing hours of the grocery store we're about to visit. This experience with the wearable smartwatch is a good example of the ways that augmented reality technologies are affecting our lives in ways that require new ideas and languages to process and understand.

Pauline: I had a unique experience with VR recently at an online event for the National Writing Project. We selected our breakout sessions from a menu ahead of time, but I was pleasantly surprised when I clicked the link and entered a Kumospace instead of a Zoom room. At first, I had no idea what I was doing; a picture of my face was floating in a bubble above a 2D layout of a room. I could move my bubble around the room by using the arrow keys, and I quickly noticed that when I moved closer to other participants, I could suddenly hear what they were talking about, just as if I were walking around a lounge or a conference space. This was my first time in such a space because our university's platform for the year of remote learning was Zoom. After a few minutes of trial and error, I quickly figured out the affordances of the Kumospace platform.

Matthew: My first foray into AR/VR in the educational space was helping support my partner who took a graduate-level course in young adult literature hosted in Second Life in the early 2010s. While the initial promise of Second Life never materialized (everyone was talking then about how surely within a few years, everyone would have access to virtual worlds), Second Life was still advanced for its time. To access the virtual classroom space, all the students had to download a program to access the university's "island" and create an avatar of their choice. Then, during class time, all the students would gather in the virtual space around a campfire where class would be held. Student presence was mediated through the avatar and audio. Back then, we were sure that this was the future!

As you read the previous paragraphs, you might have perked up and started to ask questions about privacy or the ethics of collecting biodata (e.g., heart rate and GPS location). Even creating an avatar in another world might be alarming! We think these concerns are important to keep in mind as the human and technical continue to merge, mesh, and clash. However, we would urge teachers and students, as well as parents, administrators, and other community members, to adopt a critical stance toward AR/VR to avoid discounting what they don't yet fully understand. We should absolutely be critical of the relationships between our data and privacy, but this does not mean we reject and disregard the gains and enhancements new technologies offer.

Before we go any further, we should define how we understand the terms augmented and virtual reality. AR includes the use of any sort of digital technology that mediates our experiences with the physical world. These technologies could come in the form of an app on a smartphone, a wearable device (such as a FitBit or Apple Watch), social mapping using Google Maps, and even "heads-up" displays that show speed and other data within cars. If you have perused Ikea or other furniture stores recently, you've probably noticed new features that allow you to visualize the possible placement of couches and chairs in your home via your smartphone's camera. Using the built-in camera on an iPhone, the user can use the Measure app to measure walls, distance, and even heights! In these examples, the user is not interacting with a new and different world; they are provided with a new and often enhanced way of interacting with the physical world. But by enhancing it, we are not necessarily attributing a positive evaluation to it. Enhancing in this sense indicates that we are dealing with more information, more data. What we do with this information and data is part of the multimodality question we want to focus on in this chapter.

Another example related to AR technologies might be helpful. Roughly a decade ago, Google unveiled one of its latest projects: Google Glass (see Figure 10.1). Google Glass was stylized as a pair of glasses with lenses that would create a mediated experience for the wearer. By looking through the lenses of the glasses, the wearer would see the physical world but would also receive additional information that would be projected onto the lenses from a computer built into the glasses.

For example, if you were standing in front of a popular landmark, the glasses would project additional information

FIGURE 10.1. Google Glass advertisement.

about the landmark. In the future, Google argued, the glasses would also be able to access face recognition data and integrate this into the information shared on the lenses. This mediating experience would be another example of augmented reality. While the developers and engineers imagined a

Listen to a podcast about Google Glass.

best-case scenario for the use of these devices, the public reaction to Google Glass was swift and fierce, as consumers rejected the device as an invasion of privacy and socially irresponsible. However, before we evaluate Google Glass as a technological failure, Tom Standage and Seth Stevenson of the podcast series, *Secret History of the Future*, remind us that at one time, the fork was seen as comparable to Google Glass. Why would anyone use a utensil when they had spoons and their hands?

Whereas *augmenting reality* enhances or extends a mediating experience with the physical world, VR creates a whole new world or context to explore and engage with or in. More and more people are also engaging with and living out parts of their lives in virtual worlds. Actually, it would be more accurate to say that many people have been engaged in virtual worlds for multiple decades and we are only now fully appreciating the significance of this. Perhaps the easiest example to understand is video gaming. Players of computer or video games use digital devices to enter into and play games within invented and imagined worlds, or virtual realities. Any mediated experience supported by digital technologies that provides access to an alternative world or space is what we would call engaging with VR. James Gee even defines video games as "a multimodal literacy *par excellence*" (2007, p. 18, emphasis in original). "Games . . . put people back in control, progressing toward goals . . . [and instilling] a sense of power and mastery" (McGonigal, 2011, p. 149). Ways of accessing these games include controllers and computer screens, smartphones, or even wearable headsets. Devices that provide access to new digital spaces where one can be immersed visually, such as Google Goggles (not to be confused with Google Glass), also constitute a VR experience.

Margin Memo

Belief #2: Consider literacies before technologies. *New technologies should be considered only when it is clear how they can enhance, expand, and/or deepen engaging and sound practices related to literacy instruction.* This leads us back to the NCTE Position Statement. Literacy is no longer representative of the physical and primarily alphabetic text; we must engage with literacies, the complex merging of visual, aural, and multimodal literacies that more accurately reflect our daily lives. And, with the increased access to and availability of AR/VR, we must turn to multimodality to support our work in understanding and critiquing these mediated spaces—not just in terms of their value in the classroom, but also as viable spaces and arenas where humans live out their lives. NCTE's second belief statement calls on us to consider literacies before technologies, and this is particularly true when evaluating and discussing AR/VR. While some people have been playing games in virtual worlds for many years, there are many more that have less experience and therefore less understanding of what technologically mediated spaces are all about. To fully grapple with these new and emerging realities, we should focus on the literacies before the technologies.

Gaming, as Sherry Turkle (1995) reports, began in the 1970s and expanded quickly in the 1980s with the birth of the internet. The first discussion forums and text-based chat rooms in massively multiplayer online games allowed humans to connect and interact in new ways. While these games were initially text based, they marked the beginning of digitally mediated experience with virtual worlds/realities. A key difference between augmented and virtual realities is that virtual worlds do not have to abide by the same rules and laws that dictate life in the physical world.

You might think about the difference between AR and VR in this way. In AR, it can seem as if a transparency is being laid over the physical world to give additional information about what is seen and felt, whereas in VR, a user is stepping into an entirely new experience. Tying these ideas to the ELA classroom, Arduini (2018) argues for gaming literacy as an extension of literacies that can impact multimodal composition. He specifically states that composition scholars (e.g., Gee, 2007; Hsu & Wang, 2010; Walsh, 2010) "have noted one of the biggest literacy advantages afforded by gaming literacy is a fluency in multimodal composition" (Arduini, 2018, p. 90).

AR/VR as Multimodal Texts

AR/VR technologies, including augmented and immersive spaces, are the latest and most exciting arena for exploring the possibilities of multimodal literacies. Multimodal literacies and AR/VR are positively made for each other. As the power and accessibility of the technologies supporting augmented and virtual reality become greater and more ubiquitous, it will be multimodal literacies that allow teachers and students to approach, understand, and utilize the potential of these new, digitally infused spaces. To begin, however, we will need to push your thinking beyond the familiar and the physical to the imagined and the possible.

In this book, we intentionally began by exploring visual and aural literacies individually before turning to their connection through multimodal literacies. In doing so, our hope was that by slowly considering both types of literacy on their own, teachers and students would be fully equipped to understand the power of multimodality. Multimodality gives us the tools, the language, and the concepts to understand literacies in their fullest expression. Because multimodality encompasses the visual, aural, and embodied ways we engage in our lives as a default state, we can use it to better grasp how technologies are stretching and enhancing/extending reality.

You will notice something a bit different with the examples in this chapter, and we think it would be helpful for you to be forewarned. If you go back to all of the other application chapters, it is very easy to wrap your mind around a meme, for example. A meme is an image you can look at on your phone; it can be sent via email or text message to someone else. It is very easy to think of a meme as a thing. By contrast, it is very hard to think about AR/VR in this way. Some of the examples we will talk about are experiences with AR/VR rather than artifacts. It is even hard to think about how to embed AR/VR in a multimodal text such as this one! The best that we can do is point you to a video or website about AR/VR, but we realize this isn't the same as experiencing AR/VR firsthand.

At a time when the United States is facing a reckoning of racial and social justice, museums have stepped up to offer VR exhibits and experiences to bring the struggle for civil rights to life for students and teachers. At the National Center for Civil and Human Rights in Atlanta, for example, there is an exhibit that Pauline experienced in 2016 in person but that has now, after a year of social distancing and remote learning, transitioned online.

Pauline: When NCTE was held in Atlanta in 2016, I took a group of PSTs to the National Center for Civil and Human Rights on a Sunday afternoon. We walked in unsure of what we were about to experience and left with our hearts and minds impacted. The most memorable part of the experience for me was the lunch counter simulation. I saw the counter, the seats, and folks wearing headphones, so I got in line with my PSTs. There were some informational placards along the wall about the non-violent protestors who sat and endured cruelty and humiliation. As my turn approached, I noticed people coming off the platform visibly shaken, some with tears in their eyes. I sat down, placed the headphones on my head, my hands on the outline in front of me, and the simulation began. Sounds of taunting came from all directions, and with some insults, my chair began to move as if I were being pushed into the counter. These three minutes have stayed with me, years later.
Matthew: While Pauline was sharing this experience with me, I was blown away by the emotions she must have felt. I checked the museum website to see what the exhibit was like, and we discovered that they had created a VR version. We were able to listen to the audio that was played in the headphones and see photos of the counter from the exhibit—all while remaining socially distanced during a global pandemic. Initially, Pauline thought the exhibit was limited to audio, but when she shared with me that her chair had moved, the multimodality of the museum experience became clearer. I'm looking forward to seeing the exhibit in person so that I can experience the exhibit's full VR.

Another simple way that AR has infiltrated our lives is through photo and video filters built into popular social media tools, such as Snapchat and Instagram. With the filter feature, users can add additional elements, such as images and words, to spice up a photo taken with the front-facing camera on a smartphone or tablet. We include two sample photos created in Snapchat (see Figure 10.2).

In the second image, on the right you can see Matthew with a tie-dyed hoodie and sunglasses on (the augmented elements of the filter) and the text *MONDAY* describing the day the photo was taken across the bottom portion. This is an example of AR because the image captures Matthew in the physical world but overlays additional elements to enhance and modify the picture. Consider that in the unedited photo, Matthew

FIGURE 10.2. Sample photos demonstrating Snapchat filters.

is wearing a navy shirt with an image on it, computer reading glasses, and headphones—none of which are visible with the augmented layer added.

To bring this into the classroom, consider as an example the use of an augmented reality app that could be loaded onto a smartphone or tablet that would allow the user to place a work of art or piece of sculpture into the space of the classroom via the camera on the device. We have found the Google Arts & Culture app to be an incredible resource for engaging with cultural artifacts and experimenting with augmented reality. The app is organized primarily by museum or by the location of where the artwork exists in the real world, such as by art located at the Louvre in Paris or the Museum of Modern Art in New York City. But users can also locate a specific painting or sculpture by simply searching for the artwork. Once located, the app provides additional context including photos, background information on the artwork and the artist, and often a way to explore the artwork in an augmented

Examine the Google Arts & Culture platform here.

Margin Memo

Belief #4: Technologies and their associated literacies are not neutral. *While access to technology and the internet has the potential to lessen issues of inequity, they can also perpetuate and even accelerate discrimination based on gender, race, socioeconomic status, and other factors.* Consider these options for equity and access. If a classroom had a full complement of devices so that all students could have their own, they could each place the artwork into the physical space and interact/manipulate it. If there were not enough devices for this, the teacher could cast the screen from one device to a projector so that all could see.

way. In the classroom, we might use this activity for a number of pedagogical reasons, such as the inspiration for freewriting, to explore the inspiration behind a piece of literature or text, or as an element of an arts-based mini-lesson.

We could build an entire lesson around one of Pauline's favorite paintings, *The Kiss* by Gustav Klimt (see Figure 10.3). Before introducing the technological tools that help to redefine how students engage with the artwork, we would first share a digital image on the screen. We could have students share about what they notice, *identify*, and the *impact* the artwork has on them. To push their thinking further, we could introduce them to one of the online exhibits devoted to *The Kiss*. In this presentation, students are guided through a series of approximately 15 slides that contain zoomed-in portions of the painting, added annotations in the form of text and captions, additional photographs of the artist and the painting's subjects, as well as video links. Returning to the language of FIMS, how might being able to examine the background or the clothing in the painting more directly influence students' understanding of the artwork? How can the multimodal online exhibit provided through the app activate students' *imaginations* by providing them with many more layers of meaning and significance than simply looking at an image of a painting from afar? Merely applying the visual literacy strategies (Chapter 3) does not do the job; we need the power of multimodal literacies.

To push this example even further, with smartphones or tablets, we could have students engage and approach the artwork in AR. Using the Google Arts & Culture app, users can place *The Kiss* into the room with them as a layer (recall the Snapchat example above) and see and interact with the life-sized piece of art. Without worrying about crowds or security alarms, students could navigate and orient themselves in relation to the painting via the image on the screen of the device, all the while using their body positioning to approach and frame the virtual object. By engaging with this augmented space, students would need to draw on multimodal literacies to gain access to the object—first visually and then embodied. This example focuses on consuming a multimodal text as presented by the augmented reality provided by the Google Arts & Culture app. Students (and teachers) would first have to *identify* the space they are working within (a blend of technology and physical) as well as the digital object they must apprehend.

The *impact* and *influence* of their meaning making is impacted not only by the image of the object but also by their

View *The Kiss* on Google Arts & Culture here.

embodied experience. Are they too close? Must they zoom out to see the whole object? What happens when they try to move around the object? *Influence* comes into focus once this positioning has been set as students grapple with the meaning of the object. The augmented space supercharges their *imaginations*. Students must simultaneously process their physical surroundings and the digital object available on the device's screen while recognizing that the digital object is a reproduction of a real painting that also exists in the real, physical world in a museum collection. Multimodality is the key to unlocking this abstract engagement with AR described here.

FIGURE 10.3. Klimt's *The Kiss*.

To be frank, museums and other cultural institutions are truly taking the lead in the AR/VR technology space when compared to the field of education. Many of the examples we have given and will highlight in this chapter were created by and are housed within art museums. The Google Arts & Culture app does include Google-created artifacts and experiences, but it primarily draws on and supports the work that museums have been doing around the world to find new ways to not only help their patrons engage with art and cultural artifacts but also to bring these works into homes through digital technology. As we transition to consider the use of AR/VR as multimodal texts in the university teacher preparation classroom, we will continue to share examples that were first presented and created for museum contexts.

Reflection Box

Do not operate heavy machinery after reading that last paragraph! We want to acknowledge that this activity is hard to wrap the mind around, especially since we are describing an augmented, multimodal experience while only using words. This is complex, yes, but FIMS helps to demonstrate the multimodal literacy skills that students and teachers must engage to create and understand meaning made using these technologies. AR/VR can simply be used as parlor tricks that do not add much pedagogically to the ELA classroom. How can you see AR/VR stretching our imaginations and opening up new worlds of texts and encounters with others?

Educating Preservice Teachers

Engaging our PSTs in experiences with augmented and virtual realities has challenged us as teachers. We pride ourselves on being able to use SAMR and TPACK (see Chapter 2) to help ground our own lessons and activities utilizing technologies to prepare future secondary ELA teachers. But we must also admit that integrating AR/VR as multimodal texts has stretched us as teachers and represents a growing edge of our pedagogical practice. Like some of our readers, we want to be sure we understand how to use the technologies appropriately by figuring out all the buttons and loopholes, the pitfalls and affordances. We also want to be sure we are drawing on AR/VR technologies meaningfully to engage our PSTs in ways that *modify* and *redefine* instruction (in the language of SAMR) and not just for the momentary thrill of having a new toy to play with.

Read about Google Cardboard here.

Explore the Globe's VR experience here.

One of the first times we brought AR into the classroom with our PSTs, we actually had one of our previous students, Katy, come and talk about teaching Shakespeare using a VR version of the Globe Theatre in London. For this particular activity, we split the students into three groups and had them rotate through center activities with both of us and Katy as group leaders. Katy shared how she had built an entire lesson around a VR field trip to Shakespeare's Globe Theatre in London using Google Expeditions (unfortunately, Expeditions was discontinued in 2021 as the Arts & Culture app has become more robust). Because it is very difficult to transport her 25 seniors across the Atlantic Ocean to see the Globe Theatre in person, Katy created a lesson using a class set of smartphones with Google Cardboard to allow her students to step into a VR version of the famous theater. Katy showed off a unique way to use VR to make Shakespeare more real for her secondary students. For those interested, the Globe Theatre also now has its own app that offers a VR tour.

In the Teaching Writing methods course that Pauline teaches, she typically requires her PSTs to write thematic unit plans that include a series of lesson plans as well. Drawing on many of the freely available sites and apps provided by museums around the world, Pauline showcases how to teach multimodality and the connected literacies now possible from anywhere in the world.

One museum-based, easy, and accessible example of using VR in the secondary ELA classroom would align the reading of *The Diary of a Young Girl* with the virtual tour and exhibit provided by the Anne Frank House and Museum. To be sure, the use of the virtual tour could be a simple add-on or extension to a typical lesson associated with the novel study. But we recommend that teachers consider the virtual tour as an example of VR by adopting the lens of multimodal literacies. A teacher with little fluency in navigating VR might cast the virtual experience via a projector and guide students together. A more experienced teacher, or one more at home in the virtual space, might hand over the exploration of the VR to students in small groups or individually, provided there are enough devices to go around. When first teaching with this technology, a teacher might also use a combination of these two approaches by showing the students how to navigate the basics of the site before letting students explore the various components of the virtual tour on their own.

As students and teachers explore the house in VR, this particular virtual experience provides preset pathways and clearly marked buttons that can be clicked to guide the viewer through the tour. For the experienced user, there is a button to teach you how to navigate the first-person view of the rooms included in VR, but there are also specific buttons to guide the user (see image on next page). The image shows

Review this list of museums with online and virtual components here.

Virtually visit the Anne Frank House and Museum here.

FIGURE 10.4. Landing page of the Anne Frank House AR site.

the entrance to the house and provides three options for users to click on and select to explore further. One option opens an additional layer of text while a second refreshes the page to highlight a video where the viewer can learn more about the layout of the house. The third button shifts the angle of the view toward the stairs and provides a quote from the text of the diary. Again, beyond being a way to extend a student's experience with the reading of the text, this example of a VR tour of Anne Frank's house must be seen as embodying the essential elements of a multimodal text.

Enjoy this VR retelling of *Hamlet* here.

When exploring the VR tour, students are constantly *identifying* what they are seeing in the images (some are photographs of the actual house, others are artistic interpretations), selecting their path through the tour based on the impact of the text and moving images that appear. The *influence* of the VR on their understanding of the book reverberates as they *imagine* themselves in a space they've only seen in their minds.

FIGURE 10.5. Annotated screenshot of Anne Frank house AR site.

Otto, Edith, and Margot Frank's room. Clicking takes you to the room.

The room of Hermann and Auguste van Pels. Clicking takes user to the room.

Orients the user. We are in the Entrance.

"Anne on the stairs" - clicking accesses additional information

Another example that we have utilized with our PSTs aligned nicely with the focus on *Hamlet* in the iteration of the book club assignment in Year Five, when classic mentor texts were paired with more recent and modern young adult texts. The Folger Shakespeare Library recently shared a VR version of *Hamlet* on their resources page. The website states:

> You don't need a ticket to see the Commonwealth Shakespeare Company's most recent production of *Hamlet*. You don't even need to leave your house. All you need is a virtual reality device. *Hamlet 360: Thy Father's Spirit* is an hour-long virtual reality adaptation of Shakespeare's play that puts you in the center of Shakespeare's tragedy.

Take a look at the shaded box to see how we set up the viewing experience for our PSTs. The experience of watching the *Hamlet* VR 360 is jarring for many of our PSTs. For those who are experienced online or virtual gamers, they share that they find it a bit easier to get into the headspace to understand the performance. Other students have shared that they struggled at first because they were not used to so many streams of information—images and sounds—coming at them all at once while being able to control what they see and hear. (In the YouTube 2D, or non-immersive, example, the viewer can click and drag the view to change the focus, whereas in the 3D/360 and immersive version, the viewer can move their whole body.)

Matthew: We have been discussing our assignments and your work in terms framed by visual, aural, and multimodal literacy. As we come to the end of our time together in this course, we want to present you with one more experience that really exemplifies the multimodality that is made possible by technology.
Pauline: Let's also remember that you have been working with multimodality now for a few weeks; you've created your teaching demo video, where you demonstrated a portion of your lesson plan and watched that to reflect on your practice, and you're currently working on your digital video on your teaching identity. Both of these video-based assignments have you working with multimodal literacies as you make decisions as authors about whether to integrate an image, a sound clip, a video clip, and so on.
Matthew: But we want to push this multimodality to another level for you. You may have thought we were done talking about Shakespeare and *Hamlet* since we wrapped up your book club group work a few weeks ago, but we're bringing them back again!
Pauline: A number of you used the Folger Shakespeare Library as a resource when building your lesson plans and activities, and this activity is actually one shared and produced in conjunction with the Folger.
Matthew: A theater company, paired with other producers, created a VR version of *Hamlet* that can be watched with a VR headset or even just on a normal screen via YouTube. You don't get the full experience without being fully immersed in the action, but you can still get the gist. We want to explore this VR version.
Pauline: Let's start by watching a few moments from the film on YouTube. Then, we'll check back in to see how you're doing and what you're thinking.
Matthew: They have a podcast with the producers of the VR, so we can listen to a few minutes of that.
Pauline: Yes, so we can hear their voices and get their perspective. We'll watch a bit more of the VR, but then we're going to have you watch the remainder on your own and come next time ready to talk about it.

Even though they may find it a challenge, we encourage our PSTs to embrace and sit with that discomfort. We remind them that when they integrate technologies into their future classrooms, some of their students will also experience this sort of discomfort. We asked our students to share more about their experiences with the VR version of *Hamlet*. They shared that once they *identified* what was happening and how to engage with the multimodal format, they were better able to consider the *impact* of this production. A few even shared that they were able to understand the *influence* of this scene differently because they were now seeing and hearing it.

Given the newness of this technological space, we have primarily shared areas where we are experimenting in our own teaching. We want to assure teachers that we are not experts in this area and consider ourselves advanced beginners, at best. AR/VR offers creative possibilities of immersive storytelling, and the language of multimodality can help us integrate these stories into our classrooms. The use of virtual worlds can enhance our students' understanding of place and setting within classic texts. Pauline is particularly fond of the VR Van Gogh experience that toured North America in fall 2021. After stepping into the impressionist paintings as multimodal texts, she immediately began making plans to integrate this VR experience into her future teaching.

From the University to the Secondary Classroom

We have repeatedly noted throughout this book how blown away we are with the work our ELA secondary colleagues are doing in their classrooms. We are pleased to share how three of our peers are pushing the boundaries of multimodal texts with AR/VR and stretching their own understandings of literacy, an experience we have found in our own testing of these emerging technologies. In this section, we explore VR concentration camps when teaching about the Holocaust with Julianna, see how Katy has used VR to enhance her students' understanding and engagement with Shakespeare, and meet Allison to learn about how she uses GIS (geographic information systems) and Google Cardboard to teach vocabulary and other skills.

Julianna described how she used a premade virtual tour activity with her students as they were reading Elie Wiesel's *Night*. In order to provide greater historical and cultural context, she situated *Night* within the larger narrative of World War II and the concentration camps. To help her students engage with and visualize the experiences of concentration camps, she turned to 360Cities, a website that allows users to upload 360° photographs of cities around the world. Allowing her students to step into the virtual world of the camps was sobering for her students but provided them with an opportunity to access the scene and setting of the autobiography in a way that could not be achieved except via these experiences with VR.

Earlier we shared some teaching ideas from our former student Katy, who is now an ELA teacher. When we heard about the VR work that Katy was doing with her students, we invited her to share her experience with our PSTs. In a separate class with Matthew, Katy developed an exploratory unit using Google Expeditions that used VR with her students to transport their learning to Shakespearean England. Google Expeditions allows users to create VR experiences that can be shown on a

FIGURE 10.6. Google Cardboard with smartphone.

smartphone that is placed within a Google Cardboard apparatus, which is literally a miniature headset made out of cardboard that creates the illusion of being immersed in an experience (see Figure 10.6).

Katy explained her background teaching Shakespeare based on her love of everything from the time period and how this translated into her more cultural/historical approach to teaching Shakespeare. She acknowledges that it is more time consuming to plan this way and she could see why other teachers wouldn't want to do it. There is a lot of prep time if you are creating an experience from scratch, especially as it relates to the amount of instructional time, but because she was so intrigued by the process, she said she really didn't notice the amount of time it took!

The activity itself was created as an introduction to her *Hamlet* unit. For this, Katy drew on a lot of already existing resources, such as preexisting 3D photos, but she did get pulled down the rabbit hole while creating her slides with embedded text. One thing that was different in her activity with her students was that she was the guide and she controlled the speed of what her students saw. On the day she taught the lesson, Katy described the event of getting the classroom a set of Google Cardboards. She had to drive over to a separate school to grab the devices.

The devices themselves were older, and some didn't work, so some students had to share. It was an added frustration, but her students responded positively and shared that they had never done anything like that before. A few even shared that they got a little dizzy but said it seemed to dissipate quickly. After the activity, she also encouraged the students to explore Expeditions (now Arts & Culture) further. The students appreciated doing something different.

Margin Memo

Belief #4: Technologies and their associated literacies are not neutral. *While access to technology and the internet has the potential to lessen issues of inequity, they can also perpetuate and even accelerate discrimination based on gender, race, socioeconomic status, and other factors.* What Katy's determination illustrates is that sometimes there are roadblocks when we plan activities like this. We need to plan ahead and do things that might seem like going above and beyond our job description. That said, the outcome of the experience is worth the effort.

Allison, a secondary reading teacher, has transformed her classroom with AR/VR experiences in order to connect her struggling reading students with multimodal texts. Allison stressed to us that she did not see herself as tech savvy at all, but as you will see, we weren't sure whether to believe her or not! One thing she did share was that her school provided technical support and assistance in the form of a technology coach, and this has really helped her feel more comfortable integrating AR/VR into her lessons. Because her students are struggling readers, she feels she has increased flexibility to integrate technologies to engage her students in reading in whatever way she can.

For example, in one unit on career literacy, Allison introduced her students to GIS to help them engage with maps as multimodal texts. In its simplest form, GIS is the blending of a geographical map with additional data that correlates and connects to the map. In this particular unit, Allison had her students create a GIS map of Pennsylvania with layers that included literacy rates and crime statistics. Students were then asked to analyze the data based on their understanding of its intersection. While this might seem like a lesson in geography, or even science/math, Allison argued for thinking about these maps as examples of multimodality in AR—and we would agree. The maps are multimodal texts themselves, including images, graphics, symbols, and text to communicate meaning about a physical location in the world. When the additional layers of literacy and crime data are overlaid on top of the map, and her students start to make connections between the data and the geolocation, GIS becomes an exemplar of multimodality. Because the students end up creating the maps themselves by adding data points and photographs/videos, it is a great example of composing multimodal texts as well.

Allison also shared how she used Google Expedition kits to introduce and teach vocabulary to her students. "I use science to drag them in!" she said. In the example she shared with us, she discussed how she used vocabulary around coral reefs as the foundation of her unit. To prepare, her students had already been learning about coral reefs and had watched a documentary on a scientist who worked with coral reefs. Then, when the students showed up for that day's midterm review activity, they saw the Google Expedition kits and knew it was a lesson utilizing VR. Along with her technology coach, she guided her students through a coral reef that had been layered with relevant vocabulary terms. When we asked how she had come up with all of these creative uses of VR in her classroom, Allison reflected that she had immense support from her tech coach and that she had been inspired by professional development. She noted that the latitude she has to create innovative lessons and activities to help engage her students inspires her to integrate more VR into her classroom.

Concluding Thoughts

Augmented and virtual realities will be the next space that pushes the boundaries of our grasp of multimodal literacy. In many ways, we have been inspired by our colleagues in the secondary ELA classroom and their use of AR/VR. As technologies continue to develop and AR/VR becomes increasingly mainstream, the greater impact we will feel in the classroom. As ELA teachers, we are fortunate in that we have the language of multimodality to help us appreciate the new capacities made available as our students engage with alternative worlds.

While this chapter has primarily focused on consuming AR/VR as multimodal texts, there are new spaces that are making it easier to create and produce AR/VR experiences. For example, CoSpaces allows students to create virtual worlds that can be a technological redefinition of the shadow box, representing an extension of VR that was unthinkable a few years ago. Kumospace gives teachers and students access to a VR space in which to gather and collaborate in a way that is similar to Second Life but much simpler. With AR/VR, we find ourselves turning to one another often and simply shrugging with a look of surprise as we wonder "what will they think of next?" Regardless, multimodality can help ground us in these new and emerging realities.

Margin Memo

Belief #3: Technologies provide new ways to consume and produce texts. *What it means to consume and produce texts is changing as digital technologies offer new opportunities to read, write, listen, view, record, compose, and interact with both the texts themselves and with other people.* This chapter gave us an opportunity to discuss an emerging technology like AR/VR and connect it to practical applications in the classroom by thinking about how students can produce and consume texts. This is one area that we see as exciting and brimming with possibilities for students and teachers.

Other Ways to Use AR/VR to Support Multimodal Literacies in the Classroom

- **Consuming:** Locate modern-day physical settings/locations that connect to novels and texts through VR experiences in 360Cities or Google Arts & Culture.
- **Consuming:** Explore virtual worlds, such as Second Life, to locate places and settings that would allow students to step into Shakespearean England.
- **Producing:** Have students use CoSpaces to create their own settings and scenes of a text being studied.
- **Producing:** Allow students to create presentations that can be delivered in Kumospace and invite parents and grandparents to attend virtually from anywhere with an internet connection.

Producing Multimodal Texts: Digital Video

Chapter Eleven

Introduction

Think about the incredible changes that have taken place in the world of video over your lifetime. Digital technology has advanced rapidly and so significantly impacted the ease with which we access videos that even the name of the video medium has shifted and is now known as *digital* video.

For comparison and as an example, consider the following (and see Figures 11.1 and 11.2):

- The first major innovation in video was the VHS cassette tape that let people record shows and movies from their television with the click of a button.
- VHS tapes also allowed for the development of personal video cameras that could record through a lens right onto a cassette tape that could then be viewed on a VCR in one's home.
- VHS tapes were analog, based on magnetic tape that could contain roughly two hours of footage.
- At present, the typical smartphone can easily store several hours of digital video (video encoded in digital format as opposed to on analog tape), including videos downloaded from streaming sources and self-recorded videos.

Reflection Box

What is your earliest memory of video? How has video technology impacted your pedagogy?

FIGURE 11.1. From left to right: VCR player/recorder, VHS tape, VHS handheld recorder.

FIGURE 11.2. A pictorial guide of the analog tape sizes, from VHS to MicroMV, before the leap to digital.

While this walk down memory lane might seem quaint, we think it is important to recognize just how quickly video-based technologies have changed and transformed.

Increased mobility through the use of smartphones and the internet, as well as the funny way that devices keep getting smaller while the memory capacity increases, has driven the success of digital video. For example, YouTube was founded in 2006 and was mainly used to share simple videos that could be viewed by friends. The video site was primarily accessed via personal computers (desktops and laptops) because they were hardwired into the internet and able to support the download speeds necessary to stream video.

But over the past fifteen years, the site has been purchased by Google, and news and other popular media use it in order to have a streaming presence. Using increased bandwidth and cell phone coverage, YouTube videos can be streamed on smartphones, and now you can even stream a video feed live from a mobile device onto the site. There are even individuals and groups that, with the added benefit of Google's advertising algorithms, earn large amounts of money—enough to live off of—by creating and sharing videos on YouTube. Pauline's son Robert actually has a YouTube channel with his friends where they post videos of their LEGO creations (but eight years later, he has yet to make any money from it).

Matthew: When I was an undergraduate preservice middle school teacher in the early 2000s, I picked up an hourly job in the College of Education where I helped convert analog video to digital. In those days, I had to connect the camera that had recorded the video onto magnetic tape to a huge Mac computer with a cable and sit and watch the hours and hours of video as it played and converted into a digital video file. It took a long time, and if there was a break in the connection, or the cord was finicky, you had to start all over! We don't even think about this practice today unless we're working to convert old home movies into digital format for safekeeping, but it made for easy spending money, and I learned about the basics of digital video at the ground level.

Pauline: As Matthew described what he was doing in the early 2000s, I realized I was a new mom at that time and relied on small, handheld video recorders to capture the milestones of my children's lives. One of my favorite videos is of my then two-year-old son, Robby, talking to my infant daughter, Emma. He is tenderly covering her up with a blanket, giving her a bottle, and declaring "I WUV her!" This memory lives on forever as a YouTube video thanks to my sister. It doesn't exist as any other kind of file on my phone or computer.

As access to digital video technologies has increased over the past decade, so too has the use of these technologies in the classroom. In this chapter, we advocate for using digital videos as a means of creating or producing multimodal texts with students. At their most basic, digital videos are narratives; the real work begins as students begin to compose their stories. Before our students get to work on crafting these stories, we ask them to begin by asking themselves the following questions:

- Who is the audience?
- What is the mood or tone of the story?
- Who are the main characters?
- What is the best genre to use to convey my story?

As we begin to teach our PSTs about digital video, we share a short documentary called *City Voices, City Visions* that was created in the early 2000s, chronicling an early digital video project in Buffalo Public Schools. Our PSTs comment on some of the more dated elements they spot in the footage: handheld video cameras, a flip phone, and large iMac G3, just to name a few (see Figure 11.3). Even though the devices now seem dated, the pedagogy developed through the project is still relevant today, and in some ways is even easier. In this activity, we have our PSTs consume the documentary as a multimodal text, *identifying* the middle school and high school students who are talking about their learning as it relates to the digital videos they have composed. Then these future teachers take note of the *impact* this pedagogy has had on the students. Further, our PSTs hear experienced teachers talk about the pedagogical *intentions* of embedding digital video meaningfully into the curriculum.

Watch the full *City Voices, City Visions* video here.

FIGURE 11.3. An iMac G3 that was featured in the *City Voices, City Visions* documentary we share with our PSTs.

One of the reasons we start our teaching on digital videos with the *City Voices, City Visions* documentary is because we want to show the early history of digital video in order to demonstrate how far we have come. The students notice how the teachers and researchers in the video acknowledged what students were doing outside of classrooms and felt the urge to create relevance *in* classrooms. The good news for teachers (and school budgets) now is that the equipment has come a long way. We no longer need to rent or put in a request to use the school's sole video camera, and we don't need to use our measly budgets on buying cassette tapes to make the recordings. Thanks to technology, we have everything we need on our phones and tablets to capture the raw footage, and we can use basic software on our computers to edit, revise, and polish that footage to create multimodal, digital videos.

For our PSTs, we ground our approach to digital video in years of research and application, and focus on how teachers might utilize digital videos in their classroom practice. We firmly believe that "to ensure teachers are prepared for the 21st century digital world, teachers and teacher educators must take up the pressing issue of what constitutes effective pedagogies for multimodal composing" (Miller & McVee, 2012, p. 7). The epitome of multimodal composing might just be the creation and production of digital videos.

Digital Videos as Multimodal Texts

While we have argued throughout this book that it is appropriate in some contexts to distinguish between literacies along aural and visual modes, the complexity of literacies is best acknowledged at the fusion of the two: multimodality. In this chapter, we focus on the use of digital videos in the secondary ELA classroom as multimodal texts. Video is inherently multimodal; it is a combination of moving pictures that often includes

Matthew: The first time many of my PSTs work with digital video is when I introduce the screencast assignment. Because it is now easy for the everyday user to create videos, the ability to create and share a screencast is almost expected by new and incoming teachers. A screencast is simply a video recording of a screen with a voiceover provided that narrates what is being seen on the screen. It is a simple idea that offers the possibility of making a profound impact. You have probably watched a screencast if you have typed technical questions into YouTube's search bar, such as "How do I set up the email on my phone?" or "How do I set margins on a Word doc?" Screencasts are powerful multimodal texts because they combine the visual (images and print) with the aural narration guiding the action on screen. I urge my PSTs to also imagine how they might create screencasts in the future to demonstrate the use of particular kinds of websites or software for both students and parents. Knowing how to create a screencast, upload it to the cloud, and share it with others is a technical skill that builds on multimodal literacies of the digital video.

visuals and printed text along with sounds, music, and effects that extend the aural experience. Integrating videos into the classroom for consumption is an important element of building up students' confidence to then produce these multimodal texts.

Sharing professional videos is one way to offer students an ultimate mentor text; here, we distinguish them from the movie clip examples that we talked about in Chapter 9. Those movie clips, while multimodal, are not edited or remixed to create a new or unique text. They are simply clipped from an existing long-form video. An example that is still professional and shows students what we mean by digital video could be a movie or series trailer.

As we write, the Season 4 trailer for *The Handmaid's Tale* has just been shared all over social media. Considering that the original book was written in 1985, with a film version following in 1990, you may think this story is already outdated and irrelevant, but you would be wrong. In 2013, the audiobook recording won an Audie Award; in 2019 a graphic novel version of the story was published; and, probably most impactful, in 2017, Hulu began streaming the story as a series on its platform. Building on Margaret Atwood's chilling original text, the adaptations have stretched from traditional text to an audio format (in the audiobook), to a visual format (in the graphic novel), and then to a truly multimodal text (in the form of the Hulu series). If we were teaching our PSTs and using *The Handmaid's Tale*, we would be sure to point out the ubiquitous nature of the multimodal interpretations before turning to the series' trailer.

View the Season 1 trailer for *The Handmaid's Tale* here.

The trailer for the first season probably felt familiar if you'd read Atwood's original book. Viewers might visually *identify* the dress colors—red for handmaids, blue for

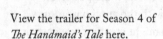

View the trailer for Season 4 of
The Handmaid's Tale here.

wives, and brown for the aunts. They would also acknowledge the *impact* of hearing specific lines of Biblical scripture and how they are taken out of context. For those who haven't read the dystopian novel, the images and music used in the video clip would be striking, maybe even terrifying. But beyond the first season, the story surpasses the original storyline laid out in Atwood's novel. Perhaps, riding on the coattails of the series' success, Atwood wrote a sequel in 2020 titled *The Testaments*. Thus, viewers of the Season 4 trailer would be moved similarly because they are coming to the experience cold, without prior understanding or expectations. By this season, viewers are feeling the *influence* of the producers to keep us watching as we cheer June on in her quest to destroy Gilead. In our *imaginations*, we want to see some restoration of a world we can actually recognize.

Movie and series trailers can be quite powerful tools for helping viewers know what to expect from the full-length product. Studying movie trailers as mentor texts helps us pivot from consumption to production. Students could also make their own movie/series trailers as an example. While consuming and producing are highly interrelated, we lean toward the production of digital videos in this chapter. Specifically, we note how the production and development of digital video can mirror phases of the traditional writing process while highlighting the capacity of multimodal literacies. This chapter builds on the work our PSTs have done with digital video and how it applies across genres.

Educating Preservice Teachers

In this section, we examine and reflect critically on guiding our PSTs to engage with digital video, primarily via producing. Our primary example describes the multimodal process of how our PSTs develop their teaching philosophy statements into digital videos. In this assignment, not only must students transform a written statement into an engaging and provoking video, they must also connect their beliefs to the NCTE Position Statement and other relevant research. We believe this complex assignment best exemplifies the focus on multimodality, not only as a strategy for literacy but also as a pedagogical tool. We don't start by jumping into creating the digital video; instead, we begin by reminding our students of the multimodal literacies required to unpack consuming digital video. We also share other examples of simple digital video authoring before returning to the teaching philosophy assignment.

In addition to creating digital videos for their own work, PSTs also need to learn how to teach students about digital videos through both critical consumption and creative production. In Pauline's Shakespeare seminar, one of the (many) multimodal choices for PSTs to make is to take a theme from one of Shakespeare's plays and create

FIGURE 11.4. Sample storyboard template.

Stockman, A. (2021). Creating inclusive writing environments in the K-12 classroom: reluctance, resistance, and strategies that make a difference. New York, NY: Routledge.

a mash-up by embedding some elements of popular culture. She provides some storyboard template examples, like the ones shown in Figure 11.4 above, and the PSTs walk through brainstorming activities in small groups.

One group took the witches from *Macbeth* and the characters from *Mean Girls* and created a news exposé about the "Witches' Burn Book" that identified the witches as wearing pink on Wednesdays. This group wrote the script, assigned parts, found costumes, and located spaces to record on campus and then went through the process of composing a digital video story.

In Chapter 4, we reported on how we challenged our students to identify three memes that reflect their teacher identity; in this chapter, we offer another example of multimodal digital video creation that builds on that introductory activity. Returning to the teaching philosophy statement assignment, we continue by having our students explore the NCTE and ISTE websites, including deep-dive analyses of NCTE policies (2005, 2016) and ISTE Standards for Students (2016). We transition from standards to explore how teachers are using new media before examining the very real challenges to technology integration. During class time, we structure mini-lessons highlighting our own experiences while weaving in critical insights from other practitioners. We also attempt to demonstrate what effective and thoughtful technology integration looks and feels like in the English classroom.

Then, instead of requiring our PSTs to simply draft a statement of their beliefs as a required assignment, we scaffold to incorporate and exemplify best practices in educational and digital literacies. We offer our own co-teaching metanarrative for these future teachers so they learn an additional scaffolding strategy that can be critical for their own future secondary students. Building on the course readings and in-class conversations and activities, we communicate our approach in such a way that we model developmentally responsive and appropriate technology integration.

Explore our brainstorming worksheet and other materials here.

After two brainstorming workshops, we require students to write the first draft of their teaching philosophy. There is a very traditional flow of writing workshops here: drafting, peer review, and conferencing with us as instructors. We then build on existing instruction on the integration of digital video into the secondary ELA classroom by introducing the culminating component of the process: the teaching philosophy digital video. We share the work of previous students so our current students can identify the connective tissue among formats. The first step in the digital video project is to translate the more philosophical written statement into a video script or storyboard. We push students by reiterating the traditional aspects of writing and urging them to consider the following questions as they work to produce their multimodal texts:

- What is the purpose of this piece? *Imagine* who will view/read it?
- What is your tone? What is the *impact* of altering your word choice when taking the traditional piece (meant for an academic audience) and transforming it into a digital video (intended for parents at Back to School Night or students on the first day of school)?

The final step is recording, creating, and editing the video that exemplifies who they are as a future secondary English teacher. Likewise, this falls into a traditional writing workshop format, with students collaborating and problem solving together.

The drafting of the teaching philosophy statement has now progressed through four multimodal stages: images (e.g., memes in Chapter 4), a written form (e.g., reflective essays), a video script (e.g., an additional mode of writing), and a published digital video. Each stage creates a learning opportunity for PSTs to express their evolving teaching philosophy statement. Specifically, what begins as a tongue-in-cheek meme describing a particular moment in teaching proves to be an essential phase in the evolution of a formal essay. What's more, the transition from images and text to a text-only format and then into a digital format illustrates a multimodal approach to the same content. Provided with critical feedback from us, the PSTs are then pressed to consider what their philosophy statements will sound like in their revisions to create a script version. The greatest evolution begins with script in hand as students select the images, music, and other audio or media components that will go into their digital videos.

Two standout videos from our class really took the assignment to a whole new level and even prompted us to consider how to get our PSTs to add the elusive X factor in their work. One example came in spring 2020, when we received an email from Aliza who asked what our thoughts were on parody-style digital videos. We encouraged her to storyboard and think about what she wanted to accomplish with the parody and how it might make her a memorable teacher candidate. In our follow-up interview with her, she shared the following:

> We went to a wedding last year, and someone did a parody in their speech, and I thought it was so fun. So, in this [digital video], I wanted to show my personality, but I also wanted to be able to use it for a project and turn it into a lesson for my (future) students. I didn't just want to share something that was my take on technology, I wanted to integrate a lesson as well.

That was something we hadn't thought of explicitly at that point; but we love that Aliza thought about situating this artifact in her classroom in a meaningful way. This was a remote semester, so she recruited some friends and family members to appear in her video as students. In the end, her parody of Will Smith's "The Fresh Prince of Bel-Air" not only entertained us but also demonstrated a unique and clever approach to our assignment. As she produced her multimodal text, she had to *imagine* the cadence of the theme song and how her teaching philosophy would fit within the rhythm and rhymes. She wanted to introduce herself to future students in a slightly humorous and memorable way, and the *impact* on the viewer was clear.

Another student who added a clever twist to the project was Rob, a nontraditional student who actually loathed his high school experience. His video starts with a wide shot of him on a skateboard with a punk rock version of the theme song to *Mister Rogers' Neighborhood*, "It's a Beautiful Day in the Neighborhood," playing in the background. To be honest, we did wonder at first where he was going with this approach, especially when his opening line was, "Hi! I'm Mr. Fitzpatrick. I'm living my worst nightmare; I'm back at high school." We quickly realized that Rob had capitalized on his unique

Watch Mr. Fitzpatrick's video here.

experience as a nontraditional student and applied it to the creation of his video. It was clear to us that Rob's juxtaposition of himself as a high school student and then as a future high school teacher showed how he hoped to *influence* his future students. This relationship made him relatable to high school students, and we were easily able to *identify* the key components of his teaching philosophy throughout his multimodal text.

From the University to the Secondary Classroom

This section presents three examples of current teachers who have taken the core ideas of multimodality from the digital video assignment in our methods course and transformed them into usable models for their secondary English students. In the first example, Talia's students consume and produce using digital video. The second example follows Tim, who utilizes multimodality in a digital video assignment where his students can choose to do scene interpretations, character monologues, or book trailers for other students. And in the final example, Samantha has her students in an urban, all-girls school tell untold stories of their lives in Philadelphia. All of these teachers integrate multimodality into their work with their students and keep it at the forefront.

In Talia's secondary ELA classroom, she uses digital video in both consuming and producing ways. Midway through the year, when she introduces six-word memoirs to her students, she uses videos to get her students' creative juices flowing. After introducing the format of the memoir, explaining the construction, and offering some examples, she has the students read the iconic example that is often attributed to Hemingway: "For sale: baby shoes, never worn." Then, she turns to YouTube to locate other six-word memoirs in digital video format as additional mentor texts for her students. Although her students write and illustrate their six-word memoirs on paper, Talia argues that the digital video examples are what unlock her students' minds as they began to draft their own memoirs.

Talia also has her students create and produce their own digital videos at the conclusion of their book club unit. She focuses on allowing her students to develop their own voices when it comes to reflecting on the books that they read in small groups. Rather than someone else telling them what the themes and significant plot points are, Talia wants her students to take ownership over these conversations. After reading their books, each book club group is tasked with using the Biteable app to create a movie version of their book. We learned about this app from Talia. Talia describes the app as "sort of when Prezi meets a short film" and assured us that the technology was easy to use.

Biteable only allows users to create short videos, approximately ten minutes long. Talia shared that she starts this activity by having her students begin playing around and experimenting with the app before looking at it together as a class. Then, she previews a sample video that she made for the students before showing them how she put the video together. After this brief demonstration, her students have no trouble jumping in and getting started on their videos with their peers. The videos are meant to be a film version of their book that highlights the major themes, conflicts, and anything else that stood out for the students. Rather than simply repeating what she told them about the books, Talia wants the digital videos that students produce to organically focus on the components of the books that are important to them. At the end of the unit, Talia has to bump her upcoming lesson plans because each group demands that their video be screened and viewed by the class. Talia and her students have ended up spending four days watching each group's video!

Tim, another of our secondary ELA colleagues, who teaches a literature and film class for seniors, tries to make his curriculum and activities "as multimodal as possible." One activity he shared with us builds on a digital video project he had his students complete after reading Mary Shelley's *Frankenstein*. Tim calls the project a proof of concept because he asks his student to pitch a film adaptation of *Frankenstein* that pushes the themes, plot, and characters of the book outside of the traditional, canonical text. What might a film version look like that emphasizes the theme of dangerous knowledge as a positive rather than a challenge? What would happen to the story if the characters were all animals rather than humans? What if the main characters were of a different gender or ethnic or racial background? Working in small groups, students must make these decisions together and create a brief digital video that demonstrates the key elements of what a full, feature-length film would entail.

Tim allows his students to choose their own groups for this project, as with other projects in his class with seniors, because he finds that it is easier for students to align with their peers in terms of scheduling considerations. Because the class is focused on literature and film, Tim also incorporates additional smaller assignments to test students' knowledge and capability with certain film and editing techniques. Even though these are only short clips (roughly thirty to sixty seconds long), these projects take about three days of class time to complete and are also completed in small groups of three or four students. Tim did share that his students are sometimes bound by the technical capacities of the Google Chromebooks that are used by his school. For example, when it comes time to edit the video for his students' projects, he books the school's computer lab so that they can use iMovie on the Mac computers to complete their editing. While not required, Tim has also provided an option for students to produce a ten-minute documentary for their final exam project.

Samantha has taken a different approach to multimodality in an attempt to immerse her students in the culture of Philadelphia using the genre of documentary. She set them up by first having them complete a WebQuest about important aspects of documentaries.

> **Margin Memo**
>
> **Belief #3: Technologies provide new ways to consume and produce texts.** *What it means to consume and produce texts is changing as digital technologies offer new opportunities to read, write, listen, view, record, compose, and interact with both the texts themselves and with other people.* This embodies the NCTE Position Statement as we "encourage multimodal digital communication while modeling how to effectively compose images, presentations, graphics, or other media productions by combining video clips, images, sound, music, voice-overs, and other media" (2018). In the teaching philosophy statement assignment, we model how to compose their statements in multiple modes, from memes to digital video.

Adding to that scaffolding, she then had them watch several documentaries and provided prompts that would help them focus on the various elements, considering the multimodal design of not just a digital video but of a documentary. Sam explained:

> They had to look for things like voiceover, the pictures, and any text that was used on the screen to explain a location or any sort of data. They had to essentially write about why the person creating that documentary was using that statistic on that specific picture or that specific voiceover and how it was contributing to informing the viewer.

In the language of FIMS, students would have to *imagine* what their final project might look like as a documentary. What images and music would *impact* or *influence* the viewer? How would they *identify* whether or not they were successful? Once they viewed and analyzed these mentor text documentaries, they were given the assignment to create their own Philadelphia-themed documentary. They could choose a historical site, a famous person from Philadelphia, or popular places like the Reading Terminal Market. Some students chose lesser-known events, like the MOVE Bombing. Sam had originally planned for her students to interview people over the phone (activating their oral literacy skills), to take a trip to the Philadelphia Free Library to explore research methodology, and to select specific filming locations around the city for their documentaries (activating their visual literacy skills). They worked in teams and wrote and revised the scripts, and Sam even recruited folks from the neighborhood to help mentor the students as they completed this important project.

The students were supposed to create their documentaries over the course of the entire school year. The culmination of the project was meant to be a film festival at the end of the school year, where they would show their documentaries to the public. Unfortunately, it did not work out as intended because of the pandemic, but Samantha cannot wait to try this large-scale project again next year!

Concluding Thoughts

This chapter focused on consuming and producing digital videos, which are powerful multimodal texts that have been made accessible by the influx of digital technologies. While consuming

---

Margin Memo

Belief #1: Literacy means literacies. *Literacy is more than reading, writing, speaking, listening, and viewing as traditionally defined.* It is more useful to think of literacies, which are social practices that transcend individual modes of communication. The use of digital video broadens our definition of literacy to include all modes of information: visual, aural, and text-based information. By having students create their own videos, they are engaging literacies' skills—not just traditional literacy—as they consume and create these multimodal texts. They synthesize all of our lessons into one engaging product.

videos within the classroom has been common practice for decades, the ability to create and produce our own multimodal texts with students has become easier and is now possible for most. With a smartphone or a tablet with a built-in camera, teachers and students can produce multimodal texts that include moving images, words and texts, video clips, sound effects, and music. Digital videos as multimodal texts represent the pinnacle of multimodal literacies.

Other Ways to Use Digital Video to Support Multimodal Literacies in the Classroom

- **Consume:** Locate excellent videos and films to integrate daily into the classroom that help to situate and unpack the texts being studied. Consider interviews with authors and poets or other arts-based reinterpretations of traditional texts.
- **Consume:** Search YouTube to find other student examples of digital video projects in the ELA classroom. You are not alone! Other teachers are having their students create and share their assignments, too. Use these student videos as mentor texts or for critique.
- **Produce:** A twist on the character study is to have students collaborate, create, and produce digital videos of either monologues by particular characters in a text or of interviews with those characters and a student interviewer.
- **Produce:** Have students create family documentaries that take audio interviews to the next level. Raise the bar to encourage students to frame and tell a family narrative through the use of collected video clips.

Part V
Final Thoughts

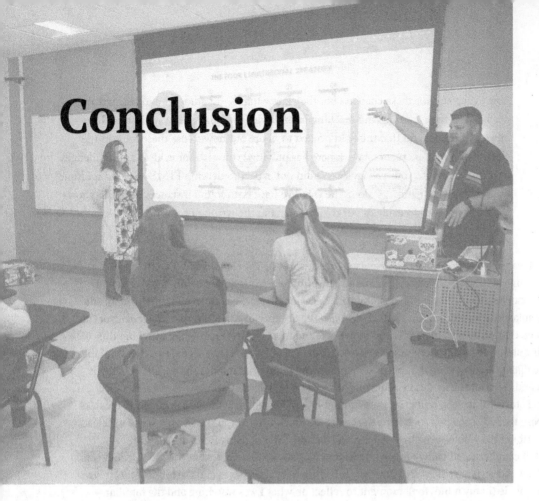

Conclusion

Chapter Twelve

Summary

To conclude our text, we want to circle back to the overarching framework for this book: the NCTE *Beliefs for Integrating Technology into the English Language Arts Classroom*. These four beliefs have informed our research and served as the foundation of this text:

1. Literacy means literacies.
2. Consider literacies before technologies.
3. Technologies provide new ways to consume and produce texts.
4. Technologies and their associated literacies are not neutral.

We are fortunate to be a part of NCTE, an organization that has always acknowledged the ever-changing landscape of classrooms, as illustrated in both the 1983 *Resolution on Computers in English and Language Arts* and the 2003 *Resolution on Composing with Nonprint Media*. Exploring these statements truly reveals both how focused NCTE (and ELA teachers) have always been on technology and also just how far we have come. They also demonstrate just how challenging it is to be an educator during these times. The authors of these NCTE statements did not necessarily know how to account for these changes, but they knew that K–12 students and teachers were engaging in their learning and teaching in multiple (newly) digital ways in their lives outside of school and that the field needed to figure out how to use these tools in the classroom. We hope that our work here has provided you with some ideas and challenges to incorporate into your pedagogy. We did not expect to develop FIMS and find multiple ways to apply that strategy along the way. We have both found instances of FIMS showing up in our work outside of our co-teaching and the writing of this book.

Pauline: I was mesmerized by a specific episode in season 4 of *The Handmaid's Tale*. The scene takes place in a sterile, all-white hospital room. The only color you can see is June's red ensemble and the black character's face in the hospital bed. Occasionally, lines of children walk through, and there are splashes of pink coats and hats. I *identified* the absence of color and then the *impact* of the three colors that stood out: red, pink, and brown. I found myself using FIMS while watching this captivating show. But, wait, there's more. Not only did I visually assess the scene, I started thinking about the dialogue and a song that plays. June is starting to lose her mind (I think), and she likens the drips and beeps of the medical equipment to the tune of Belinda Carlisle's "Heaven Is a Place on Earth" and starts to sing the lyrics. So, then I found myself considering the influence of the creators to juxtapose the lyrics of a pop song from the 1980s with such a horrific and terrifying scene in Gilead. I was describing the whole scene to Matthew, and he said, "You're using FIMS in real life!"
Matthew: I caught myself using FIMS while watching Disney's *Cruella*. Just as the movie producers intended, I was drawn into the story narrative, pulled along by the images and the music. I took myself out of the movie (in my mind) for a moment to reflect on what I was watching and the familiar became strange—why was everything so dark? Everything was shades of black and gray, with pops of red. The *impact* of these images, colors, and the background music *influenced* and engaged my emotions, and my brief reflection allowed me to ponder the *influence* of the producers. My imagination immediately drew me back into the story; I was going to have to watch this more than once!

Reflection Box

Have you found yourself listening to or watching something and applying FIMS? Have you considered the ways that you're going to incorporate what you've learned from this book into your classroom?

Final Thoughts

And so we reach the end of our journey, for now. We hope that we have created a useful resource for teachers and PSTs to push their pedagogical praxis to think in new, multimodal ways via digital technologies. We will continue to share our work on our podcast and on our website, and we will keep the QR codes up to date as well.

Annotated Bibliography

Compiled by Jen Rodgers

Introduction

As in other texts in the series, below we share a teacher-friendly listing of resources.

Visual Literacy

Adobe Spark

Teachers can use this multimedia tool within the classroom to help students create quality graphics, short videos, and single-page stories. This is an easy-to-use tool that offers a new creative format for the students to use when working on projects. This helps students and teachers create visual stories within the classroom while incorporating educational value. Students and teachers can use this as a tool to expand the concept of posters and make them into stunning visually interactive designs that are easy to share.

Canva

Teachers can use this powerful website to help students engage in rich and authentic learning experiences by reflecting on the real world around them. The drag and drop tools help alleviate the stress of creating posters for the classroom and make displaying visuals in the classroom easy. Students are able to respond more effectively and interact with their learning, and students and teachers can create infographics, websites, and more with Canva's ready-to-use templates.

Coggle

Students can use this as a web-based tool to allow them to create mind maps easily. Users sign in with their Google account and can instantly start designing their maps. This site does not offer any premade templates, so students must get creative right from the start. There are helpful self-guided tours that offer tips and tricks on how to utilize every aspect of this site. Users have the ability to share their maps with others and even comment on the maps of others.

Aural Literacy

Anchor

Teachers can use this tool to help students create quick and easy podcasts for projects in the classroom. Teachers can use this to create steps for assignments and projects for students to listen to as well. Parents can interact with this tool if teachers use this to provide information on what they are doing in class, what the students are working on, and upcoming activities within the classroom. The tool is there to promote a new type of assignment that teachers can use to emphasize a newer experience for students to discuss and participate rather than writing an essay.

GarageBand

This app allows students to record and layer up to eight tracks of loops, instruments, and vocals to create original songs and soundscapes. The visual interface can help students learn how to create multitrack recordings and songs. Virtual instruments can reinforce music theory. Students can also use this to record voice only for podcast use, poetry readings, etc. Students can easily share what they create using this app via email.

Jamboard

This is a digital interactive whiteboard where students and teachers can collaborate with each other. This helps with discussion posts or warm-ups, where teachers can have students interacting with one another digitally.

Multimodal Literacy

Animoto

Teachers can use this website to quickly create introductions to the course, lesson recaps, and educational videos. Students can use it to create videos when working on projects or assignments that promote digital storytelling. Teachers can assign projects and establish higher-order thinking as students are able to create unlimited videos. Teachers and students can use this to their advantage to emphasize the importance of storytelling and incorporate student learning through digital media.

Biteable

Teachers can suggest students use this tool to create multimedia reports and presentations. This interactive website helps teachers plan engaging videos for students to watch and can provide examples for students to be able to produce their own videos for assignments in the classroom. This web-based tool can help teachers create more engaging lessons for students to be able to interact with.

Edpuzzle

This is a web-based interactive video and formative assessment tool that allows teachers to edit existing online videos and add content to target specific learning objectives. Teachers are able to search the library or upload their own video to customize with voice-overs and audio comments, and they can add questions and additional resources. Also, the site offers options to assign due dates and prevent students from fast-forwarding through the videos. Teachers are also able to view student progress over time and see how long the students spend completing the assignment. Edpuzzle offers a community approach to share creations to spark inspiration or for classroom use.

Educreations

This is an iOS app that makes it simple for students and teachers to create multipage presentations or lessons that can be easily shared. Teachers can begin creating a whiteboard-style slide by adding images or text. There is an option to record audio over the slides, as well as some simple video editing tools.

Evernote

This note-taking tool offers companion apps for web clipping, drawing, and scanning. Students are able to create notes, snap images, hand-write notes, make checklists, or record audio on their mobile devices or computers. Students can search notes by keywords or customizable tags for easy retrieval. Multiple notebooks appear as Stacks to make it easy to drag and drop content between them. Students can download apps like Scannable and Skitch, which will allow them to import documents or annotated images.

Flipgrid

Teachers can use this app to quickly assess how students are connecting to new information. Flipgrid allows for an entire class (of any size) to present quick, short videos to respond to teacher- or student-generated questions. The classroom can interact with each post and send short messages to each other. Flipgrid can be used for classroom discussions, feedback on questions, etc.

FluentU

Teachers can use this application to find real-world videos in an online, searchable format. This is used for language classes especially because teachers are able to search for videos by language topics. The videos include real sources like actual ads, real movie trailers, etc. in whatever language the teacher chooses.

Google Sites

This website creator sponsored by Google can help teachers create website-based projects. This allows students to build websites from scratch or by using a template. This can be used for projects and other assignments as a creative outlet. This is a structured wiki and webpage creation tool. This app allows students to collaborate together to create and edit websites.

Kahoot!

This website provides a game-based learning platform for teachers to embed in their daily lessons. The digital game resource allows teachers to develop and research quizzes, surveys, and discussions to be used to assess student knowledge in the classroom. Students are provided a chance to compete in real time with their classmates. The website provides data for the teacher to reveal how many questions students answered correctly following the end of each game.

Nearpod

This website helps teachers creatively incorporate interactive presentations for their students either virtually or in the classroom setting. The teacher is able to create polls, videos, collaboration boards, quizzes, and more into a presentation where the teacher will get instant feedback from the students. The website can help liven up the classroom setting and fosters a more student-centered environment.

Pear Deck

This is an interactive presentation tool used to actively engage students in individual and social learning. Teachers create presentations using their Google Slides and this tool turns a Google Slides presentation into a more engaging lesson for the students to learn from.

Screencastify

This program lets students record video from their devices to replay later and share. They can even edit the video before they put it to good use. That means they are able to give a presentation across multiple websites with highlights on the screen and their face in the corner via their device's webcam, to name just one option. Teachers can use this to record lectures and post them to their learning management system (LMS).

Seesaw

This is a simple way for teachers and students to record and share what's happening in the classroom. Seesaw gives students a place to document their learning, be creative, and learn how to use technology. Each student gets their own journal to which they will add things like photos, videos, drawings, or notes.

Wix

This is a website design tool that is easy to use and can help students build their own websites. Wix offers the possibility to use premade templates or build websites from scratch. This can be helpful for teachers who are using this tool for student projects or even their own websites.

Managing the Classroom

Actively Learn

Teachers can use this website to help monitor and manage students' reading progress. The website is a tool that can help teachers to emphasize discussion-based learning and encourage some of the more reluctant hand-raisers to participate in reading. Teachers can use the questions that the website adds for them or they can create their own questions to help break the reading into bite-sized sections. The website helps build more student-centered and student-led reading strategies as they interact with the texts.

ClassDojo

Teachers can connect with their students and parents through this website and build amazing classroom communities. For teachers, this app/website helps them promote a positive creative culture through its mainframe system. Teachers are able to give students a voice through this tool as students can share their work with the rest of the class. Students can share photos and videos to their portfolios as a way to communicate their discoveries in the classroom. The app/website also gives teachers the opportunity to share with parents the classroom learning that is taking place.

Class Tree

Teachers can use this web and mobile app to communicate with students and their parents. Teachers can create class sections with students and parents one by one or by adding an entire roster. They share their class code with the parents and students. Teachers can use this app to send direct messages to individual students and parents. Teachers can collect permission slips and go paperless with this app.

E-hallpass

This allows teachers and administrators to provide hallway permissions to students and to track activity in a school. The tool is implemented to improve the accountability of students and staff. It is also there for student security. Students are able to access this app via any web browser and make a request to leave the classroom. The request includes both their intended destination and why they are leaving the classroom. Students show the teacher, who approves it by entering their unique pin number. A timer tracks how long the student spends between being checked out and the check-in time. Finally, staff can receive alerts if the student never checks into their final destination, thereby improving school security.

Edmodo

This free Facebook-like LMS can help teachers manage online instruction. Teachers can create an account and classes within this site. Also, teachers are able to invite students and parents to join via a class code, email, or a handout. Once students join, they can see the content, manage deadlines, submit assignments, and interact with the classroom community. Students can participate in activities and write posts that include embedded files, links, and media. Teachers can use the discover page to find apps, games, and student-focused news to add to their assignments. The reports feature allows teachers to track the assignment grades.

Google Classroom

Teachers can use this free web-based service to simplify creating classes to share files between their students. Teachers can set up a Google Classroom for each of their classes and share it with their students via a classroom code. Students are able to submit assignments and write discussion posts through the Google Classroom website.

Quill: Interactive Writing and Grammar

This website provides free writing and grammar lessons to early education, middle school, and high school students. This web-based tool provides personalized lessons for each student and aligns with Common Core standards.

Remind

Teachers can use this app to efficiently reinforce communication systems they already have in place. In addition to a class website, LMS, and student agendas, teachers can send or schedule a text message (including attachments) to remind students and families about important due dates, upcoming tests and quizzes, schedule changes, field trips, or other pertinent information.

Schoology

This is an LMS that schools use to post all of the work for classes and how they organize all of their classes. Students are able to access homework assignments, their class notes, and other materials that teachers post to the LMS website.

Socrative

This is a formative assessment tool that helps teachers and students assess their understanding

and progress in real time in class through the use of quizzes, questions, and reflection questions.

Cloud-Based Storage Solutions

Dropbox

Teachers interested in setting up cloud-based storage and organized files can use this application. Students can create shared folders with documents for their groups to work on collaboratively and can turn in assignments to an assigned folder through this application. This can also serve as a storage system for syllabi, notes, assignments, rubrics, and other files. All of these files can be accessed from home or school and on tablets and phones.

Google Drive

This cloud-based storage system is supported by Google. It allows files to be saved online and accessed from anywhere from any smartphone, tablet, or computer. Teachers can use this to collect assignments and organize notes and other files. This makes it easy to collaborate in class and edit other people's work.

Digital Resources

360Cities.net

Teachers could use this to show students panoramic pictures of cities and other types of photography. This could be used in student projects and in the classroom as part of the background knowledge for a lesson. It has global licensing agreements with a number of the world's largest photography licensing companies, including Getty Images, Alamy, and others.

Journeys in Film Website

In some cases, an English teacher will actually be assigned a film class. We see this as an exciting opportunity to interact with several films as multimodal texts. But these texts are unique in comparison to the physical novel, and therefore teachers will need other resources. We have identified the Journeys in Film website as an excellent place to start; a teacher can search through themes and lesson plans and in some cases access the film itself on the platform. The website makes the case that students can engage with the content in accessible ways and then have meaningful and critical conversations about a variety of topics.

Project Gutenberg

This is a collection of e-books that teachers can use in their classrooms for free. It is a website dedicated to classics for students to read. This could be helpful if students need to read a chapter at home and teachers only have a class copy. This could also be a way for students to access books without having to worry about checking them out and teachers not having to stress about books being returned.

TED Talks

This informative video series offers a virtual library of professional speakers who discuss certain topics and issues that are relevant to the world around us. It offers categories for teachers to be able to view and implement TED Talks in their classrooms.

Scholarly Books

Workshopping the Canon (Styslinger, 2017)

In *Workshopping the Canon*, Mary E. Styslinger introduces practicing and preservice English language arts teachers to a process for planning and teaching the most frequently taught texts in middle and secondary classrooms using a workshop approach. Demonstrating how to partner classic texts with a variety of high-interest genres within a reading and writing workshop structure, Styslinger aligns the teaching of literature with what we have come to recognize as best practices in the teaching of literacy.

The Art of Comprehension: Exploring Visual Texts to Foster Comprehension, Conversation, and Confidence (Bryan, 2019)

In *The Art of Comprehension*, Trevor Bryan describes nine "access lenses" that can be used to focus students' attention when examining the visual: facial expressions, body language, colors, distance, alone, silence, big things/little things, zoom in/zoom out, and symbols/metaphors. His text goes into detail about how to examine artwork through those lenses, and he even uses illustrations from the picture book Ish by Peter Reynolds as a sustained example throughout the text.

References

Arduini, T. (2018). Cyborg gamers: Exploring the effects of digital gaming on multimodal composition. *Computers and Composition, 48*(1), 89–102.

Atwell, N. (2014). *In the middle: A lifetime of learning about writing, reading, and adolescents* (3rd ed.). Heinemann.

Baker, F.W. (2012). *Media literacy in the K–12 classroom.* ISTE.

Ball, C, Sheppard, J., & Arola, K. (2018). *Writer/designer: A guide to making multimodal projects.* Bedford/St. Martin's.

Beers, K. (1998). Listen while you read: Struggling readers and audiobooks. *School Library Journal, 44*(4), 30–35.

Bellingham, R. (2020). *The artful read-aloud: 10 principles to inspire, engage, and transform learning.* Heinemann.

Brookfield, S. (2017). *Becoming a critically reflective teacher.* Jossey-Bass.

Bryan, T. A. (2019). *The art of comprehension: Exploring visual texts to foster comprehension, conversation, and confidence.* Stenhouse Publishers.

Cahill, M., & Moore, J. (2017). A sound history: Audiobooks are music to children's ears. *Children and Libraries, 15*(1), 22–29.

Chen, S-H. L. (2004) Improving reading skills through audiobooks. *School Library Media Activities Monthly, 21*(1), 22–25.

CNN.com (2016). *25 of the most iconic photographs.* CNN. https://www.cnn.com/2013/09/01/world/gallery/iconic-images/index.html

Dail, J. S., Witte, S., & Bickmore, S. T. (2018). *Toward a more visual literacy: Shifting the paradigm with digital tools and young adult literature.* Rowman and Littlefield.

Eisner, E. (2002). *The arts and the creation of mind.* Yale University Press.

Fletcher, R. (2019). *Focus lessons: How photography enhances the teaching of writing.* Heinemann.

Franklin, A. [@alexisvicki]. (2020, December 30). Still can't believe I got to do all of this, this year.... I'm excited for next year! [Tweet]. Twitter. https://twitter.com/alexisvicki/status/1344349610362372096/photo/1

Gander, L. (2013). Audiobooks: The greatest asset in the library. *Library Media Connection, 31*(4), 48.

Gee, J. P. (2007). *What video games have to teach us about learning and literacy.* Palgrave Macmillan.

Golden, J. (2001). *Reading in the dark: Using film as a tool in the English classroom.* NCTE.

Helsper, E. J., & Eynon, R. (2009). Digital natives: Where is the evidence? B*ritish Educational*

Research Journal, 36(3), 502–520.

Hertz, M. B. (2013, March 13). How teachers use technology: The latest research. *Edutopia.* https://www.edutopia.org/blog/how-teachers-use-technology-mary-beth-hertz

ISTE. (2016). ISTE standards for students. *ISTE.* http://www.iste.org/standards/standards/for-students

Jewett, C. (2008). Multimodality and literacy in school classrooms. *Review of Research in Education, 32,* 241–267.

Journell, W., Ayers, C. A., & Beeson, M. W. (2014). Tweeting in the classroom. *The Phi Delta Kappan, 95*(5), 63–67.

Knowyourmeme.com. (2013). *Ducreux.* Know Your Meme. https://knowyourmeme.com/memes/joseph-ducreux-archaic-rap

Kress, G. (2010). *Multimodality: A social semiotic approach to contemporary communication.* Routledge.

Kress, G., & van Leeuwen, T. (2001). *Multimodal discourse: The modes and media of contemporary communication.* Arnold Publishers.

Learning Network. (2014, August 29). From article to infographic: Translating information about "sneakerheads." *The New York Times.* https://learning.blogs.nytimes.com/2014/08/29/reader-idea-from-article-to-infographic-translating-information-about-sneakerheads/?searchResultPosition=1

Levin, K. R. (2016). Arts education: Systemic change and sustainability. In G. Humphries Mardirosian & Y. Pelletier Lewis (Eds.), *Arts integration in education: Teachers and teaching artists as agents of change* (pp. 433–462). Intellect.

Macro, K. J., & Zoss, M. (2019). *A symphony of possibilities: A handbook for arts integration in secondary English language arts.* NCTE.

Marshall, J., & Donahue, D. M. (2014). *Arts-centered learning across the curriculum: Integrating contemporary art in the secondary school classroom.* Teachers College Press.

McGonigal, J. (2011). *Reality is broken: Why games make us better and how they can change the world.* Penguin Books.

Miller, S., & Bruce, D. (2017) Welcome to the 21st century: New literacies stances to support student learning with digital video composing. *English Journal, 106*(3), 14–18.

Miller, S., & McVee, M. (2012). *Multimodal composing in classrooms: Learning and teaching for the digital world.* Routledge.

Mills, H., & O'Keefe, T. (2015). Why beliefs matter. In M. Glover & E. O. Keene (Eds.), *The teacher you want to be* (pp. 31–49). Heinemann.

Mirra, N. (2018). From connected learning to connected teaching: Editor's introduction. *Contemporary Issues in Technology and Teacher Education, 18*(2), 200–202.

Mishra, P., & Koehler, M. (2006). Technological pedagogical content knowledge: A framework for teacher knowledge. *Teachers College Record, 108*(6), 1017–1054.

Morrell, E. (2012). 21st-century literacies, critical media pedagogies, and language arts. *The Reading Teacher, 66*(4), 300–302.

Moyer, J. E. (2011). What does it really mean to "read" a text? *Journal of Adolescent & Adult Literacy, 55*(3), 253–256.

NCTE. (2005, November 17). *Multimodal literacies.* NCTE. http://www.ncte.org/positions/statements/multimodalliteracies.

NCTE. (2016, February 28). 2016 *NCTE education policy platform.* NCTE. http://www.ncte.org/positions/statements/2016-policy-platform

NCTE. (2018, October 25). *Beliefs for integrating technology into the English language arts classroom.* NCTE. http://www2.ncte.org/statement/beliefs-technology-preparation-english-teachers/

Nicosia, L. (2013). Educators online: *Preparing today's teachers for tomorrow's digital literacies.* Peter Lang.

Penrod, D. (2008). Web 2.0, meet literacy 2.0. *Educational Technology, 48*(1), 50–52.

PodcastInsights. (2022). *Podcasting simplified.* PodcastInsights. https://www.podcastinsights.com

Prensky, M. (2001). Digital natives, digital immigrants. Part 1. *On the Horizon, 9*(5), 1–6.

Rowsell, J. (2013). *Working with multimodality: Rethinking literacy in a digital age.* Taylor & Francis.

Rubery, M. (Ed.). (2011). *Audiobooks, literature, and sound studies.* Taylor & Francis.

Schmidt, P. S., & Kruger-Ross, M. (2021). Shakespeare versus the homo sapiens agenda: Exploring gender in *A Midsummer Night's Dream* and *Simon vs. the Homo Sapiens Agenda.* In V. Malo-Juvera, P. Greathouse, & B. Eisenbach (Eds.), *Shakespeare and young adult literature: Pairing and teaching* (pp. 135–152). Rowman & Littlefield.

Shirky, C. (2014, September 8). *Why I just asked my students to put their laptops away.* Medium. https://medium.com/@cshirky/why-i-just-asked-my-students-to-put-thei-laptops-away-7f5f7c50f368

Shoffner, M. (Ed.). (2016). *Exploring teachers in fiction and film: Saviors, scapegoats and schoolmarms.* Routledge.

Shulman, L. (1986). Those who understand: Knowledge growth in teaching. *Educational Researcher, 15*(2), 4–14.

Spanke, J. (2007). The trouble with teaching stories. *English Journal, 106*(6), 84–87.

Sterne, J. (2003). *The audible past: Cultural origins of sound reproduction.* Duke University Press.

Sterne, J. (Ed.). (2012). *The sound studies reader.* Routledge.

Takayoshi, P., & Selfe, C. L. (2007). Thinking about multimodality. In C. L. Selfe (Ed.), *Multimodal composition resources for teachers* (pp. 1–12). Hampton Press.

Turkel, S. (1997). *Life on the screen: Identity in the age of the internet.* Simon & Schuster.

Wiggins, B. E., & Bowers, G. B. (2014). Memes as genre: A structurational analysis of the memescape. *New Media & Society, 17*(11), 1886–1906.

Yang, G. (2016, November). *Comics belong in the classroom* [Video]. TED Conferences. https://www.ted.com/talks/gene_luen_yang_comics_belong_in_the_classroom?utm_campaign=tedspread&utm_medium=referral&utm_source=tedcomshare

Index

Authors

Pauline Schmidt, PhD, is a professor of English education in the Department of Secondary Education at West Chester University of Pennsylvania. She is also the director of the West Chester Writing Project. Her teaching and research interests include the infusion of the arts in English education, diversifying the canon of literature for children and young adults, and the impact of new literacies on curriculum and teacher preparation.

Matthew Kruger-Ross, PhD, is an associate professor in the Department of Educational Leadership and Higher Education Administration at West Chester University of Pennsylvania. He teaches graduate courses on educational technology, curriculum, and research methodologies. Matthew's research interests include the philosophy of education and technology and its impact on educational practice, curriculum theory as it relates to teaching and being a teacher, and the intersection of philosophy of education and the hermeneutic phenomenology of Martin Heidegger.

Contributors

Julianna Balmer graduated from West Chester University in 2018 and now teaches tenth- and twelfth-grade English at Downingtown High School West in Chester County, PA. She is an active NCTE and PCTELA member, passionately invested in building authentic, lasting relationships with her students and colleagues, and will always listen to any music her students say she must check out.

Haley Bauer is a 2021 graduate of West Chester University. She studied English literature in secondary education and hopes to work with her cooperating teacher after graduation.

Talia Borochaner has been teaching for almost a decade in the Bensalem Township School District. During this time, she has taught English literature and writing at middle school and high school. She currently teaches ninth-grade elements of literature and academic writing. She also coaches mock trial, is a student activities advisor, and co-leads the Sew What's Up Club. She has a BA in English literature from Arcadia University and an MS in education from the University of Pennsylvania, focusing on literacy and social justice.

Siena Catanzaro is a third-year eighth-grade English teacher at Garnet Valley Middle School in Garnet Valley, PA. She is a proud 2019 West Chester University alumnus. She is an active NCTE member and co-advisor for Garnet Valley Middle School's Drama Club.

Katie Cooney is a 2022 graduate of West Chester University who studied English secondary education. She is planning to further her education in literacy and become a reading specialist in a middle school.

Jennifer DiCriscio is a 2022 graduate of West Chester University who studied English secondary education. For her final year at West Chester, she participated in a year-long student teaching program and hopes to apply for a permanent high school teaching job.

Julie Mihalic DiNaples is a graduate of Slippery Rock University. She has been teaching for eighteen years and has been teaching at PA Cyber Charter School for fifteen years. She currently teaches two young adult literature courses that she created several years ago.

Sam Dugan is a former high school English teacher who spent four wonderful years at John W. Hallahan Catholic Girls' High School. Sam is currently working on her master's degree in English and a certificate in gender and women's studies at Villanova University. When she's not doing schoolwork, you can either find her giving ghost tours in Old City, Philadelphia, podcasting, or cuddling with her two cats.

Rob Fitzpatrick is a graduate of the secondary English education program at West Chester University.

Deanna Gabe has deep roots in the West Chester community. She is a two-time alumnus of and an adjunct instructor at West Chester University. Deanna is also the parent of two children who have gone through the West Chester Area School District. She has been both frustrated and pleasantly surprised by the promise and reality of technology in her classroom.

Heather Harlen, MA, MEd, is a proud public school teacher with over two decades of experience in the classroom. She is a National Writing Project fellow and a founding English teacher at Building 21, a competency-based high school in Allentown, PA. Her main professional interests are curriculum decolonization and instructional design.

Allison Irwin is a reading specialist and English teacher from Berks County who has been teaching for over ten years. She is grateful for the professional development opportunities provided by organizations like NCTE, PCTELA, WCWP, and National Geographic, which have greatly influenced her instructional philosophy.

Sophie Koval is a 2022 graduate of West Chester University. She graduated with both a BSED in secondary English writing and a BA in languages and cultures in French, with a K–12 teaching certification.

Dan Lonsdale has taught English language arts in the Souderton Area School District for the last six years. He completed his undergraduate degree at West Chester University of Pennsylvania in 2015 and completed his master's degree in English in spring 2021.

Hailey Lucas started her career in education by teaching seventh-grade English language arts at South Middleton School District. She currently works as a higher education curriculum consultant and LMS administrator. In 2015, Hailey earned her bachelor's degree from West Chester University and completed her master's in 2022.

Molly Mangan is a proud West Chester University alumnus both at the undergraduate ('13) and graduate ('18) level and is a fellow of the National Writing Project ('17). Molly teaches ninth-grade English in the Bensalem Township School District where she also serves as a class advisor, tennis coach, and staff-wide instructional coach.

Katy Mills is in her seventh year of teaching English at Avon Grove High School. She is a two-time West Chester alumnus, graduating with both her bachelor's degree and a Master of Science in transformative education and social change. Additionally, she completed her educational technology certificate at WCU and is currently using that in her temporary role as a teacher on special assignment this year, helping to support other teachers with ed tech needs during remote and hybrid learning.

Aliza Mulloy is a lead expressive arts teacher with an organization that provides a variety of trauma-sensitive programming for youth in care with the Chester County Youth Center. She is excited to begin her next chapter as the middle school special education teacher at Avon Grove Charter School.

Tim Patton has been an English teacher at Unionville High School since 2011. An NWP and WCWP fellow, he brings a love of technology, writing, literature, and film to his classroom every day. He currently teaches twelfth-grade comparative literature.

Bobby Rea is a West Chester graduate with a Bachelor of Science in English education who is now working toward a master's in English literature. Currently, he is in his first year of teaching as a long-term substitute at Unionville High School.

Jen Rodgers completed her graduate studies at West Chester University in the Master of Science in transformative education and social change program in 2022.

Justin Thomas received his Master of Education and his teaching certification in grades 7–12 ELA in May 2021. In the winter and spring 2021, he spent his time as a student teacher at Springton Lake Middle School in Media, PA, teaching seventh-grade English language arts. He hopes to teach ELA, theater, and journalism.

Abigail Turley is a 1999 West Chester University graduate and a 2019 National Writing Project teacher consultant. She is beginning her twenty-third year of teaching high school English language arts in the West Chester Area School District where she serves as department chairperson and advisor to the literary magazine and creative writing club.

Erin Umpstead is a writer, thinker, speaker, highly effective educator, cat enthusiast, and fiber artist. She teaches seniors at the North Campus at Holt High School in Michigan and is in her thirteenth year of advising the Gay/Straight Alliance. She is making room for all students as she learns to be an antiracist teacher.

Brett Vogelsinger is a National Board Certified Teacher who leads ninth-grade English classes at Holicong Middle School in the Central Bucks School District. He enjoys starting class with a poem each day, studying and creating infographics with his students based on their research, and matching great books with great students. His annual blogging project, Go Poems, looks at how teachers can bring poetry into their daily practice with just a few minutes at a time during National Poetry Month.

Ashley Wakefield is a West Chester University alumnus and completed her master's in education at Holy Family University. She has taught at Renaissance Academy Charter School in Phoenixville for the past eleven years, where she teaches tenth- and eleventh-grade English language arts and advises the high school's Gay–Straight Alliance.

Hana Wiessmann graduated in 2022 with a BSED in secondary English education at West Chester University of Pennsylvania. She is currently working as a substitute teacher and writing tutor.

This book was typeset in Adobe Caslon Pro and PT Serif by
Cynthia Gomez.

Typefaces used on the cover include
Chronicle Display Semibold, Avenir Next Medium, and Formata Light, Medium, and Bold.

The book was printed on 50-lb. white offset paper by
Sheridan.